'Reading the story of Reg Chard and his fellow servicemen only reinforces how grateful we all should be to the soldiers who sacrificed everything in order for us to have the privileged life we often take for granted. These men were full of bravery, courage and conviction yet were regularly battling against the odds in the knowledge they may not see out the day. Every word of this story has meaning, importance and impact and I for one am indebted to those who have served our nation to make it what it is today.'
STEVE WAUGH AO, former Australian Cricket Captain

'*The Digger of Kokoda* is a gripping read about an all-Australian hero, Reg Chard, who like so many of that WWII generation had greatness in him, only revealed when he was called on to put everything on the line for his country. This biography evocatively portrays the hardships of the Kokoda campaign, the sacrifices made, and the irrepressible spirit of the Australian soldiers and nursing sisters. Bravo the lot of them, and this book.'
PETER FITZSIMONS AM, journalist and author of *Kokoda*

'The lessons and life experiences of Reg Chard are ones all Australians today could learn a lot from. *The Digger of Kokoda* was very honest and gave me a new perspective and understanding of what they went through and why. Warm, moving, heartbreaking and inspiring in equal measure. The greatest lesson I take from Reg is his quote: "Make the most of life, because no matter how bad something may seem, life goes on – just make sure you go with it."'
EMMA McKEON AM, Australian Olympic gold medallist

'I have an immense respect and admiration for Reg Chard – the Digger of Kokoda. He's a genuine Australian hero whose story could help teach our nation's youth the importance of resilience, grit, and mateship. Reg, and others like him, should be honoured in our school system to ensure the ANZAC/Kokoda spirit thrives . . . reading this man's powerful story is a perfect start to guaranteeing that.'
DANNY GREEN, former World Boxing Champion

'A lifetime ago, no series of battles were more critical nor horrendous than those of the New Guinea campaign – Kokoda and the likes of Sanananda. Reg Chard was a typical and thus extraordinary digger who fought in those battles and survived, to this day mourning and honouring his many mates who fell. This brilliant account by Daniel Lane, of Reg's war service, reminds us all of the price of peace so many of our predecessors have paid. A great story.'
GENERAL THE HONOURABLE SIR PETER COSGROVE AK, AC (MIL), CVO, MC (RET'D), former Governor-General and Chief of the Defence Force

'Reg Chard's biography transported me straight back to the jungle in New Guinea and rekindled memories of walking the Trail later in my life. The written word of the Kokoda Trail will last long into history like the track itself. *The Digger of Kokoda* is essential reading for any Australian.'
KEITH PAYNE VC, AM, Australian Army veteran, Victoria Cross recipient and author of *No One Left Behind*

'At the end of the Kokoda Trail stand four granite pillars, each inscribed with a single word – Courage, Sacrifice, Endurance and Mateship. Values informing our national character given to us by Reg Chard and this nation's finest generation. They gave their youth and many, their lives for one another. *The Digger of Kokoda* offers a deeper understanding of what it means to be an Australian and the inspiration to be a better person.'
DR BRENDAN NELSON AO, former Director of the Australian War Memorial and Minister for Defence

'In a world where an internet outage is deemed a catastrophe, *The Digger of Kokoda* is a masterclass in perspective and relativity. If this book doesn't get you to the Dawn Service on ANZAC Day, nothing will.'
JOHN SCHUMANN AM, lead singer of Redgum and songwriter of 'I Was Only 19'

'Courage, endurance, mateship and sacrifice are qualities synonymous with Kokoda and Australia's national identity. They embody, too, the service and life of Reg Chard. His is a story that will inspire.'
DR KARL JAMES, Head of the Military History Section, Australian War Memorial and author of *Kokoda: Beyond the Legend*

'Grittily honest, told with great sensitivity, this is the finest account of Kokoda by a front-line soldier that I've read. Reg Chard, only 18 when he fought the Japanese in Papua, tells much more than another "mud and blood" story. Now 98, he shows how the experience touched his life and, in an extraordinary twist, saved him from his own demons after his wife died. The true story of a boy soldier who faced some of the worst battles of the Pacific War.'
PAUL HAM, author of *Kokoda*

'Raw, vivid and searingly honest, Reg Chard's personal account of Kokoda is one of the most moving I've ever read. From the nightmare of Eora Creek to the terrible swamps of Sanananda, I felt I was right there, and it's not a pretty place. One of the last true voices, Reg reaches across the decades to remind us of what our men did, and how much they endured.'
MICHAEL VEITCH, bestselling author of *Flak*, *Barney Greatrex* and *Turning Point*

'A behind-the-curtain look into some of the toughest battles Australians have faced, in some of the toughest terrain. Reg Chard, a soldier's soldier, shares insights into the graphic, brutal and confronting scenes endured by Australians on the infamous Kokoda Trail. Reg's memoir reminds us of all the extraordinary acts committed by ordinary people and fills a Digger like myself with pride in the honour of donning the same badge they wore.'
DAMIEN THOMLINSON, 2nd Commando Regiment veteran, actor and World Ranked Disabled Golfer

'The realities of war are best understood by the soldiers who fight them. In Reg Chard's compelling account of Kokoda, we gain a unique insight into war's madness. We not only advance alongside him in the mud and blood of the trail towards a ruthless enemy; he also invites us to join him as he retreats deep inside himself to the comfort of home, family, and his beloved Betty. More than a book about stoicism, survival, and forgiveness, *The Digger of Kokoda* is a modern digger's time capsule full of the human lessons of war and soldiering that never change.'
ANTHONY 'HARRY' MOFFITT, Australian SAS veteran and author of *Eleven Bats*

REG CHARD grew up amid the hardship of the Great Depression before volunteering to fight in the Australian Army during World War II, where he served at Milne Bay, the Kokoda Trail and Sanananda. Upon his return from the battlefield, Reg married his childhood sweetheart, Betty, and he worked multiple jobs as he raised his family in Sydney's south-west. These days 98-year-old Reg helps to keep the spirit of the diggers and army nurses alive in his role as a guide on the Kokoda Track Memorial Walkway at Concord. His community service was recognised with an OAM in 2021.

DANIEL LANE has been a sports journalist for over 30 years, including time with Australian Consolidated Press, AAP, Network 10 and the *Sydney Morning Herald*. He has written 18 books, and scripts for three televised documentaries/shows. He has visited the battlefields of Gallipoli, the Western Front, El Alamein, Singapore and Malaya, and for decades has interviewed veterans of the Boer War and both world wars, including Kokoda. The biography of Reg Chard, *The Digger of Kokoda*, is his first military memoir.

The DIGGER *of* KOKODA

THE OFFICIAL BIOGRAPHY OF REG CHARD

DANIEL LANE

MACMILLAN
Pan Macmillan Australia

Pan Macmillan acknowledges the Traditional Custodians of country throughout Australia and their connections to lands, waters and communities. We pay our respect to Elders past and present and extend that respect to all Aboriginal and Torres Strait Islander peoples today. We honour more than sixty thousand years of storytelling, art and culture.

Some of the people in this book have had their names changed to protect their identities.

First published 2022 in Macmillan by Pan Macmillan Australia Pty Ltd
1 Market Street, Sydney, New South Wales, Australia, 2000

 A catalogue record for this book is available from the National Library of Australia

Typeset in Bembo Std by Midland Typesetters, Australia

Printed by IVE
Cartographic art by Laurie Whiddon, Map Illustrations

The author and the publisher have made every effort to contact copyright holders for material used in this book. Any person or organisation that may have been overlooked should contact the publisher.

Aboriginal and Torres Strait Islander people should be aware that this book may contain images or names of people now deceased.

 The paper in this book is FSC® certified. FSC® promotes environmentally responsible, socially beneficial and economically viable management of the world's forests.

To Betty, a beautiful woman and loyal wife who won
my heart the day she rode her bike past my place
when we were kids of 16. I miss you every day, Betty.
For my sons, Robert and Garry, I love you very much.
This is the story I kept to myself for far too long.
This book is also my heartfelt dedication to the men
and women who didn't return home from the war.
Rest in peace, you are Australia's greatest heroes.
Reg Chard

To my wife, Camille, a constant source of love and
inspiration; to my late mother, and hero, Carol,
and my grandfather Richard Feint NX 88777 –
while Nan told me some stories I wish
I could've heard them all from you.
Daniel Lane

Contents

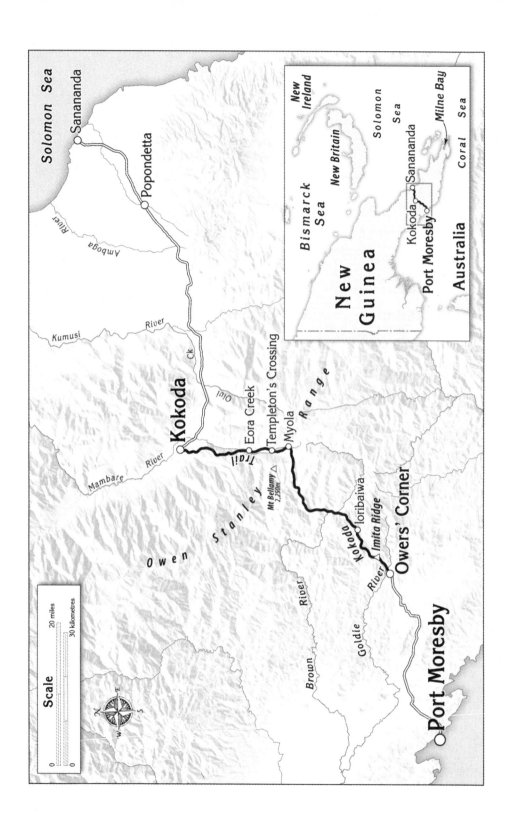

Solomon Sea

Sanananda

Popondetta

Amboga River

Kumusi River

Ck

Oivi

KOKODA

Eora Creek

Templeton's Crossing

Myola

Mambare River

Owen Stanley Range

Mt Bellamy △
2,250m.

Trail

Ioribaiwa

Kokoda
Imita Ridge

Owers' Corner

Brown River

Goldie River

Kokoda River

Port Moresby

Scale

20 miles

30 kilometres

0

0

New Ireland

New Britain

Bismarck Sea

Solomon Sea

New Guinea

Kokoda
Sananda

Port Moresby

Australia

Coral Sea

Milne Bay

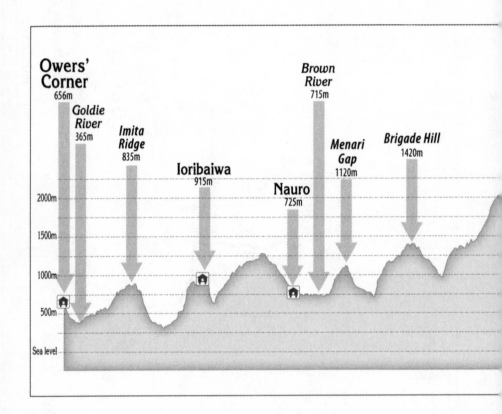

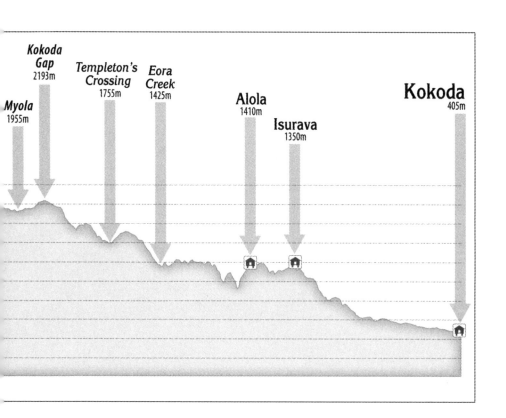

Myola
1955m

Kokoda Gap
2193m

Templeton's Crossing
1755m

Eora Creek
1425m

Alola
1410m

Isurava
1350m

Kokoda
405m

Author's Note

Over the years there's been passionate debate as to whether the foot route over the Owen Stanley Range in Papua New Guinea should be called the 'Kokoda Trail' or 'Kokoda Track'. As the World War II campaign has become even more prominent in Australian history, many people have demanded it be called 'track' because they consider 'trail' to be an American term. Reg Chard has insisted that it be called a trail in his story because, in Reg's words: 'The land belongs to the Government and people of Papua New Guinea and they call it the Kokoda Trail, and so do I in order to respect their wishes.' Please note that 'track' is used in the Kokoda Track Memorial Walkway because it's the name of the place.

Introduction

You have seen things at this place that no man should witness. Some of these things you must forget. But history will remember you, and in the years to come others will wish that they had your conviction . . .

Lieutenant Colonel Ralph Honner's address
to the 39th Australian Infantry Battalion
after fighting on the Kokoda Trail

The idea to write the biography of Reg Chard OAM came on 3 November 2019 – Kokoda Day – when I stood among a crowd of 500 people who listened in silent awe as the 96-year-old veteran provided his recollections of fighting in the Kokoda and Beachheads campaigns.

We, the crowd, had gathered for the 77th anniversary of the Kokoda village's recapture by Australian troops from the Japanese who'd retreated after coming within 60 kilometres of Port Moresby. This day was a time to remember people like Reg – an apprentice pastry chef before the war, who'd met the love of his life, Betty, when they were both 16 – who'd made all number of sacrifices to ensure Australia's freedom.

On this particular afternoon, the Kokoda Track Memorial Walkway, based in the leafy Sydney suburb of Concord, dripped with sentiment. The Corrective Services NSW band played haunting hymns and patriotic anthems;

politicians and dignitaries made rousing speeches; and schoolchildren read emotive poems they'd written about the deaths of boys not much older than themselves in a jungle hell.

A group of young soldiers, some bearing their Afghanistan and/or Iraq campaign medals, re-enacted the raising of the Australian flag over Kokoda village in 1942. An old woman who clutched either her husband's or brother's medals in her hands sobbed as she watched the solemn ceremony. By the end of Reg Chard's Kokoda Day Address, others joined her in dabbing away tears from their eyes.

Reg seemed like a grandfather who was asked to make a speech at his grandson's wedding as he thanked everyone for taking the time out of their day to attend the ceremony. The more he spoke, the more he sounded like the Australian of long ago – the quiet achiever who'd done his bit – and while he'd done it well, he was uncomfortable to be the centre of everyone's attention. Perhaps that was the reason why Reg was quick to point out there were other Kokoda veterans present, Ray Gentles, Lloyd Birdsall and Dick Payten.

After speaking of the mateship that helped him survive his time at Kokoda and Sanananda, and detailing the savagery of the enemy, Reg focused much of his speech about the importance of the Kokoda Track Memorial Walkway on the mangrove-studded banks of the Parramatta River and across the road from Concord Hospital, where Reg spent too much time as a young man battling the wicked bouts of the malaria he brought home from the jungle.

In simple, old Aussie straightforwardness, Reg explained

the importance of the Walkway, which commemorates such battles as Milne Bay, Eora Creek, Templeton's Crossing, Gona, Buna and Sanananda. As a 'living memorial' he hoped people would continue to visit it in 50 years' time 'long after we're well and truly gone' to remember the people who'd served during World War II, just as generations had made the pilgrimage to the Anzac Memorial at Hyde Park in the middle of Sydney's CBD to remember those who'd fought and fell at Gallipoli and other World War I battlefields.

He told the crowd that at 96 he was happy to drive his car (he still does at 98!) from his home in Sydney's south-west to the Walkway where, as one of its volunteer guides, he helps educate schoolchildren and visitors of the campaign's place in history as the battle that saved Australia. And then, after pausing, Reg revealed how, eight years earlier, the Walkway saved him when he planned to end his life following Betty's death from cancer. After being married to her for 66 years he'd thought his life was over. However, the decision to make one last visit to the Walkway where he and Betty had lunch after she received her medical treatment actually gave him a new lease on life and reason to keep living . . .

After talking to Reg about his experiences it was obvious there was an important story to tell.

While *The Digger of Kokoda: the official biography of Reg Chard* is rich in anecdotes about the men he fought along-side, battles with the military police and dealing with pompous officers, it also details the horrors of war, including being led to a massacre site, having friends die in front of his eyes, the savagery of the enemy, the darkness that lies within even the best of men, the trauma of PTSD and adjusting to the responsibilities of civilian and family life.

For me this was also a special project because Reg's memoir could well be the last first-hand account from somebody who fought on Kokoda and then at the bloody Beachheads – regarded as the worst of the battlefields any Australian fought on during World War II.

Something that never failed to amaze me while working with Reg was his remarkably clear, consistent and lucid memory, from the intricate details of the men who he fought alongside to *everything* you could possibly want to know about the ovens he used as a 16-year-old apprentice pastry chef. I also welcomed during the fact-checking process that if Reg wasn't 100 per cent correct about something, he was very close to it.

Reg's account of the unorthodox manner he was sent to fight at Kokoda – his 'mob' was divided in two with a wave of an officer's arm at Owers' Corner with his half ordered to march until they found the frontline 'somewhere up there' – emphasises the desperate need for extra Aussie boots and rifles to combat the Japanese. It remains Reg's hope that revealing one of Kokoda's untold stories honours his mates' courage and resilience.

There are only a handful of Reg Chards in Australia these days, and I believe we're poorer for it.

If Reg's story – *their* story – teaches us anything, it's the importance of having the courage, and finding the sense of purpose needed, to keep going when it'd be easy to give up.

Daniel Lane, January 2022

1

A Soldier's Son

We could not believe that we were expected to attack in such appalling conditions. I never prayed so hard in my life. I got down on my knees in the mud and prayed to God to bring me through.

Private Pat Burns, 46th Canadian Infantry Battalion, Passchendaele, November 1917

My father, Herbert Hercules Chard, was wounded twice in the space of eight days during one of World War I's bloodiest battles, Passchendaele. He never spoke about any of his experiences on the Western Front and the reason I never asked him about them was because I didn't need to: his drinking said more than enough about the horrors he'd witnessed.

While I loved my father, he had some terrible flaws. As a result of his war service, he became an alcoholic and, sadly, he could be a violent one. There were times when he'd return home from a drinking session and need no excuse to start on my poor mother, Annie. It was dreadful.

I thought that maybe I could prevent him from lashing out if I knocked him onto the floor. I remember once trying to wrap my arms around his legs to tackle him, but my father was too strong, and too wild, for a boy of my small build to stop his violence.

Dad worked as a carpenter to provide for our family, and there were also moments where he showed kindness – but they were few and far between. I suppose that's why one of my most enduring childhood memories of Dad is of him sitting alone at home and smoking his pipe while he brooded. We kids left him in peace on those occasions because we'd learnt – the hard way – that Dad had a short temper. We realised that when aggravated he could snap without warning.

The entire household was on edge whenever my father returned home, but rather than feel sorry for ourselves my brothers and sisters and I (there were nine of us in total) got on with life the best we could. Obviously, we knew Dad's behaviour was wrong, and it was due to the ugly scenes we witnessed that all but one of my four brothers and I never touched alcohol or smoked. I even promised myself from an early age to be nothing like my father when I grew older. Sadly, the brother who drank only started because, like Dad, he was scarred by his military service during World War II.

Of course, ours wasn't the only family who lived with that unspoken curse of the Great War. There were thousands of soldiers like my father who returned from the trenches with demons that made life hell for their wives and kids in the form of drunkenness, uncontrollable rage, savage out-bursts and domestic violence.

The government's approach towards its veterans in those times was completely different from how they're managing the effects of war on today's generation of diggers. While the men who came back from the Great War with obvious injuries such as lost limbs or blindness were given extra assistance on top of their war pension, no-one in power during the 1920s and '30s seemed concerned about the soldiers who'd suffered 'invisible wounds' brought on by the nerve-shattering experience of battle – let alone their dependants. With no offer of psychological help or access to other effective treatments, my father was one of many returned servicemen who reached for the only means of dulling the pain readily available to them: they self-medicated with alcohol, even though it was self-destructive, and damaged their families.

Fortunately for me and my siblings, Mum was as big-hearted as she was brave. Besides doing an incredible job of shielding all of us children from Dad's dark side, she also did everything within her power to help him. She was caring and patient, but despite her best efforts my father was a lost cause. While they remained married until Dad's death in 1968 – 60 years after their wedding in 1908 – Mum had made me, my sisters and brothers her life's focus when she realised Dad couldn't let go of the ghosts from Passchendaele.

Dad's alcoholism is a memory I don't like to dwell on because even now, at 98 years of age, it's still hurtful to think of the dreadful impact it had on our household. However, Mum's efforts to try and keep the family as happy and functional as possible despite her own health problems is a tribute to her character. Indeed, she provided me with a lifelong lesson about the importance of having resilience: the inner courage to keep going when it'd be so much easier to just give up. I know I speak on behalf of all of my siblings when I say the love she gave us was more than enough compensation for Dad's struggle to show us any affection.

I can't tell you what motivated Dad to drop everything and front up at the Army Recruitment Office in Bondi in 1917 because he made his war service a taboo subject. He might've been looking for adventure, or maybe he felt obliged to enlist because of the shocking number of casualties our army had suffered at Fromelles, Pozières, and in other battles. Perhaps he just wanted to do his bit, but, given his character, it wouldn't have surprised me to learn Dad volunteered just to get square with the Germans for a mate who'd been killed 'over there'. This much I *do* know: on 8 January 1917 Dad left Sydney with the 35th Australian Infantry Battalion, which consisted mainly of men from the dairy farms, coalmines and steel mills around the Newcastle district. I also know that when Dad marched up the gangplank to the HMAT *Anchises*, he left Mum on her own in the Sydney suburb of Waverley – near Bondi Beach – to fend for their three children: Edna (born 1908), David (1911) and Myra (1913).

Regardless of his reasons for sailing away, 30-year-old Private Chard, serial number 3502A, arrived in time to join his battalion when they were sent into Passchendaele, a series of battles where half a million men were either killed, wounded, or went missing in a bloodbath described by British historian A.J.P. Taylor as the 'blindest slaughter of a blind war'. The heavy rain that fell at the beginning of the battle added to the nightmarish scenes, creating a sea of mud that was said to have 'sucked' men into its great nothingness, as though it were a monster straight from the pages of one of the science fiction comic books I read as a boy. Indeed, there are numerous reports detailing how some men, and even some poor horses, fell into that Belgian sludge and sank to what I can only imagine must have been a dreadful death.

It was amid this chaos that on 12 October 1917 Dad took part in the 35th Battalion's disastrous assault on the German lines. The battalion's official war diary documented the extent of the mauling, noting that only 90 of the 508 men who started the battle escaped being wounded or killed. I don't know how badly Dad was injured during that first attack, but his records show he was pitchforked into the next suicidal charge on 20 October with other survivors and hastily drawn reinforcements. As Dad ran towards the Germans' defences, he was knocked flying into the mud by a chunk of shrapnel that ripped through his chest before lodging itself dangerously close to his heart. After lying for Lord knows how long among his dead and dying comrades, he was eventually carried from the battlefield and transported by lorry and ship to the Australian Hospital Camp in Salisbury, England. Surgeons there left the shrapnel where it rested because they decided any operation to remove it was too risky. While my father was told he'd have a normal enough life upon his return to Australia, the shrapnel inside him was a ticking time bomb. The surgeons warned him that if it moved even slightly it could sever an artery and kill him. While Dad never spoke about it, I'm sure there were many times he lay in bed worrying that the shrapnel from Passchendaele could end up killing him.

My mother was advised of Dad's injury on 11 November – one year to the day before the Armistice was signed – but it wasn't until 10 December 1917 that news of his fate appeared in *The Daily Telegraph*'s list of men who'd been Killed in Action; Killed Accidentally; Died of Wounds; Died of Illness; Wounded; Wounded and Missing; Missing; Ill; Injured or Taken Prisoner. It's a shocking commentary on the carnage on the Western Front that in the brief time between *The Daily Telegraph*'s Saturday edition and their Monday publication which carried details about Dad's status, 155 men from New South Wales were reported killed, and 393 wounded. The page Dad's name appeared on also carried photographs of such men as Trooper G.A.S. King of Balmain who was Killed in Action; Lieutenant George Burrows from Penrith receiving the Military Cross for his bravery at Polygon Wood; and the heart-wrenching news that Mrs S.E. Nolan of West Narrabri had lost her son Peter, Killed in Action, while her other boy, Jack, was wounded.

Dad received his second mention in the newspaper a few weeks later, this time in a small article which was accompanied by yet another long list of wounded officers and troops:

RETURNING SOLDIERS ON TROOPSHIP L
Following is the nominal roll of sick and
wounded soldiers who will return to Sydney
by the troopship 'L', which has already left
for Australia. A notification as to date of arrival
will be given later.

After spending months recovering in England, Dad was ruled medically unfit for active service and sent home. He returned on HMAT *Llanstephan Castle*, which the military censor had referred to as *Troopship L* in an attempt to deny the enemy any intelligence about Allied ship movements.

Dad's soldiering days officially ended on 29 July 1918 when he received his discharge papers in Sydney. The war was over for him, but it was only the beginning of a long and weary battle for Mum. I'm afraid whatever joy she may have felt to have the man she loved return safely after 19 months away was cruelled the first time my father showed how the war had changed him.

One night after Dad went on one of his rampages, I asked Mum to describe what he was like before becoming a soldier. I couldn't wrap my head around how such a loving and kind woman as Mum had ended up with *him*. Mum painted the picture of a model husband who had abstained from drinking alcohol, who was hardworking, full of life, and who'd happily devoted himself to his family. He was apparently a cheerful bloke, slow to anger, a man who'd found pleasure in life's simple things. By the time she'd finished I couldn't help but feel sad because my first thought was: *Geez, I would've loved to have met that Dad.*

My next was to wonder how terrible a thing war must be if it could damage its survivors beyond recognition.

When the family moved to Marrickville in Sydney's inner west before I was born, Dad's sanctuary became the ANZAC Memorial Club at Garners Avenue. It was a place where veterans of the Great War met – and drank, and drank – as they tried to forget both the past and the many problems they had on the home front. It was also a boys' club; the only time Mum and the wives of the other members were permitted inside its doors was for the night of the annual ball.

For quite a while I was confused by Dad's need to be at the club so often because it seemed as if he was clinging to the very bloody things that had ruined him: the army and the war. Besides the many hours he spent there, Dad *never* missed an ANZAC Day March or any of his regiment's drunken reunions that were held in the city. On every 25 April he'd polish his shoes, have Mum press his suit, and wake before 5 am to leave for the march with his medals and Returned from Active Service badge displayed proudly on his coat. Indeed, he was so keen to be among it all he would've, as a saying from the time suggested, 'climbed out of his grave to be there'. During my youth it upset me to think that my dad felt as though the group of men he drank with were his 'real' family, which is how it seemed to me because he spent so much time with them.

However, what I couldn't possibly have understood was that my father and his mates *had* to go to Garners Avenue. I'd appreciate one day that it was there – and only there – where Dad could speak comfortably about what he'd witnessed on the Western Front and the experiences that had scarred him. And those men who propped up the ANZAC Club's bar with him – the very blokes who I'd curse when I'd think that my father considered them his 'real' family – were all returned servicemen. That meant they understood Dad in a way that we, his own family, could not. Like him, they were navigating their way through their own hell.

It's been 105 years since Dad fought in the war, but even now I can't help but think that Passchendaele possibly robbed my family of a very different sort of life. To this day, I sometimes still find myself wishing, for my mother's sake, my sake, my siblings' sakes – and especially for Herbert's sake – that our mutual relationships could've been different from the ones the Great War shaped.

2

Life's Early Lessons

There is no tragedy in life like the death of a child. Things never get back to the way they were . . .
Dwight D. Eisenhower, 34th President of the USA

The best way to describe my mother's resilience and her capacity to love is that during the 24 years between 1908 and 1932, Mum gave birth to ten children. She devoted her life to making sure each of us was happy and healthy despite the hardships that were brought on our family by Dad, the Great Depression and her annual battle with pneumonia. She was a remarkable woman, without doubt the shining light in my childhood.

On 31 October 1923, I became Mum and Dad's seventh child when a midwife delivered me in Ramsay Street in the suburb of Haberfield in Sydney's inner west, almost six years to the day after Dad's close call at Passchendaele. By the time my baby brother Ken was born in 1932 the Chard tribe consisted of (in order) Edna, David (dec. 1932), Myra, Leila (dec. 1918), Herbert Jnr, Jack, me, Ray, Jean

14

and Ken. I still have no idea how my parents managed to feed, clothe and care for us during a time when money and opportunity were hard to come by. While Dad was on a minimal war pension because of his injury, it wasn't enough to cover the cost of raising a large family so he worked as a carpenter. It's a credit to his work ethic that even after a big night of drinking, he always rose bright and early to attend work. As for Mum, with so many children to look after, she never had any time to herself. It helped that she was very resourceful – she could make a nutritious meal that filled all of our bellies with only a few shillings – and she also knew *everything* that was going on in the household.

However, her bitterest blow of all was having to endure – on two terrible occasions – the worst pain that any parent can face. To this day, I still admire her for being able to summon the strength to survive it. My sister Leila, a sister I never met, passed away eight months after her birth in 1918 from an illness my mother could never bring herself to discuss. For better or worse, I was an inquisitive child who wanted to know everything about everything. However, I eventually stopped asking about Leila because, even though it certainly wasn't my intention to upset Mum, and it had been many years since my sister's death when I asked about her, I saw that my questions made Mum's eyes fill with tears.

Unfortunately, Leila's death wasn't the only time my parents needed to cope with the tragedy of burying a child. In February 1930, two burly police officers knocked on the door of our rented home at Beauchamp Street, Marrickville. They arrived just on dusk to notify the family that my oldest brother, 19-year-old David, had been killed earlier that day in a motorcycle accident. The news devastated all of us. Even though I was only seven at the time, I was old enough to feel a sense of waste and loss. While there was a 12-year age gap between Dave and me, he was a terrific big brother; always cheerful and easygoing. He had also become a third-generation carpenter when he followed our grandfather Gilbert Chard and Dad into the trade. It's strange what stays with you throughout your life, because after more than 90 years since that dreadful day, something I clearly recall about Dave is his favourite shirt. It was white with a distinctive blue lining stitched around the collar, and he'd wear it on special occasions, such as when he'd take his sweetheart – a lovely girl named Jean Vincent who lived nearby – out on a date.

Mum always did the best she could to protect me and the other little ones from the bad things that surrounded us, and, needless to say, Dave's death was one of those. However, inquisitive as I was, I managed to piece the story together. In the hours before their accident Dave and his mate, Alfie Dawson [not Davies, as the newspaper reported] – who worked at Dairy Farmers and owned a motorbike – had spent their day off at the beach. During their ride home the driver of a motor car failed to brake in time after the boys came to a lawful halt at a junction in Rockdale, a suburb which was only six lousy kilometres from the safety of our home. Without warning the car ploughed into them, and Dave, who was perched on the back of the motorbike, had no hope of surviving – as the *Sydney Morning Herald* noted in its report on 24 February 1930:

YOUTH KILLED AT ROCKDALE
David Chard, aged 19 years, of Beauchamp St,
Marrickville, while riding pillion on a motorcycle
in Rockdale, on Saturday afternoon, was killed
instantly when the cycle came into collision with
a motor car. The rider of the cycle Alfred Davies [sic]
suffered minor injuries only.

Something those few lines didn't capture was the deep grief that accident caused my entire family, as well as Dave's girlfriend Jean and, of course, Alfie. My mother was an emotional wreck. She cried for months, and yet, despite being overwhelmed by her loss, she somehow managed to rally each day to care for us little ones.

Then, of course, there was the impact the accident had on my father, a man who struggled to show his emotions at the best of times. Sadly, he retreated further into his shell and became even more distant. Dave's death was even tougher on Dad because in the weeks leading up to it he'd been mourning the loss of his own father, Gilbert Henderson Chard, who had passed away at the end of January. He and Dad were very close, and up until my grandfather's death at 84, he'd made the long trip from his place in Sydney's eastern suburbs to visit our home at least once a month. Dad enjoyed having his father around, but I didn't. Actually, it was through Grandpa Gilbert's visits that my father realised that even though I was a painfully shy child, I possessed a stubborn streak that was a few miles wide. You see, whenever my grandfather came to our house he greeted all of us kids in a way that I hated – he kissed us on the cheek! While it was unusual in Australian culture for a man to do that, there was nothing sinister in his actions. He was affectionate and unafraid to express his love for each of his grandchildren with a quick peck on the cheek. While none of my siblings was too bothered by it, the idea of being kissed by my grandfather didn't sit well with me because, due to my shyness, it felt like unwelcome attention. As a result, whenever I heard him knock on our front door I'd bolt into the backyard and climb to the highest branch of our tallest tree! Whenever the old bloke peered out the window to see what I was doing, he must've thought his grandson was part-monkey because rain, hail or shine, I'd sit on that branch for as long as he was inside our place. Of course, Dad knew there was more to it, and throughout my grandfather's visits he'd storm towards the tree scowling that I was acting like a spoilt so-and-so. He'd order me to climb down and do the respectful thing and greet my grandfather – *or else*. Now, if experience had taught me anything it was that Dad wasn't bluffing when he'd threaten that I was going to really 'cop it' later that night. However, belting or no belting, I refused to climb down because there was no way I was going to be kissed!

What I learnt after Dave's – and my grandfather's – passing was that even when people experience the toughest of tragedies, life carries on. Even though Dad probably just wanted to lock himself away in his room to drink and grieve, he still had to rise early to go to work because there were bills to pay. Mum soldiered on heroically, caring for us through thick and thin. However, her sorrow eventually became so profound that she couldn't stay at Beauchamp Street. It was too hard for her to accept that Dave wouldn't be coming home there ever again. This was one occasion when Dad showed his kinder side. He didn't argue or dismiss Mum's plea for us to move into a new home. We simply packed up our belongings and relocated to nearby Francis Street, Marrickville. While it was only a kilometre away from our old place, it gave Mum enough distance to better cope with the despair of burying a second child.

Despite all that was going on at home, life continued much as it always had for seven-year-old me. While my childhood burdens didn't compare to those of my parents, I still dreaded having to attend Marrickville West Public School. From the moment Dad accompanied me on my first day when I was five, I hated the place. Indeed, it took less than five minutes for me to do a runner after Dad introduced himself – and me – to my teacher, the stern-looking Mr Walsh. I followed the other kids as we were ushered into the classroom, took one look at the rows of desks, the blackboard and the teacher's cane resting ominously against the side of his desk, and baulked. That instant confirmed that school wasn't for me, so I leapt to freedom through an open window. I left behind me the din of the kids who cheered me on, and the sound of Mr Walsh's booming voice yelling for me to return to class. I ran so quickly I even beat my father home! However, as you can imagine, he was far from pleased to be greeted by the unexpected sight of me sitting with my arms folded on the kitchen table and grinning from ear to ear. After receiving a solid belting, Dad frogmarched me back to my classroom where an unimpressed-looking Mr Walsh accepted custody of me until 3.05 that afternoon.

Of course, school had its benefits. I made some friends, and I really enjoyed Fridays because that was sports day. Whenever we played cricket, I pretended to be one of my childhood heroes, the great Australian batsman Don Bradman, taking strike against England's fearsome pace attack at the Sydney Cricket Ground; when we played rugby league I imagined I was a member of our local team, the mighty Newtown Bluebags (now Jets), and playing against the likes of the Western Suburbs Magpies, North Sydney Bears, Balmain Tigers and Eastern Suburbs Roosters at Henson Park, their nearby home ground. However, the school day that made the biggest impression on me (apart from my last one when I was 12) was in April 1932, when we kids from Marrickville West Public School were taken on an excursion to walk across the brand new Sydney Harbour Bridge, just a few weeks after it opened on 19 March.

I was hugely excited because I desperately wanted to see the bridge that was described as one of the world's greatest engineering feats. It would also be the furthest I'd been away from home without my parents.

The bridge lived up to all my expectations, and I remember how I stared at it in amazement. When Mr Walsh rattled off a series of facts and figures about 'our' bridge, it was probably the most attentive I'd ever been. I was fascinated to hear the Sydney Harbour Bridge needed 20 years of planning; eight years of building; 95,000 cubic metres of concrete; 17,000 cubic metres of granite; 52,800 tonnes of steelwork and around six million rivets to construct it. I also remember being mesmerised by the sight of the steam trains that crisscrossed its span. In addition, I was in awe of the panorama my schoolmates and I enjoyed as we walked across the bridge. Although we were on the walkway that overlooked the 'working-class' Darling Harbour side of Sydney, and not the 'million-dollar view' which faces where the Opera House now stands on Bennelong Point, it was still wonderful to watch the many boats and ships which made the harbour a busy port. I have no doubt that one of the reasons that day made such an impression on me is because it provided a welcome reprieve from the grim times we were experiencing during the Great Depression.

3

The Hungry Mile

They tramp there in their legions on the mornings dark and cold
To beg the right to slave for bread from Sydney's lords of gold;
They toil and sweat in slavery, 'twould make the devil smile,
To see the Sydney wharfies tramping down the hungry mile.

'The Hungry Mile', Ernest Antony (1930)

At the height of the Great Depression in 1932, I'd some-times be woken by the sound of my father leaving home long before sunrise to start his 11-kilometre journey on my prized Paragon pushbike from Francis Street to the wharves at Hickson Road in East Darling Harbour.

Waterside workers dubbed that part of Sydney 'the Hungry Mile' because it was there where hundreds of unem-ployed men, all desperate for work, crowded around the dockyard gates before dawn to try and get a 'work ticket' – a prized piece of paper that guaranteed the holder a day's wage.

During the dry spells when Dad couldn't get work as a carpenter, he'd stand outside those gates dressed in his collar, tie and vest, hoping he'd be picked for a shift. Occasionally his persistence was rewarded with two consecutive days of work as a labourer, but the downside was it could be many weeks before he'd get another go.

Labouring on the wharves was tough, but Dad was well suited for it. Despite being short in stature and weighing just a shade over eight stone, my father lived up to his middle name of Hercules because, even when he was in his late 70s, he was still as strong as a bloody ox.

Something I didn't ever think about as a child was how difficult it was for men like Dad to get a shift on the Hungry Mile, or what they might have gone through to get a work ticket. However, historians have documented the shoddy way these men were sometimes treated by the more arrogant of the foremen – and it sounds appalling.

Apparently there were occasions when these foremen wouldn't even bother to take the time to select their workers, they'd simply throw fistfuls of job tickets into the air for cheap entertainment and laugh loudly at the sight of the quicker blokes ducking between the legs of others to pick one up off the ground, or at the bolder ones who'd snatch them out of other men's hands. Those who weren't as swift were said to have traded heavy punches and kicks as they brawled among themselves for the paper, looking like wild dogs fighting over a bone.

My father never mentioned experiencing that during his time at the Hungry Mile but, as I've mentioned, he rarely spoke to us about much at all. It is certainly possible he might have found himself having to brawl with other men for work because he had to make money to keep us going.

Dad found 'bits 'n pieces work' to see us through the Depression. For a while he enjoyed solid employment when he worked for my uncle Sydney Strugnell (who'd married Dad's sister Maud in 1906) who owned the Rose Bay Ice Works in the city's eastern suburbs. After a lot of hard work to get established, Uncle Sydney's business boomed and he decided to build a new house that was large enough to park his business's three trucks underneath it.

It was quite a large project, but once the job was finished Dad found himself back in the unemployment queue until he secured 'relief work' in the second half of 1932 as a tradesman with the Public Service. Relief work was a government initiative which allowed people to work for a minimum payment rather than languish in the dole queues. However, while Dad waited for his application to go through, there were many times when his only chance of making some money was to turn up at the Hungry Mile and hope for the best.

I was six years old when the New York Stock Exchange collapsed in 1929, wiping the equivalent of $26 billion off the world's markets. One of the reasons why Australia's financial system crumbled so quickly was because the international demand for our commodities, such as wheat and wool, plummeted in the second half of the 1920s due to competition from Argentina, Canada and the United States.

On top of that, Australia's federal and state governments had incurred an incredible amount of debt with overseas financial institutions, including the Bank of London. They needed that money to finance public works because besides supplying the nation with much-needed infrastructure – including roads and bridges – the public works also provided people with employment. However, when the world's economies slowed down and we couldn't repay our debt, Australians from all walks of life, and of every age, found themselves up the proverbial creek without a paddle.

It was the workers and their families who paid the highest price. While my family faced a never-ending struggle to make ends meet, there were plenty who suffered far worse fates. By 1932 our official national unemployment rate was 32 per cent, one of the highest on earth, making the so-called 'Lucky Country' – as Australia was known – not so lucky. At the height of the Depression, it was estimated that 40,000 men were moving around the bush in search of work. Due to evictions or houses being repossessed by the banks, tin and canvas shanty towns sprang up at such places as 'Happy Valley' on the shores of Botany Bay. The poorest of the poor even tried to subsist in the caves that honeycombed the coastal cliffs south of Sydney. Food was scarce and expensive; over 60,000 men, women and children relied upon the 'susso'; a state-based 'sustenance payment', and soup kitchens were set up in the hardest-hit areas. Suicide rates soared as more and more people saw no other escape from their woes.

My own family's struggle wasn't a reflection of my father's work ethic. While Dad was as moody, hard-drinking and short-tempered as ever during the Great Depression, he was always hunting for work. However, I do know this period in our nation's history left Dad and many other veterans feeling disillusioned. They became even angrier as they were turned down for job after job, because they found their military service – and the politicians' solemn promise that it would never be forgotten – counted for nothing.

In May 1932, Dad applied for a carpenter's job in the public service, but the penpusher who was in charge of employing tradesmen insisted Dad had to contact the Officer in Charge of Military Records to get a copy of his discharge papers. The reason? To prove he really was a returned soldier. Unfortunately for Dad, his original papers had been stolen three years earlier, along with other personal documents, when someone ratted through his coat pockets while he worked on a job site.

However, the bureaucrat would not accept Dad's three medals as proof of his service, nor the Returned from Active Service badge he always had pinned proudly to the lapel of his coat, or even the jagged scar next to his heart. Instead, the man demanded what he called 'proof' that Dad wasn't a fraud. That must've been humiliating for someone who was so proud of his military service, and I imagine the only reason why my father didn't do his block was because he needed a wage to look after his family.

Indeed, his desperation is reflected in the hand-written letter he eventually penned to Military Command when he requested a copy of his lost paperwork. My younger brother Ray discovered the letter a few years ago when he obtained my father's full military record from Canberra. It's because I remember the hardships of the time that I understand the reason for the anxious tone in my dad's note.

Francis Street
Marrickville
Sydney
NSW
27 May 1932

To Officer in Charge,
Dear Sir
Would you be so kind to forward me a statement of my war service as I have put in an application for work in the public service here and they have answered I am not considered a returned soldier until I get this statement from you and also a copy of my discharge as I had my discharge stolen. If you will oblige me in this I will be thankful.
I remain yours,
H.H. Chard
PS my number was 3502A of the 35th Batt.
Left Sydney Jan 1917.

Dad was eventually given relief work by the government not long after the army mailed him a Commonwealth of Australia Statutory Declaration Form which, when signed by a Justice of the Peace, verified that he was a returned veteran. Even though he was paid the bare minimum, Dad was happy to be working. As a matter of fact, I clearly remember the time he was assigned to work for the Department of Education because I received a hell of a fright one morning when I was in my school's playground with some friends.

I heard a worker on the roof of one of the buildings, and he was making an almighty racket as he hammered away.

When I looked up, I almost fell over because there was my father, dressed in his hat, collar, tie, vest and a white apron, and puffing away on his pipe. He hadn't told me he'd been assigned to work at my school, and when I saw him peer down at me from his vantage point, I made a mental note to be on my very best behaviour for Mr Walsh – and anyone else – that particular day.

It's impossible to explain to people who didn't live through that era how tough a time it was. I had no shoes, so I walked barefoot everywhere I went. That was fine in summer, but in winter – when the occasional frost covered the ground – it was terrible. But I wasn't alone, because I still have a school photograph in which the girls in the front row have their feet covered by little pairs of cotton socks, and we boys are all standing behind them, shoeless.

The kids in our neighbourhood who owned one pair of shoes – usually kept for Sunday School – were considered 'lucky'. It didn't matter if their shoes were a size too big for them, or if they had some carefully concealed cardboard covering the holes in their soles, we all considered those children fortunate because at least they owned a pair!

Our clothes were little more than rags, and each of the garments I had were hand-me-downs that'd been put through the wringer by my older brothers. Actually, you didn't really own clothes, you were just using them until you outgrew them and passed them on to your younger siblings. All of the kids I played with also had the holes and rips on their shirts or shorts covered by patches that had been taken from such things as old flour sacks. There was no shame in that, because at that time the people who lived in the house beside you, in front of you, and behind you, were in the same, dirt-poor boat.

During this time of going without and simply making do, my mum always went to great lengths to make each of our Christmas Days during the Great Depression special. We'd wake to find that she'd filled our individual pillowcases with a handful of nuts, some cherries, a small bottle of drink, and an inexpensive toy. We thought it was marvellous, and I don't think you would have found a happier group of children as us while we ate our treats and played with the toy Mum had most likely bought from the Friday night markets that were held every week at the Newtown Tram Sheds.

Food, however, was all anyone thought about because there was never enough. Many families, mine included, were dependent on the state government to supplement our pantry. I was nine years old when Dad assigned me the job of collecting the family's weekly food supplies from the town hall. He took me aside one morning and said: 'Come on, we're going for a walk.' That was always his way of saying there was a special task that he and I needed to do. Every Monday morning before school after that, I joined the droves of people from my neighbourhood who queued outside the Marrickville Town Hall for fruit, vegetables, sugar and vouchers for fresh bread, milk and meat. The quality was excellent; the only problem was that because the government needed to provide for thousands upon thousands of people, they could only offer each family the bare minimum.

Getting to the front of the queue was a slow, long and boring process, but I didn't mind because every minute

I spent there was time I didn't need to spend in the class-room. It could be hours after the 9 am bell before I took my seat in the classroom. However, on the first day I made the mistake of thinking my father and I were working together. But once we reached the front of the line he pocketed his government-issued two ounces of tobacco and took off! He offered me a cursory nod before leaving me on my own to get the food and then drag our supplies home. I can still picture him heading off down the street to search for casual work before meeting up with his mates from the ANZAC Club!

The one thing my father did teach me through this behaviour was to be resourceful. And I'm grateful for it, because at 98 I'm still living independently and I couldn't imagine getting by any other way.

4

The Marrickville Brawler

Most of us, I suppose, will have our regrets; regrets at unavoidable happenings; regrets at things, which we, had we known better, might have avoided. We have made our mistakes, every one of us, else we would not be human . . .
Prime Minister Joseph Lyons's 1934 New Year's Address

When I was 11 years old, I discovered that despite my acute shyness I had a dangerous temper. I'd lost control of my senses when a boy picked a fight with me. While I belted him quite badly, that wasn't the worst of it; I was so enraged by what he'd said to start the punch-up I had no intention of simply ending it with a handshake. Instead, I wanted to throw him from a bridge – one with a 40-foot drop – onto the train lines below . . .

In the winter of 1934, I'd been given a lot more responsibility after my family left Francis Street for our new home at Wardell Road, Dulwich Hill. Dad had called our family physician, Dr Harper, to make a home visit because the onset of the annual illness that had knocked Mum around in previous winters was more severe than ever. When he finished his examination Dr Harper confirmed that Mum had pneumonia and added that her best hope of making a complete recovery from the illness, which had a high mortality rate in the 1930s, was to have complete bed rest and to take two Aspros of a morning.

About five minutes after Dr Harper drove off in his 1927 Chevrolet Tourer to continue his rounds, Dad laid down the law. He said because I was 'responsible', I'd take over the bulk of Mum's household duties until she recovered. Although I'd have some help from my older sisters, who'd married and made their own lives with their husbands, wherever possible, I'd cook; make breakfasts; cut lunches; dust; polish; mop; sweep; wash the clothes; send my school-aged brothers and sisters to school; see my older brother Jack and Dad off to work; and help Mum to look after my infant brother, Ken.

The bad news was, I still had to attend school! And while it didn't take very long for me to get my routine for the housework in order, my schooling remained its usual mess. I was always late to class, and rather than focusing on my algebra and English lessons, my mind was always preoccupied with the never-ending list of jobs that waited for me back at home. One of the reasons I hated being in that classroom was because sitting there stopped me from helping my mother by doing the things she couldn't – although, I did my utmost to be in two places at once.

As soon as the lunch bell sounded I was off like a flash, running the one-and-a-half kilometres to our house to ensure Mum and Ken were okay, and also to get a head start on preparing that night's dinner. After that, I'd race back to school, doing my best not to be late for class. Then, when the final bell sounded at 3.05 pm, I'd dash home again to give the house a quick dust and clean before putting dinner on the stove. It was a regimented routine, but it was one that worked well enough for me to feel as though I was doing a good job of keeping the house running smoothly.

This went on for months, and it was during one of my mad after-school dashes that I came close to throwing a loud-mouthed kid named McIntosh to what would have been his certain death. The crazy thing is that I barely knew him (I can't recall his first name, but I'm certain he was nicknamed 'Hughie' after the old Sydney sports promoter) because he was at least two years older than me and we mixed in different groups. On this particular afternoon I noticed McIntosh was holding court and speaking to a group of girls near the Livingstone Road overbridge which still spans the railway lines. All I wanted to do was get home to do my chores, but McIntosh decided he'd show off to the girls by talking tough and making a disparaging remark about my mother.

'Hey, Chard,' he yelled, with a smug look on his face as I ran past him. 'Your mother's a fucking bitch!' While at least one of the girls giggled at his brazenness, a rage that I'd never before experienced consumed me. My head felt like it was going to explode. I wheeled around and, without saying a word, I knocked the smirk from McIntosh's face with a stiff, straight punch that landed squarely on his chin. If there's a 'violent switch' in the human mind, mine had flicked on, and – except for remembering what I wanted to do to McIntosh to end the fight – I have no idea what happened from that point on. My temper had taken control of my mind, my fists and feet, and I was on a different planet. All I wanted was to punish him for disrespecting my mother.

Something I do remember is that when I had McIntosh backed up against the bridge's fence I grabbed him in a bear hug and started to lift him with the intention of tossing him over the railing – just like a piece of rubbish. He must've realised my plan because I do remember the look I saw in his eyes: it was one of sheer terror. Thankfully for both of us, a man who worked across the road at Cyril Cooper's Milk Depot arrived on the scene at that very moment. I can only suppose he was alerted to the fight by the screams from the girls. However, even though the man was quite strong and he managed to separate us, I continued to lash out at the sore and sorry show-off. The man could tell I was far from finished and he very wisely kept hold of me as McIntosh was given a head start to get home and escape another hiding.

When I finally calmed down, I realised that what I'd intended to do was crazy, not to mention criminal. I felt grateful the man had intervened because if he hadn't, I would most likely have been charged by the police with McIntosh's murder. If the fall hadn't killed him, I have no doubt the train to Bankstown would have finished him off. However, while the Cooper's Milk Depot man had saved me from making a mistake that would've ruined my life before it had even started, I felt no remorse about belting McIntosh because he'd asked for it. While I don't know what became of him in later life, I do remember how, on the few occasions we crossed paths after that fight, he wouldn't even give me as much as a sideways glance.

I had a different reaction, however, after my next blow-up, because that fight was against my brother Jack in the backyard of the family home. When the dust settled I was overcome by both a sense of deep remorse and a terrible realisation. All Jack had done to trigger my temper was take the pedal off my prized Paragon bicycle to use on his without asking me. When I saw what he'd done I went bananas. I grabbed him and pounded him. The rage was exactly the same as I'd experienced when I fought McIntosh; I was so far 'gone' I was oblivious to my actions. In the end it took my father, two brothers and my brother-in-law Clarrie Surridge, who was visiting with Myra, to drag me off Jack. They bundled me into the bathroom to give me time to calm down, but I was far from finished. Before they'd even locked the door I had climbed out of the window and resumed my assault on poor Jack.

When I finally regained my senses, the feeling that consumed me was guilt, sorrow and also a bitter disappointment in myself. Even though Jack was three years older than me we were the best of mates. We did plenty of things together, including riding the 140-kilometre round trip from our home to visit Myra and Clarrie, at their place in Woonona in the Greater Illawarra. We'd ride along Heathcote Road until it joined the Princes Highway. When we reached the Sublime Point Lookout we'd have a break to take in the view before following the Bulli Pass to Myra's place, where we'd stay the night. The other reason

I felt so terrible about the fight was because Jack had a much gentler nature than I did. I know the last thing he would've ever wanted to do was fight anyone, let alone his kid brother.

Surprisingly, my father appeared horrified to see that I'd inherited his temper, and it was almost ironic to hear him shout at the top of his voice for me to 'calm down' and 'stop it' because they were the kinds of pleas we'd all scream to try and pacify him during his violent rages. It speaks volumes for how highly I regarded my mother because when my blood was boiling and I was out of control, she was the only person who could make me calm down. All she ever needed to say to restore peace and order was: 'That's enough of that rubbish.' And that was it.

What hurt most after I attacked Jack was the realisation that of all my father's children it was me who'd inherited his temper. It was a bitter blow because I was determined I'd grow up to be nothing like him. While I couldn't help my genetics, after that episode I worked hard to try and do what I could to avoid blowing up. In my heart I knew my true nature wasn't a violent one because my interests as a boy included growing flowers in the garden, breeding finches in the aviary Dad had built for me, cooking and helping Mum. I also spent time caring for my much-loved little dog, a Pomeranian named Trixie. Whenever one of my older brothers brought home a Buck Rogers comic book, I enjoyed reading those. I knew I wasn't a bad kid, I just had a bad temper when – and if – I was provoked.

There was another reason I knew I wasn't really a vicious little thug. Every week I attended Sunday School at St Clement's Anglican Church, a landmark building on the corner of Petersham and Marrickville Roads. While my motivation for attending the scripture classes had nothing to do with any great interest in religion, my intentions were still pure. Every Friday afternoon Canon Denman, who was in charge of the church, held a race for the parish's children, and the winner won half a pound of chocolate. The only rule of entry for the race – and they were quite strict about enforcing it – was that a child had to have attended the previous week's lesson. I realised early on that it was worth my while to sit in Sunday School for the hour or so it took, because I was much faster than any of the other kids who attended and was always odds-on to take home the chocolate!

The six kilometres I ran to and from school every day when I looked after Mum had helped me develop into quite a handy runner, and that showed whenever Canon Denman or one of his assistants dropped their flag for us to race the 800 metres around the block. I don't want to boast, but with that prize on offer those other kids didn't have a prayer against me. However, I didn't race to win the chocolate for myself, as much as I liked eating it. I received much greater pleasure in taking the prize home and telling Mum it was hers to enjoy.

5

Billy Tea and Fresh Scones

Pass the billy round, my boys,
Don't leave the pintpot stand there
For tonight we drink the health
Of every overlander . . .
'Queensland Drover' aka 'The Overlander'

When I turned 12 it was my father, of all people, who made me the happiest kid in Sydney when he decided my school days were over. Dad made the right call because towards the end of 1935 I was only ever turning up to school once a week – on a Friday. Not surprisingly, Mr Walsh – who taught me in my first and last year of school – was never impressed by my cameo appearance because he knew why I was there, and it had nothing to do with mathematics or English. As soon as he found me at my normally unoccupied desk he'd point at me, and then, with a dramatic loop of his index finger, he would direct me to the door. 'You're only here to play sport, Chard, so wait outside until later.' As I made my way out of the room he'd say: 'And don't you dare disrupt my class!'

The reason I couldn't argue with Mr Walsh about the way in which he dismissed me was simple: he was right. So, I'd leave his classroom quietly and behave myself while I waited outside until I could have some fun with my friends.

Even though Mum had recovered from her bout of pneumonia, most days I stayed at home to help her with the housework instead of going to school. If I had to offer one reason for why I hated school, I'd say it probably stemmed from my shyness. Every day I was there I dreaded the prospect of being called upon to read aloud a passage from a book or to answer a question. Somewhere along the line I'd disconnected with it all because no matter how hard I tried, school wasn't for me. When Dad caught wind of how much time I was spending at home, he chose my 12th birthday – the age at which children could get fulltime employment – to say it was time that I contributed financially to the household. 'If you're going to wag school, you can start work with me on the building site tomorrow as our billy boy,' he said in his typically blunt fashion. 'We have no room for no-hopers in this house.' I knew the jolly swagman from Banjo Paterson's famous ballad 'Waltzing Matilda' sang as he waited for his billy to boil, but I had no idea what a 'billy boy' did.

Even though I was at the dinner table where we children knew to mind our manners and keep any thoughts to ourselves, I'm certain that I whooped loudly from the relief of knowing I didn't have to worry about school anymore.

Dad's decision coincided with Australia's slow but sure recovery from the Great Depression. By 1935, the wheels of industry had started turning again as money and, just as importantly, confidence, was returning to the economy. There were few areas in Sydney that reflected the improvement in the nation's economic health quite like Marrickville, which saw a boom in local industry with more than 130 factories and some woollen mills back in full operation, manufacturing everything from fishing line, pots and pans, boots and shoes, chocolate, radios, heavy-duty machinery, margarine, lawnmowers, and even cast-iron bathtubs. After five years of men and women humbling themselves to get even the most menial jobs to make just a few shillings to get by, there was finally a demand for labour. My older brother Herb followed Dad into carpentry, while Jack was employed as a plumber at the Australian Woollen Mills on Sydenham Road. As for Dad, he secured a fulltime job with one of the district's most respected builders, Bill Drinkwater. I'd find out for myself over the next three years that Mr Drinkwater had earned that respect by doing quality work and having high, but not unrealistic, expectations for his employees. Mr Drinkwater put me on to boil the tea for his team's morning 'smoko' and lunch after Dad asked whether he had any work available for a kid of 12. While the billy boy was the lowest rung on the ladder, I was full of excitement to head off for my first day of work. As we made our way to the building site, Dad ran through what the job involved and what the crew would expect of me. He paused briefly before revealing what he insisted was the most important point of all: 'Just make sure the billy's ready for their morning tea at 10 am and lunch at noon,' he said while puffing on his pipe. 'Remember . . . *10 am and noon . . .* if you're even thirty seconds late the bastards will most likely riot.'

The building site I worked on was also familiar territory. It was a double block in Beauchamp Street, the street where I'd lived for the first seven years of my life. While the men hadn't clocked on when we arrived, it was still a hive of activity as some of them prepared for the day ahead by either mixing the mortar, stacking small piles of bricks, or shifting the lumber to wherever it would be needed. Mr Drinkwater was talking to some of his men when Dad introduced me, and it felt very grown up to have the boss greet me with a firm handshake. Once the formalities were completed he repeated almost word for word what my father had already said about the role, and he, too, emphasised the importance of having the tea ready when the men took their two breaks: 'They get 15 minutes for morning tea, and half an hour for lunch,' he said. 'I'm not joking when I say this to you, young Reg, but they'll be very bloody grumpy if their brew isn't ready on time.' I simply nodded my head to acknowledge that I understood.

One of the men who seemed to understand all there was to know about making a billy of tea said the trick was to make sure the fire was 'red hot'. He advised me to go on a scavenger hunt and find scraps of 'tongue and groove flooring' – cypress pine – because it really burns. And he was right, because once the cypress ignited it was very similar to the fierce heat and flame you get from throwing petrol on a fire. However, after having both

Dad and Mr Drinkwater impress upon me the importance of ensuring the tea was ready bang on time, I spent most of that first morning constantly checking the clock, terrified of what would happen to me if I was as much as three seconds late.

After boiling that first billy can, I relaxed. It was straightforward work, and nowhere near as challenging as the chores I did when I filled in for Mum when she was bedridden. Even so, I took the job seriously, and the men made it known they respected that. It didn't take long for me to realise that I worked with a tremendous crew. They were all good-humoured and, as a shy child, it did wonders for my self-esteem to realise they were happy to have me around – and that helped when it came to being paid, too. Even though I worked on the building site, I wasn't paid directly by Mr Drinkwater. It was up to the men to pay me out of their own pockets for my services, and each individual determined how much they paid me at the end of the week. While some handed me a threepence (three pennies) coin for my efforts, the more generous of them rewarded me with a shilling. Although, it didn't matter how much – or even how little – I made, because all of my earnings went towards our household. And the reason that never worried me was because I was pleased to be able to contribute something.

It was interesting for me to watch Dad as he worked. I believe he was a good carpenter, but I noticed that while some of the other men had a quick joke and a laugh, he just put his head down and went about his business quietly. However, he was very popular with the workers who liked to have a beer, because more often than not, Dad led the charge to the pub to knock over a few 'frosties' after clocking off. He may not have been very sociable on the job, but he was always among the last to leave the pub.

Something I tried to do from my first day as billy boy was to show initiative. After I'd boiled the last billy of the day, I scoured the building site for offcuts of cypress to use to start the following day's fires. Even though I wasn't paid to do it, I'd also do what I could to help tidy up the site by picking up rubbish and by doing any other menial tasks that helped the men, such as stacking bricks. My enthusiasm was rewarded because I eventually received a fulltime job carting bricks. It was hard work, but Mr Drinkwater proved to be as kind as he was tall – he stood well over six foot – because he showed tremendous patience while I developed the strength that was required to move the bricks from one spot to the other. I started out by carrying just one in both hands, and, as I grew stronger, I carried one in each hand. After a while my father made me a V-shaped pod from two pieces of broomstick that allowed for me to cart up to seven in one go.

While moving hundreds of bricks a day was tiring, I enjoyed the three years I worked for Mr Drinkwater. The camaraderie among the team was tremendous, and I liked that we were always busy. However, just after my 15th birthday in 1938, my career path took an unexpected turn when Clarrie Surridge – my brother-in-law who'd helped drag me off Jack when I saw red over my bike's pedal – suggested I visit a former colleague of his from the bakery department at the David Jones department store in the city. The man, Harry Fleming, had opened his own shop along Marrickville Road called the Dundee Cake Shop, and he was looking for an apprentice pastry chef.

Meeting Mr Fleming changed my life. He was a cheery, short, roly-poly Scotsman from the coastal city of Dundee. As much as I hate to say it because it doesn't reflect well on my dad, he actually became more of a father to me than Herbert was. He was nurturing, encouraging, and took an interest in mentoring me about life. Clarrie had said Harry Fleming was a good bloke, and my first impression when we met at his store was that Mr Fleming would be hard not to like. He had a great sense of humour, but the one thing about him that took me aback was that he swore like a trooper. When my job interview began, one of the first questions he asked was what I did at home. I noticed he seemed to give a slight grin of approval when he heard that I helped Mum around the house and that I also really enjoyed cooking. In between expletives he explained that it was a six-day-a-week job from Monday to Saturday; the starting time was 4 am, and the apprentice was expected – among other things – to scrub the utensils, clean all of the bowls, mix the ingredients, prepare the fruit and vegetables that would be used in the baked goods, and, on occasion, bake some items. In return, Mr Fleming said he would teach his apprentice all he knew about the trade, as well as sharing the recipes and methods used to cook a variety of cakes, pies and pastries. In his next breath, he said the apprenticeship was mine if I wanted it, and that I could start the following morning – at 4 am . . .

At 3.30 am the next morning I pedalled my bike down Marrickville Road, immaculately dressed in my pristine white shoes, white trousers, a white shirt, and wearing a white baker's skullcap that my parents helped me to pay off over a number of weeks. As soon as I stepped into the baking room, I was warmly greeted by Mr Fleming, who was holding a tray of eight freshly baked apple pies – and they smelt delicious. After saying 'Good morning, young Reg,' he asked if I was ready to start work – and I remember nodding enthusiastically in reply. Mr Fleming then said something else and his accent was so thick that I couldn't understand a single word. I must've looked like a stunned mullet as my new boss repeated the instruction two or three more times, becoming ever more frustrated the longer I stood there looking bewildered. I finally piped up: 'I'm sorry, I can't understand you.' Well, he wasn't happy! He was still holding the pies and I watched as he lifted his arms back and threw all eight apple pies at me! However, the only words that I understood as the pies flew across the room were the expletives! I quickly apologised, saying that I didn't mean to offend him by saying I couldn't understand him. I think Mr Fleming could tell I was being sincere because after that he made the effort to slow down and speak more clearly whenever he spoke to me.

That was the only misunderstanding between us, and as the months went by Harry Fleming not only lived up to his promise that he'd teach me the secrets of the baking and pastry trade, but he also taught me a lot about life away from the ovens. It was through him that I realised how important it is for a boy to have a father figure in his life.

6

Beautiful Betty Banham

No sooner met but they looked; no sooner looked but they loved . . .

William Shakespeare, As You Like It

One afternoon in the early months of 1939, I was sitting on the veranda with Mum when a girl zoomed past our house on her Speedwell pushbike in a blur of curls and colour. I was so taken by her – she was beautiful – that my reflex action was to blurt loudly enough for my mother to hear: 'Gee, she's a nice-looking girl.' A few days later, at around the same time, she rode past us again, and after watching her disappear down towards the Wardell Road shops, I turned to Mum and said: 'I'm going to marry that girl.' While I'd never been more deadly serious about anything in my life, my mother's reaction was to roll her eyes and laugh before saying: 'Stop talking rubbish and get inside, you bloody idiot.' However, I meant every word of it. I *was* going to marry that girl; my first task was the minor matter of finding out who she was.

Our next-door neighbour was a fellow who my father called 'Noggin'. They worked on Bill Drinkwater's building sites together where Noggin's job was to nail down the floors. Noggin had a daughter named Dorrie, and while she was a likeable girl, she could talk the leg off a chair! One evening after I'd returned home from a long shift at the Dundee Cake Shop, Dorrie bailed me up to ask whether I was free that weekend to catch the ferry to Manly with her and another girl. She didn't say much about her friend except that I'd probably get along well with her. Even though I was fast approaching 16 and had been working alongside adults for almost four years, I remained terribly shy. However, on this particular day, I surprised myself by replying to her invitation with a slight shrug of my shoulders and the words: 'Why not!' I figured that even if things with Dorrie's friend went badly I'd still enjoy the outing.

In the 1930s Manly was one of Sydney's most popular seaside resorts. The Port Jackson and Manly Steamship Company, which owned the ferries *South Steyne*, *Dee Why* and *Curl Curl* that transported daytrippers from Circular Quay to Manly, captured the spirit of the place through their famous advertising slogan: 'Seven miles from Sydney and a thousand miles from care'. Manly was a place where people escaped the everyday grind because it boasted all manner of amusements including aquariums, fairgrounds, a miniature train, dance halls, merry-go-rounds, and a giant water slide into the free harbourside pool which was protected by a shark-proof net. However, when the day arrived I hardly took any notice of those attractions, because before we caught the train from Dulwich Hill station, Dorrie introduced me to her friend, Betty Banham – and my heart skipped a couple of beats. She was the girl on the bike; the girl I'd told Mum I'd marry one day! Thankfully, it took only a few moments for me to realise she was as gorgeous as I'd imagined. We were so comfortable in one another's company that by the time the *South Steyne* docked at Manly Wharf we'd hatched our plan to give Dorrie and the fellow that she was with the slip so we could be by ourselves. While it later took my usually talkative next-door neighbour some time to come around, she eventually understood the reason for Betty's and my apparent snub!

Money was still tight in those days because the main dough an apprentice pastry chef made was whatever they rolled for cakes and bread. Nevertheless, Betty and I still had a marvellous time that day at Manly, strolling along the harbourside promenade and then crossing through the Corso to admire the Pacific Ocean. I remember shaking my head in disbelief at the sight of the boys who were crazy enough to surf what I thought were towering waves on their longboards.

I learnt a lot about Betty during that day out. I found out that like mine, her father was a carpenter. She had an older brother named Jack who was a fitter and turner, and another called Bruce who was around my age, and while he was a quiet bloke, he was a heavy smoker. There was also a younger sister named Beryl. Betty worked on the counter for Alfred Saunders, a well-known clock and jewellery maker whose shop was on George Street opposite Railway Square. It was famous for its window display because it was crammed with all sorts of treasures and riches from around the world. However, it felt to me as though Betty was sharing a secret she hadn't told anyone else when she admitted she hated the job. When I asked why she didn't just leave, Betty said that was hard because her father knew one of the bosses at Saunders.

We saw a lot of each other in the weeks that followed our trip to Manly. While we went to the movies on a Saturday night at the Hoyts De Luxe Theatre on Illawarra Road, my tight finances meant that most of our time together was spent doing what most other people did in those days: going for walks or taking long pushbike rides. Sometimes we'd head to Centennial Park on the other side of the city, or we'd pedal the 32-kilometre round trip to Bondi. On those days, even if it was sweltering, nothing on earth could tempt me to dive into the surf because as a non-swimmer I knew I'd sink like a lump of lead.

It was a common practice during this era for men to buy their girlfriend or wife a corsage of frangipani for one shilling and sixpence — about 15 cents in today's money. Betty would proudly pin her corsage to her dress, and it wasn't long before that became our special thing. Indeed, when I returned from New Guinea in 1942 I smiled to see that in the stack of mail that had accumulated for me while I was fighting in the jungle, Betty had sent a copy of the portrait she posed for at Sidney Riley Studio in Marrickville. It pleased me to see she wore a corsage of frangipani pinned to her dress because I knew that was her way of letting me know that she loved and missed me.

Even though I was comfortable enough in Betty's company to talk about things I'd never before shared with anyone else, I hadn't completely overcome my shyness, especially when it came to the delicate matter of saying 'good night' after we'd been out. No matter how much I wanted to, I was just too terrified to try and kiss her! However, even in the early days of our relationship, Betty knew how to make me get over myself. One Saturday night after we saw a movie I walked her to the front door of her family's house as usual. After saying 'good night' I turned to head home – but by now Betty must have been tired of my being as slow as a wet week to pick up on her signals. As I started to walk away, I heard her say something that stopped me dead in my tracks. 'Reg,' she said. 'If you don't kiss me good night, I'll find someone who will!' With that threat hanging over my head, Betty and I shared our first kiss! And, yes, I've never forgotten either it or the fireworks that exploded in my head and seemed to light up the Dulwich Hill night sky . . .

From that night on I proudly introduced Betty as 'my girlfriend' to everyone. Mum, who hadn't forgotten my vow to marry 'that girl' after I watched her ride past our house, adored her; my siblings thought the world of her, and even Dad said he thought Betty was lovely! Mr and Mrs Fleming were so taken with her that they insisted she drop into the shop anytime to get a (free) cake for her morning tea. I was also pleased that her father, Eric, who everyone knew as 'Ike', and Mrs Banham approved of us going out together. Mr Banham had a less complicated disposition than my father. He was quite bright and cheery, and I always suspected that was a result of his being too young to fight in the Great War. Betty's mother was happy that I had no interest in drinking alcohol because she had been brought up in the pub her parents owned in the New South Wales town of Orange until she was married. I can only imagine that she saw the terrible things people are capable of while under the influence of grog because she loathed it as much as I did.

That period was a very special time in my life for so many reasons. Besides it being the beginning of my life with Betty, everything was going well for me on the work front. After working at the Dundee for more than a year my responsibilities increased, and one of my most important duties was being in charge of firing up the shop's ovens at 4 am. The ovens were manufactured at nearby Petersham by a bakery engineer and machine merchant called Brown & Kidd. They operated in a similar manner to a steam loco-motive because you built the heat up by feeding the fire with coke (coal). It normally took 45 minutes to have the fires roaring, and once they were ready, I'd go to the flat above the shop where Mr Fleming and his family lived to wake him up. The first words that came out of his mouth when I shook him awake were: 'Ah, is the oven already ready, Reg?' Something else that meant a lot to me was that the trust the Flemings placed in me went well beyond work, because whenever they went out with their Scottish friends I'd babysit their two toddlers, Jean – who was named after her mother – and Bruce.

There were three other cake shops along Marrickville Road – Kewpie's, Sargent's and, near where the trams turned left to head towards the city, Len Storey's shop. Of all his competitors Len was Harry's greatest rival, and it was funny to watch them interact because while they were cordial to one another at the numerous trade shows they attended, there was no love lost between them in business or in life. Len spent far too much time wondering why Harry's business had flourished when the reason people lined up outside the Dundee's door was straightforward: it was due to the blue-ribbon quality of Mr Fleming's food. Throughout my apprenticeship he emphasised that I was only to use fresh ingredients, and I noticed that the fillings he used in his pastries – whether it was cream for the cakes, jam for the tarts, or the beef in his pies – was always the best available.

His pies became so popular that scores of people would wait in his shop while they cooked, although I often wondered if those customers were also there for the panto-mime show Mr and Mrs Fleming would unwittingly put on. With the store overflowing with hungry patrons, Mrs Fleming would stand at the door and sing out in her distinctive Scottish accent: 'Harry, how long the pies?' Without fail he'd reply with the same response every time: 'The pies aren't long, Jean, they're *fucking* round! Ten more minutes.' As he went back to the business of baking them I'd quietly say, 'Mr Fleming, you're swearing again,' and I'd watch as he'd drop his head in what was mock disappoint-ment with himself and moan: 'Why, Reg, *why* didn't you tell me?'

The couple had another funny ritual at the end of each day which always made me grin. Harry would hand me a bag full of pies in a manner that suggested they were a stash of priceless diamonds. As I took them he'd say in a hoarse whisper: 'Don't tell Jean.' Then, when I went to the front of the store to bid Mrs Fleming good night she'd have a quick look behind me before pressing a bag of pastries into my hands while saying quietly: 'Give these to your mother, Reg, but don't tell Harry!'

While this was a joyful and fulfilling time in my life, I was naïve because I thought the feeling that had enveloped Betty and me as we experienced the wonder and adventure of falling in love was bigger than anything else in the world. Of course, it was a different story elsewhere. Ominous clouds were forming on the horizon as military aggression from Germany in Europe, Italy in North Africa, and Japan in South-East Asia again put the world on a war footing. It soon became obvious the desperate diplomacy missions by politicians from Great Britain and the United States appeared doomed to fail in changing the destructive course that had been set.

7

A Melancholy Duty

May God in His mercy and compassion grant that the world may soon be delivered from this agony.
Prime Minister Robert Menzies
on declaring war on Germany

Most people remember where they were when the major world events of their lifetime occurred. Indeed, I have no problem recalling where I was at 9.15 pm on 3 September 1939, the night Prime Minister Robert Menzies declared war on Germany. I was tucked under my bedcovers and sound asleep! As Menzies told his 'fellow Australians' of his 'melancholy duty' to commit yet another generation of young men to fight – and possibly die – on foreign soil, members of my family sat in the living room and listened to our radio set with a sense of what was almost disbelief. The reason why I slept through one of the most notable speeches in the country's history was because it was a work night, and I needed to be awake by 3 am to report for duty at the shop. It's also interesting to think that despite the gravity of the news, neither of my parents woke me to listen to it. I suppose they were happy for me to be one of the few people in Australia who'd enjoy a peaceful sleep that night.

Menzies joined Great Britain in declaring a 'state of war' with Germany when the Nazi leader Adolf Hitler refused to withdraw his force that had invaded Poland two days earlier. When Mr Fleming told me the next morning that we were at war, the news didn't come as a complete surprise. In the weeks leading up to the declaration, most of the city's newspapers had carried cables from their overseas correspondents indicating that a showdown was inevitable. Nevertheless, it hit me quite hard to hear Mr Fleming speak about the challenging times that were ahead, and also of the grave concern he had for the safety of his family in Scotland. He said it made him feel sick to the stomach to think about what would happen to his relatives in the British Isles if Germany somehow succeeded in doing the unthinkable and conquered them. I remember that Monday as among the most solemn of all the days I ever worked at the cake shop.

Even though Menzies didn't discuss his decision with Parliament, let alone debate his decision with the Opposition, most of the Australian population supported his call to arms. The reason why it was so willingly accepted was because Aussies were a different people back in those days. Many considered themselves British subjects, although I certainly wasn't among their number. Even from a young age I was always first and foremost a proud Australian. However, I concede that as a nation we gripped tightly to the ties that bound us to the 'Motherland'. As descendants of the 'Brits' we cherished the Royal family, the Westminster system of parliament, and all other elements of their civilisation. It was due to that sentiment that Menzies, who was a living and breathing example of the old saying 'he's British to his bootstraps', knew that regardless of the cost to them, Australians would stand by Britain in its hour of need. Indeed, he made that clear when he said in his speech: 'I know that in spite of the emotions we are all feeling, you will show that Australia is ready to see it through.'

It is probably obvious that I was not a fan of Menzies, and I don't mind admitting I've judged his two stints as our nation's leader quite harshly. Of all his decisions, the one that infuriated me most was his ignoring sound advice about selling pig iron (scrap metal) to the Japanese in the late 1930s. At the time, Japan was involved in a terrible war with the Chinese – hundreds of thousands of Chinese people died – and there was a growing concern that Australia's shipments of metal would be used by Japan to manufacture weapons and munitions. Even the waterside workers realised it, and they refused to load the Japanese vessels that were transporting the stuff back to their munitions factories. Even when Menzies' own military advisors warned him that it was likely Japan would one day attack Australians with the bombs made from our own metal, Menzies did not act. The one concession I'll give 'Pig Iron' Bob is that I don't doubt he meant these words when he declared war: 'No harder task can fall to the lot of a democratic leader than to make such an announcement.' So, while I'll never be accused of being a supporter of Menzies the politician, I wouldn't wish on anyone a responsibility as dreadful as sending other people's sons and daughters off to fight in a war.

In the days that followed the declaration, there were scores of old-timers from World War I who confidently predicted that 'the show' would be over long before the Australians even arrived. Nevertheless, there was no shortage of men from Marrickville and Dulwich Hill who travelled to Victoria Barracks in Paddington to volunteer for the 2nd Australian Imperial Force. Among the first wave of recruits were men aged in their mid- to late 20s who'd struggled since the Great Depression because they were members of the long-term unemployed. Regardless of what they may have thought of actually fighting the Germans, I don't doubt many viewed the promise of three square meals a day, a regular pay packet, plus having their dependants cared for by the authorities should anything bad happen to them, as the best deal to fall into their laps in quite a long time. Among the first diggers to leave for overseas were three men who lived near us at our old house in Francis Street. They were assigned to what would become the famous 6th Division, the men who, in January 1941, provided Britain with its first victory of the war when they routed the Italians during the Battle of Bardia, in Libya. The Aussies captured 40,000 prisoners of war there, but it came at a price. Tragically, two of those three men never returned to Marrickville.

It was plain to see that Mum was terrified by the prospect of her sons being dragged into the fight. She knew only too well that if the war didn't kill soldiers, it could still destroy those who survived. Knowing Mum, she would've lain awake at night tortured by terrible thoughts of what awaited Herb, Jack and possibly me on the battlefield if the war didn't end quickly. It was a small mercy Mum didn't have to worry so much about Ray or Ken being called upon to serve because they were aged 15 and nine respectively. As for Dad, he may have brooded more than usual, but he still didn't talk much about his own experiences at the front, or even his thoughts on what was happening around him. However, he told me later as my 18th birthday approached that he'd sign my papers for me if I wanted to fight! I think he suggested that because I was underage, and he thought I might get it in my head to try to join up under an alias if I couldn't obtain his consent. Of course, Betty was worried that I'd want to fight, and even though I was a month away from my 16th birthday when war was declared – and still four years too young to be eligible – she told me not to join. She needn't have worried herself because the last thing I planned to do was leave her. I was too deeply in love and happy with my life to exchange my time with her for an army uniform.

However, my eldest brother Herb joined the queue of volunteers. He and Jack were members of the pre-war Militia, which became known as the 'Army Reserve' in 1980. However, and I do say this respectfully, for anyone to consider Herb, Jack and their mates hardened soldiers based on their limited training would be as sensible as entering a nag used to plough the back paddock into the Melbourne Cup. Ironically, though, it was probably my eldest brother's desire to risk his neck on the frontline that actually saved it.

In the early days of the war Australia's military was quite strict about the medical and health criteria it had set for volunteers to be passed fit enough to join the army. They only wanted the cream of the available men, and the doctors ran a fine-tooth comb over each recruit. Eventually, as the war took its toll and the military needed to push more men to the front, they dropped their standards, and dramatically in some cases. Herb passed all the tests, but his first few weeks of army training were plagued by constant bouts of sickness. The army doctors couldn't work out what was wrong, so they sent him to a specialist named Dr Fervour, and the diagnosis wasn't good. Herb had stomach cancer. Not only was he declared unfit for military service, Dr Fervour decided to operate immediately. Before performing the surgery the doctor told my mother and Herb's wife Dorothy – or 'Dot' – that he wouldn't know the full extent of the cancer until Herb was opened up. After a long wait, a nurse was finally sent from the theatre and she advised Dot and Mum that Dr Fervour had two courses of action available to save Herb's life. The first was cutting out his bowel, but that meant Herb would require a colostomy bag for the rest of his life. The second option was far more complicated, and while I don't remember the exact details it posed a serious risk to Herb's life. Both women needed little time to agree upon the safer of the choices. To our great relief, the procedure was successful. While Herb needed the colostomy bag for the rest of his life, it didn't hold him back in any way. He and Dot enjoyed a long life together. An interesting sidelight to Herb and Dot's story is that her father, Frank Leonard, became a local celebrity during the 1930s when he wrote the 'Aeroplane Jelly Song' that's still used to this day.

Despite everything that was happening in the world around me – German troops marching virtually unopposed through Poland, Mr Fleming's fears for his family in Scotland, Herb's terrible battle with cancer, as well as watching more and more men from our neighbourhood leaving to join the army – my life remained much the same. You could have been forgiven for thinking there wasn't even a war on. It was the same in England; because nothing had happened since Poland was invaded on 1 September, people were apparently lulled into such a false sense of security that the children who were evacuated from major cities such as London to the countryside started to return to their families. However, after eight months of the inactivity the Brits called 'the Phoney War', everything exploded. In April 1940, countries began to fall to Germany like dominoes: Denmark, Norway, Belgium, the Netherlands, Luxembourg and France were overrun when the Germans unleashed their frightening *Blitzkrieg* – or lightning war – tactics. Without question, the most morale-shattering moment for the British Empire during the spring of 1940 was the news that over 300,000 British, French, Canadian and Belgian troops needed to be evacuated from Dunkirk in northern France after retreating to escape what would have been a rout. The war was now a deadly serious business, and all of those people who'd predicted Germany would be easily subdued suddenly had second thoughts. However, Australia would eventually face challenges of its own when we were forced to stand alone against a savage foe to our north.

It would be a time when men and women would need to put their own interests aside and make tough decisions, including whether they were prepared to defend Australia to their death. While I was not scared to do that, the thought of telling Betty of the plans I was starting to consider terrified me.

8

The Toughest Talk

SPIRIT OF AIF TO WIN AGAIN
'Out of the jaws of defeat, the AIF
once before plucked victory. We beat
the Germans and we shall beat them
again,' said the Minister for the Navy
(Mr Hughes) in a fighting speech at the
Legacy Club Luncheon to-day.
Faux text on 1940 Australian Army recruitment poster

A few weeks before I celebrated my 18th birthday on 31 October 1941, Betty and I went to watch the Saturday night movie at the Hoyts De Luxe Theatre at Marrickville – and to this day I have no idea of the name of the film we saw, let alone what it was about. While Betty seemed to thoroughly enjoy it, I sat through that film with my mind in a tangle. It was impossible for me to relax because I was agonising over how to tell the girl I loved that I planned to leave her behind for God only knew how long to fight in a war that wasn't going in Britain's favour.

In 1940, Australians could serve in three branches of the army. The lowest rung was a national Home Guard, which I joined when I turned 17. For months I drilled every Friday night alongside a collection of kids who, like me, were too young to enlist and men who were deemed by the government to be too long in the tooth to serve overseas. They were a bunch of decent blokes who just wanted to do their bit if ever they were needed. While I never pretended to know much about the military, I was certain that the training we did under the watchful eye of our ancient sergeant was nowhere near enough to prepare any of us for the business of fighting – and defeating – Hitler's crack units.

The second branch was the Citizen's Military Force (CMF). This was what Herb and Jack joined before the war, and besides attending the Addison Road Drill Hall in Marrickville every Thursday night they also spent one weekend away each month at the army camp at Singleton, near Newcastle. During the war it was simply called 'the Militia', but due to government legislation, members of this force could not serve outside Australian territory. There were two ways to join the CMF during the war: by volunteering or through being conscripted by the government. While I volunteered, the government forced many men into khaki.

The third arm was the Australian Imperial Force (AIF) – the nation's all-volunteer force. These were the 'glamour boys' – the heroes of Bardia, Tobruk and El Alamein. They were regaled in the newspapers as the 'sons' of the original AIF that distinguished itself so well in World War I, and cables from overseas regularly celebrated both their fighting prowess and their 'high spirits' while on leave in Cairo, Jerusalem, Damascus, and other ancient Middle Eastern cities where they were based.

I was stunned the day Jack returned home dressed in the uniform and slouch hat of the AIF's 2/3rd Pioneer Battalion. The reason was because he'd said nothing about volunteering to fight overseas when he left for work that morning. I hadn't really thought too much about joining the army until that day, but from that moment I devoted myself to following my brother's lead. I joined the Home Guard and went overnight from being a carefree 17-year-old who was madly in love with the girl of his dreams to a would-be recruit whose sole focus in life was to get overseas and get stuck into whoever I came across first, the German Afrika Korps, or their allies, the Italians. I didn't care which army it was, I just wanted to fight them.

Whenever I thought of Jack becoming a soldier I'd tell myself: 'If he's going, I'll join him.' Even though I'd foolishly lost my temper with him that time he took a pedal from my bike, we remained close and I would've done anything for him. The last thing I wanted was for Jack to march off to war on his own. I was, however, still too young to enlist officially in the AIF, whose lower age limit was 19 in 1941. (It had been 20 when war broke out in 1939, and was lowered again to 18 in 1943.) Once I turned 18, I was eligible for the Militia, and I figured once I was accepted I'd transfer to the AIF so I could fight alongside Jack.

I took a keener interest in the news from the front, and surprisingly enough, I also noticed for the first time the number of recruitment posters the government had plastered in public places – there were thousands of them. Of course, they were propaganda in its most basic form, and their purpose was simple: to compel all able-bodied men to drop everything in their life and fight. The posters portrayed the soldiers as the most masculine of men with big chests, square jaws, broad shoulders, and women hanging off their arms. They were seen as the pride of a grateful nation. While they also had any number of slogans printed on them, the poster that rang home to me simply said: *JOIN THE AIF – THIS IS SERIOUS!*

However, if a would-be soldier's bravery was measured by how willing he was to have a tough conversation with his girlfriend, I'd have failed the test miserably. I was confused by my reluctance to tell Betty. After all, we'd never kept any secrets from one another, and the reason we were so close was because we could speak openly about everything and anything. However, the idea of me telling her I planned to enlist was incredibly tough; without a doubt it was the hardest thing I'd needed to do up until that point of my life. Later, with the clarity that hindsight brings, I didn't need to scratch the surface too deeply to understand why it was so difficult. I knew that no matter how I worded it, my message was going to hurt her terribly. I just didn't want to break Betty's heart. Even though I had so much conflict whirling around my head as I sat in the cinema, I sneaked a few peeks at Betty as she watched the flick. When I saw her face illuminated by the glow from the silver screen, I was, yet again, struck by just how beautiful she was. However, in the next instant, when I realised what the coming talk would do to her, I felt a pang of . . . well, I don't exactly know what it was: sorrow? Heartache? Remorse? The need for Betty to forgive me? Whatever the feeling, it stabbed me violently in the chest.

I continued to rehearse 'the talk' in my mind, drawing inspiration by thinking of the thousands of other men and women in the forces who'd already had the same difficult conversation with their sweetheart. The movie dragged on and on, but I told myself that was good because it gave me extra time to think about some other things I could tell Betty when she'd ask me to explain why I felt the need to fight. I made a mental list: London had been reduced to rubble by the German *Luftwaffe* (its air force) during the Blitz; the brave little island of Malta threatened to sink beneath the Mediterranean Sea after being targeted for constant bombing raids by Hitler's warplanes; Australian troops were among those holed up, like rats, in a Libyan coastal fortress called Tobruk, while almost 20,000 ANZAC troops had been taken prisoner in Greece and Crete. I supposed that I could also add that Australia was involved in a war that needed to be won despite the costs, and to achieve that victory it was up to all people – including me – to do our bit. Of course, I realised that my signing up as just one man wasn't going to change anything, but I figured if thousands of us did, together we could make one hell of a difference to stop Hitler's wickedness and hatefulness from conquering the world. I'd also tell Betty that once peace was won, we could get married and raise our family in a world that was free of such an evil as the Nazi threat . . .

When the movie finally ended, Betty and I held hands as we walked along Marrickville Road towards home. It was a typically busy Saturday night with the shops and cafés doing a roaring trade, but every time I passed a soldier or sailor – and there were lots of them on leave at that time – the voice in my head that was demanding that I tell Betty what was on my mind became even more strident. Finally, as we walked past Marrickville Town Hall I thought, *It's now or never*, and I heard my voice say Betty's name aloud before blurting out: 'I'm thinking of joining the army.' Betty always read me like a book, and I should've realised she'd been anticipating this moment for quite some time. Instead of appearing even the slightest bit shocked, she replied with a logical question. She asked me why I couldn't wait until my apprenticeship finished because, as she rightly pointed out, I only had six months to go before I had a trade under my belt. The answer I gave implies plenty, but it mostly suggests I was a young kid who was a tad too eager to enter the fight. It was also the most honest response I could give her at that moment. I said, 'I don't know, Betty; we might all be dead by then . . .'

Talk about a poor choice of words! The temperature under the light on that street corner instantly plummeted to minus 50 degrees. My answer left poor Betty feeling mortified, and I sensed it. She realised my view of our immediate future was poles apart from what she'd pictured. However, I also think that was the moment when Betty realised I couldn't – or wouldn't – be swayed from the idea I had of fulfilling my 'soldierly duty'. Rather than implore me not to join, or threaten to break up with me if I did,

Betty made only one request, and it knocked the wind out of me: 'If you're going to join the army, Reg,' she said with tears welling in her eyes, 'I'd like to get married before you go away.'

I didn't know where to look, and my throat felt unusually dry. However, incredibly enough, it was my father, of all people, who had helped prepare my response to that very question when I'd discussed my plan with him and Mum the previous night. I'd carefully considered every word with the same intensity as a man stuck in a minefield sweating over every step he took. I knew I was in danger of deeply hurting Betty, but, as was the way of that night, it took only the first few words for me to stuff it up completely. I started my reply by saying I'd already spoken to Dad about us. Upon the mention of him Betty put her hands on her hips and asked quite pointedly: 'And what did he have to say?' Betty knew the kind of man my father was. However, when it came to Betty, my father had all the time in the world. He knew she was special, and that view was certainly reflected in the advice he'd given me the previous night. I should add that his view on the unfairness – and dangers – of wartime marriages was one of the only good pieces of advice my father shared with me.

'Betty,' I said, trying to redeem myself, 'Dad has warned me that my life is most likely going to be spoiled one way or another by fighting in this war. Dad says you're "soft" – which you are, and as you know – so he's not having a go at you. He said if something happened to me while I was fighting, and if you had a child on the way, your life would be ruined. He said it'd be destroyed, Betty, because he says you're not the sort of person who'd grab somebody else. And, you know what? I believe that, too . . . I know my father's right.'

While Dad's words were a compliment to the esteem in which he actually held Betty, nothing I said from that point, not even my stuttering some of the lines I'd rehearsed ad nauseum in the Hoyts De Luxe, could rescue me from the hole I'd dug for myself. I swore to Betty we'd be married the moment I returned, and while I had never spoken a greater truth in all of my 18 years, she was still fuming when I walked her to the front door of her home. I'm quite certain it was the first − and only − time she slammed the door shut on me.

Something that would undoubtedly have played on Betty's mind that night was that she knew through her younger sister, Beryl, that local men were being killed and maimed in the fighting. Beryl was employed by the General Post Office, and her job was to deliver telegrams to the next of kin of those men who'd been either killed, wounded, or taken prisoner of war. It was by no means an easy job for a girl so young, because Beryl carried with her the heaviest of burdens every time she pedalled off on her bike to inform the young wife or the parents of a fallen soldier's fate. Sometimes she'd sit with them and do her best to comfort them despite having no idea of what to say. However, it didn't help my cause at all that she'd told Betty how those poor women broke down. It appeared to Beryl as though their own lives had also ended.

Now that Betty was aware of my plan, the next person I needed to inform was Mr Fleming, who by now felt like the father I should have had. I'd hoped that task might have been easier than talking to Betty, but it proved to be another hard and terrible conversation. It cut me deeply to see Harry's reaction. Over the three-and-a-half years I'd worked for Mr Fleming we'd taken to breaking up our routine of working from sunrise until late afternoon six days a week by picking an occasional Sunday to go rabbiting at Ingleburn, a Sydney suburb on the banks of the Georges River. I considered those 80-kilometre round trips in Mr Fleming's car to be very special. We spent the time talking about how things were going in my life, his stories of growing up in Scotland, and also any Dundee Cake Shop business that might make us laugh – including my first day of work when he threw the tray of apple pies at me! The interest Mr Fleming had showed in me from the beginning was what underpinned the bond I enjoyed with him. He listened to what I said and his advice was never judgemental or critical. It meant the world to me that I knew his responses came from a good place in his heart, even if I didn't always agree with him.

The first time we went to Ingleburn in 1939 I would've sworn we were in the middle of Burke and Wills–like bush. However, by 1941 the war had changed so much of the world, and not even the tranquil forests of tall eucalyptus trees in that remote part of Sydney could escape its destructive reach. The Ingleburn Military Camp was constructed in 1940 after the Commonwealth Government acquired 684 acres, almost three square kilometres, of land. The bush that had once teemed with rabbits – and was invaded each summer by squadrons of cicadas that made a deafening racket whenever they hummed – was now overrun by battalions of soldiers and their noisy weapons of war. Fortunately for us, there was still enough unadulterated bush in the area for a baker and his young apprentice to go rabbiting, and so I had decided to break the news to Mr Fleming on one such trip.

On the day in question, I wrestled with exactly the same nerves that had plagued me as I'd worked up the courage to tell Betty. I didn't want to disappoint Mr Fleming because he'd been such a wonderful mentor and staunch friend to me for almost four years. Of course, I knew he needed to know about my decision to join the army because my departure would affect his business.

'Mr Fleming,' I said, spitting the words out as fast as a machine gun, 'I want you to know that I'm going to join up.'

'*YOU'RE WHAT?!*' he said in a voice that boomed so loudly it must have made any rabbits within a five-kilometre radius run for their lives.

'I'm going to join up. You know my brother Jack has enlisted . . . and I think it's high time I did, too.'

It's fair to say Mr Fleming was aghast. He tried his best to dissuade me, pointing out that I was only 18 and not old enough yet to enlist in the AIF. He reminded me, as Betty had, that I only had six months to go before I finished my apprenticeship, which would give me a trade to come back to. He asked me to at least consider what he and Betty had to say, as they had my best interests at heart.

Mr Fleming's concern made a deep impression on me, but I stuck to my guns. I was determined to do my bit.

Something I vividly recall is how deathly quiet that car trip home from Ingleburn was. Normally we'd laugh about that one rabbit that invariably escaped, but on that trip Mr Fleming wasn't in a talkative mood. As I sat there looking out the window, I realised his silence wasn't born of anger, or even any disappointment he might have felt in knowing I wanted to break my apprenticeship after all those years and all the knowledge he'd instilled in me. Instead, I knew his silence was because he was concerned about my welfare. It upset him to think I was willing to risk my life fighting in a war thousands of miles from home when he believed I had no need to. While Mr Fleming had been too young to fight in World War I, he had friends back in Dundee whose lives reflected how war kills dreams and can break even the strongest of men. I politely listened to him as he spoke about those friends who were now little more than zombies, but I already knew for myself the price men could pay for fighting in a war; I saw it in my father's eyes every day. In spite of all this, in my mind I was already headed overseas on a troopship, and Harry's heart-felt appeal for me to 'stay and wait' had no hope of swaying my conviction.

While it was always my intention not to allow Jack to march off to war on his own, unfortunately when the time came that's exactly what happened. The military's powers that be sent my brother to Egypt on the mighty British ocean liner, RMS *Queen Mary*, along with the other reinforcements for the 2/3rd Pioneer Battalion which was attached to the now famous 9th Division. While Jack's Pioneers didn't play a role in the defence of Tobruk, the

9th's campaign in the desert – which included the victori-
ous Battle of El Alamein – is remembered for them being
a mighty bloody pain in Rommel's backside!

Before Jack shipped out, Dad took me aside and suggested that if I was planning to join the army I ought to do
it as soon as possible, because he believed my older brother
could 'claim' me, which would allow both of us to serve in
the same unit. For that to happen Dad said I would need to
simply fill out the paperwork to transfer from the Militia
to the AIF. My father's logic was if we were together, we'd
at least always have someone watching our back when
things got 'hot'. Dad scribbled me a note which gave me
his permission to join up because I was still too young to
join legally of my own accord. This was the pass I needed
to obtain the 'freedom' – if you can call it that – to join up
and fight the Nazis and Italians alongside Jack. I planned
to put it to immediate use, but I would hit an unexpected
roadblock. At a time when the government was screaming
for men to volunteer for active service, becoming a soldier
would prove to be not as easy as I'd thought. I soon discovered that the government's laws actually prevented me
and Jack from having any chance of meeting up in Egypt,
and all because I was learning to bake pies and pastries for
a living.

9

The Infanteer

He is born to the earth; on the day he enlists
He is sentenced to life on the soil,
To march on it, crawl on it, dig in it, sprawl on it,
Sleep on it after his toil.
Be it sand, rock or ice, gravel, mud or red loam
He will fight on it bravely, will die,
And the crude little cross telling men of his loss
Will cry mutely to some foreign sky.

Captain Philip Geeves,
2/5th Australian Field Regiment, The Infanteer (1944)

A few mornings after I'd revealed my plan to Mr Fleming, I took my best set of clothes into work with me. By then I'd turned 18, and because Harry knew I intended to fight it wasn't a problem asking him for permission to slip into town later that day to enlist. By this time Mr Fleming had accepted my decision and had stopped trying to talk me out of fighting in the war. He simply nodded his head and said that would be fine. However, he gave me a gentle warning that once I was accepted into the army the law required him, as my employer, to officially inform the government's Manpower Department that I'd gone 'missing'. In 1939 the Commonwealth had introduced a series of stringent regulations to manage the conflict of demands between the military and industry. Because the Australian government had the important job of supplying our forces fighting overseas with food, clothing and the equipment they needed, there had to be enough men and women manning the factory floors and working the farms.

In 1940, the Minister for State of Defence Coordination compiled a list of 'reserved occupations' to prevent the voluntary enlistment of skilled workers from services deemed crucial to the war effort, and among their number were wharfies, farmers, agricultural workers, ship builders, doctors, teachers and railway workers. Not surprisingly, police weren't allowed to leave their jobs for the military because they were needed to uphold law and order. As the war progressed and Australia relied even more heavily upon the local manufacture of supplies for our troops and allies, the restrictions escalated to the point where the Director-General of Manpower, John Dedman, had extraordinary powers. Indeed, he became known as head of the 'ministry for austerity', and was at one point accused by the public of 'stealing Christmas' when he banned department stores from using images of Santa Claus or Rudolph the Red-nosed Reindeer in their advertising material because he said it encouraged 'wasteful consumerism'. Dedman also had the authority to exempt any person from military service if they worked in essential services.

During this time in Australia's history, workers were in the previously unimaginable position of not being able to change their job without first obtaining the government's permission, and there were some cases where bosses had all but lost the authority to sack their staff. So dealing with the Manpower Department was a serious business for people such as Mr Fleming, and when he shook my hand to wish me luck as I headed for the tram stop, he said I had one full week before he filed his report to the authorities. Of course, I thanked him because he was putting himself out for me, but in all honesty, the Manpower regulations were the last thing on my mind as I took my seat on the tram. I just wanted to get into the army, and when I saw a group of soldiers who were also travelling to town I felt excited to think that in a few hours' time I'd be serving alongside them.

The army recruiting hut based at the Castlereagh Street end of Martin Place in the city centre was surprisingly small. There was only enough room for one man to enter at a time, but as I made my way towards the front of the queue I realised that the sergeant in charge had a mega-phone of a voice, so anyone standing within earshot could hear him grill the latest would-be digger. When I found myself in front of the sergeant he fired off his questions with the authority you'd expect from a person of his rank and intimidating stature. I even felt myself straighten as if at attention as he addressed me.

'How old are you, son?'

'I turned 18 on 31 October this year.'

'You married?'

'No.'

'Do you have your parents' permission to join?'

'Yes. I have my father's written consent here.'

'Any military experience?'

'Yes, I'm in the Militia (Home Guard).'

'Where do you do drill?'

'The Addison Road Drill Hall in Marrickville.'

'Good. So, what do you do for a living?'

'I'm an apprentice baker and pastry chef.'

The sergeant paused. 'So, you're telling me you're an apprentice? You're, what, learning to make pies and cakes?'

'Well, I only have six months to go.'

The sergeant wasn't having a bar of it. *'PUSH OFF, YOU DRONGO! WE DON'T TAKE APPRENTICES IN THE ARMY. WHEN YOU GET YOUR BLOODY TRADE COME BACK AND TRY AGAIN.'*

'But, I *want* to fight . . .' I spluttered.

'I SAID, PUSH OFF! THERE ARE SOME RULES I'LL BEND, BUT THERE'S OTHERS I WON'T DARE TOUCH – AND SHOVING APPRENTICES INTO THE ARMY IS ONE OF THEM. GO NOW! I'M SURE YOU NOTICED ON YOUR WAY IN THAT I HAVE A LINE OF MEN WANTING TO JOIN THE ARMY! THEY HAVEN'T GOT ALL DAY TO WASTE, AND NOR DO I!'

Obviously, I was crestfallen, and the men who'd heard what happened grinned and laughed as they watched me leave, because I must've looked every bit like a school-boy who'd been chastened by his headmaster. Eventually, I made my way back to the shop to help Harry clean up, and while I'm pretty certain he stifled a smile of relief when he heard I'd been rejected on account of my apprenticeship, he winced when I explained I had no intention of taking the sergeant's advice to stay put. You see, I had a plan. On the tram ride back to Marrickville, I realised it was quite easy for me − or any apprentice − to get around the government's red tape regarding our 'untouchable' status. It was clear the army didn't give two hoots about the men who were employed in menial work, so I knew what to do.

Two days after being ordered away by the recruiting officer, I changed my career and started work as a storeman at the Egg Marketing Board at Wattle Street in inner-city Ultimo. It was easy to get the job because they were short-handed on account of many of the men going off to fight. For the rest of that week, I lifted and shifted and heaved crates which each held 30 dozen eggs. It was hard work, and the older men who I slogged alongside advised me to get ready for the egg-laying season, because they said it was quite possible I could be working 24-hour shifts to keep up with demand. While they obviously welcomed the overtime because of the extra money, I just smiled and nodded. Despite the promise of a fat pay packet in the not-too-distant future, I was determined to fly the coop! The manager, a fellow named Haynes, wouldn't have realised it at the time, but when I offered him a cheery 'good night and see you later' as I walked out the door at the end of that week, I really meant 'goodbye, and nice knowing you!'

The following day, armed with my payslip from the Egg Marketing Board, I returned to Martin Place dressed in exactly the same clothes I'd worn the previous week. After standing in line for the better part of an hour, I arrived before the same sergeant wearing my best poker face. He narrowed his eyes until they squinted while he sized me up. There was a flicker of recognition in his eyes when he stared at me, but after a few seconds he gave up and began to rattle off the same questions.

'How old are you, son?'

'I turned 18 on 31 October.'

'Are you married?'

'No.'

'Do you have your parents' permission to join up?'

'Yes. I have my father's written consent here.'

'Any military experience?'

'Yes, I'm in the Militia.'

'Where do you do drill?'

'The Addison Road Drill Hall in Marrickville.'

'And what do you do for a living?'

'I'm a storeman,' I said, and triumphantly threw my payslip clearly marked *Storeman* onto his desk.

That was how one week after he'd told me in no uncertain terms to get lost, the same man handed me my attestation form to sign and congratulated me on becoming a member of the army. He advised me that the training camp I'd be sent to wasn't quite ready, so I was to wait at home until the army notified me with further orders. However, he repeated in his loud parade-ground voice that I was now a soldier and could expect to be paid until I was called up. As I made my way home to Mum and Betty that day, I felt as though I'd transformed from my five-foot-six, ten-stone self into a six-foot-two, 15-stone – and bulletproof – monster.

★

Despite my best efforts I still hadn't completely found my way back into Betty's good books, and this latest development didn't help my cause. We were still as madly in love as ever, but I knew she felt I'd let her down badly by not agreeing to marry her when she'd asked. It was a tough situation – of course I wanted to marry Betty – but my gut instinct assured me that Dad's advice was correct. There was no way I'd risk Betty's life being ruined if anything happened to me on the battlefield. However, no matter how hard I tried to explain that to her, she just couldn't find it within herself to agree with me.

While I waited for the army to send me further orders, I stayed at home helping Mum. I tended the garden and the lawn, and I also pitched in with the housework. As you'd imagine, my mother wasn't too excited that I'd volunteered, but as we drank a cup of tea one morning, she revealed she was more concerned about Jack being on the frontline. 'Reg,' she said, 'I know you'll be able to look after yourself, and that you'll handle whatever happens over there. But I'm worried about Jack; he has a different character to you and he really shouldn't be in the army.' My mother knew her children well, because if Jack was anything at all he was a soft-natured fellow. In a different time, I'm sure the military would've turned him away. However, from what I would later see, Jack wasn't the only man who shouldn't have been put in the thick of the fighting. I'd meet dozens of men of a similar makeup to his throughout the course of the war, and the toll their experiences took on them was shocking. Like my father, the war broke them.

The decision to fight in the war was taken out of all of our hands on 7 December 1941 when 353 Japanese aircraft launched a sneak raid on the US fleet anchored at Pearl Harbor, Oahu, Hawaii. The American president called it a date that 'will live in infamy', and he vowed vengeance for the 2403 American service personnel and 68 civilians who were killed there when he said: 'No matter how long it may take us to overcome this premeditated invasion, the American people in their righteous might will win through to absolute victory.' That air raid was the catalyst for hell to be unleashed in South-East Asia and the Pacific. Within hours of their warplanes returning to their six heavy aircraft carriers, the Japanese also attacked Nauru, Wake Island, Guam and Malaya. While declaring war on Japan, Australia's Prime Minister John Curtin noted: 'The Pacific Ocean was reddened with the blood of the Japanese victims. These wanton killings will be followed by attacks on the Netherlands East Indies [Indonesia], on the Commonwealth of Australia; on the Dominion of New Zealand, if Japan can get its brutal way . . .'

In the weeks that followed, Australia was alone and defenceless. As Emperor Hirohito's army prepared to assault Hong Kong and seize it from its British, Indian and Canadian defenders, I received my 'further orders' when a letter from the Department of Defence was delivered to Wardell Road. It was from Captain Martin, who ran the Marrickville Drill Hall, a 'warning notice' that spelled out everything I needed to know about the next steps involved in starting my military career. It carried every possible detail, including the need for me to take my own soap, hairbrush, comb and even *sandwiches* to camp!

Chard, Reginald James
Area 53A Drill Hall Marrickville.

Captain W.H. Martin
Office 53A Drill Hall, Marrickville

Prepare to proceed to camp for continuing training at [indecipherable]
Free issuing of following articles in addition to uniform
- 2 singlets
- 2 pair of underpants
- 2 pair of socks
- 2 towels

The following articles will not be provided by the Defence Department, and if you are in possession of them you should bring them with you: knife, fork, spoon, mug, hairbrush, comb, toothbrush, shaver, shaving brush, razor, razor strop, small padlock and key for kit bag, piece of soap, shaving soap, toothpaste, pair of braces or belt, cardigan or sweater, 1 pair of sandshoes or light shoes.

When uniform is issued all of your plain clothes will be despatched to your address.

You will report to Captain W.H. Martin, area officer Addison Road, Marrickville, at a time and place and date to be notified to you later. Prepare to proceed to camp for continuous training.

Show this notice to your employer immediately if you
receive it. Bring two cut lunches with you. This notice is
subject to medical fitness.
Captain W.H. Martin

Three days later, I stood next to a bricklayer from Beverly
Hills named Thomas Claude Whitney as we waited in line
to be poked and prodded in our 'medical'. We hit it off
immediately, and 'Titch' became the first friend I made in
the army. Our first challenge was to be passed fit for active
service, and I had my concerns because I was cursed with
feet flatter than the back veranda! It worried me that an
overzealous doctor might consider that to be enough of
a flaw to end my war. However, I needn't have worried
because it soon became obvious even to blind Freddy that
the examination was little more than a charade.

The first test the army put us recruits through was to
measure our height and weight. The bloke in charge made
it clear he was uninterested in his job as he instructed us to
stand against the wall to be measured. Regardless of whether
you stood six-foot-four or four-foot-six, he'd say with a
slight yawn: 'Yeah, mate, you're tall enough. NEXT!' I then
saw a fellow who later became a great pal of mine, 'Pee
Wee' Corr, step up to the scales. He looked better suited
to life in the saddle as a jockey than to life as a soldier, but
a little trick the army had learnt ensured he passed. Before
Pee Wee was weighed, he was told by the man in charge
that he didn't need to take off his heavy boots; he just had
to 'hop on' and then 'get off'. As for myself, while I was
happy to have breezed through all of the criteria, I bounced

from one flat foot to the other with nervous energy as I waited for the chiropodist (known as a podiatrist these days) to inspect my feet. However, when my moment of truth came, he took a quick glance before giving me a wink and declaring to my great relief: 'You'll be right, cobber.'

We were then paraded before the doctors who got straight to work examining us for piles, tonsillitis, any heart defects, decaying teeth or other dental health problems, and they also took a sample of our urine. Ultimately, what we all realised was that if you had two arms, two legs, and could look them in the eye, you were fit enough to become a soldier. I didn't see anyone in our group fail, and there were a few who I'd have been willing to bet at the start of the day were long odds to get in.

The reason we were all passed was simple enough. The government and the army knew Australia was in danger of being invaded by Japan, and so anyone willing to pick up a rifle was considered capable enough of serving at the front. What's scary is that as the war dragged on and Australia's situation to the north became even more dire when the Japanese reached Rabaul, Timor and Papua New Guinea, the army dropped its standards even further. The orders from on high, I believe, were that they didn't give a toss about how it was done – or who they used to do it – but the army needed to fill an ever-growing number of holes on the frontline.

After Mum had shared her fears with me about Jack, I hoped that he'd be able to claim me for the 2/3rd Pioneers, AIF, so I could keep an eye on him. However, that possibility was dashed the moment I was classified as infantry. The army desperately needed riflemen in the jungle, and once you were pencilled in for an infantry battalion you had no hope of being transferred to the engineers (Jack's unit, the Pioneers, came under this umbrella), supply units, artillery, or whatever you might've wished for. It was cruel to think that the army prevented me and Jack from serving together on a bloody technicality. The Pioneers had also trained to fight as infantrymen – Jack and his mates were used as such during the famous Battle of El Alamein – but the powers that be refused to budge. That was a damn pity because I believe if I'd served alongside Jack, he might've returned from his experiences in far better shape than he did.

10

Cut Lunches and Broomsticks

Animo et Fide

'By Courage and Faith',
the 2/55th Australian Infantry Battalion's motto

When the Japanese bombed the US Pacific Fleet anchored at Pearl Harbor on 7 December 1941, Australia was a nation on its knees. We were so bloody helpless it was pathetic. One of the reasons for our perilous state was that our best trained men were fighting overseas for British causes. We had 181,129 AIF troops in North Africa, Syria, Greece and Crete, and there were also those who were urgently despatched to Singapore as part of the 130,000-strong Commonwealth garrison there. Added to that were 12,000 pilots either flying or training abroad, while the 'heavy hitters' of our tiny navy – six ageing destroyers – were under the command of the British Admiralty and patrolling the Mediterranean Sea. What this meant was that when the Japanese started their rapid southward thrust towards Australia, the nation's seven million people were defended by 32,000 AIF soldiers and 200,000 ill-equipped and poorly trained Militia troops.

However, having troops away on 'active service' only scratched the surface of the reasons for our troubles. Much of our vulnerability came as the result of the government's unwillingness to spend money on defence during the Great Depression – even though they were aware Japan posed a threat to the region – combined with the unhealthy belief in Canberra that Great Britain would drop everything to save us from an invasion. It meant that when we came under fire in '41 we didn't have the firepower needed to defend the country. Believe me, I'm not joking when I say we were an army armed with broomsticks!

Australia's new Prime Minister, John Curtin, inherited an impossible situation. His nation's vast coastline – all 34,000 kilometres of it – was protected by a handful of minesweepers and patrol boats and a seriously ill-prepared air fleet. Indeed, the Royal Australian Air Force would've represented mere target practice for the Japanese Zero fighter planes because all we had on the tarmac were 101 Wirraways (a training and general purpose aircraft that recorded just one 'kill' during the entire war); 53 Lockheed Hudson bombers; 12 Catalinas, and a dozen obsolete Seagull amphibian flying boats. When you compare that to the Japanese task force of six state-of-the-art aircraft carriers and 353 combat planes that king-hit Hawaii, we were going to need more than raw Aussie grit to save our country.

It chilled me to the bone when I read Paul Ham's excellent book *Kokoda*, in which he detailed how deeply rooted our defence problems were. While there was no lack of willingness among the Australian people to fight (including the 16-year-old boys and grandfathers who enlisted), Ham noted that we simply didn't have the 'tools' that were needed to provide genuine resistance. Even though we had fewer than 200 warplanes, the country didn't have enough aviation fuel for a sustained aerial war. In addition, the government was powerless to prevent the modern combat planes it had ordered from American factories being redirected to Britain's war effort. Of the 200 Vickers machine guns produced each month at the Lithgow Arms Factory over the Blue Mountains, 125 were sent to British troops based in India while a mere 20 made their way into Australian hands. There were no sea mines to protect our ports, there wasn't a single anti-aircraft weapon to be found anywhere in the country, and at a time when Hitler's tanks had blitzed their way through Europe and North Africa, Australia had just ten light-training tanks to defend the entire continent! We had, however, produced 80 per cent of the bullets that would have been needed to make a stand – except that we didn't have the rifles or machine guns needed to fire them! If the situation we found ourselves in wasn't so serious, it would've been laughable. It's because of this that I understand why Prime Minister Curtin lay awake in a cold sweat at night until the Americans came to our rescue by providing us with their weapons and troops.

Of course, none of us knew at the time how precarious the situation was. The politicians, bureaucrats, and especially the military censors, kept it all a very closely guarded secret so as to avoid mass panic. It was in this state of relative ignorance that I returned with the other recruits to Addison Road on 21 December 1941. It was the morning after our medicals and we each turned up with our suitcases crammed with the items the army had advised us to pack. The only thing from their long list that I left behind were the two bath towels, because I couldn't fit them into my bag. When Mum suggested I repack it, I couldn't be bothered because I was certain the army would have millions of towels!

I met up with Titch and we joined one of the huddles of men that had formed on the parade ground. While I was certain we'd leave that day to start basic training – and it was only a gut feeling based on our orders to bring along our packed suitcases – a few of the fellows were adamant we'd have Christmas at home with our families before being recalled for duty on Boxing Day. I conceded they might be right because after Jack had completed his medical he was sent home for a week before being shipped off to train at Bathurst. However, I didn't share that information with these blokes, because as far as I was concerned, Christmas Day 1941 could wait. All I wanted to do was get cracking and start my training. I was determined to get to the front-line before the war ended.

We must've resembled a mob of sheep as we milled about chatting because when Captain Martin addressed us, he ordered us to form lines and stand to attention 'like bloody soldiers!' Once we were in formation, he announced that we now belonged to the 2/55th Australian Infantry Battalion. He added that the army expected each of us to emulate the honour and courage of the 'original' 55th, who fought at Villers-Bretonneux, an action that is ranked as one of World War I's mightiest feats of arms. As a teenager who didn't know better, I couldn't have been happier. I'd joined to fight, and now that I was about to, I was very pleased with the cards I'd been dealt.

We were then allocated to our companies. A company (written as Coy) is a subsection to a battalion. During World War II the typical Australian battalion had four companies – A, B, C and D – and they could each comprise anywhere between 100 and 225 men. However, the 2/55th had so many men the brass created a fifth company, E Coy. While I wasn't too bothered about where they shunted me, it pleased me to learn Titch and I would serve together in C Coy.

After we joined our companies, Captain Martin stood in front of the 2/55th, waving his arms like a windmill. After shouting for everyone to 'PIPE DOWN!' he issued what I think was the first order the Battalion received during the war: 'Sit the bloody hell down and eat your sandwiches!' It was then we realised that the reason we went to war with our mothers' cut lunches was because it spared the army the job of having to feed us! About ten minutes after we finished eating, the sergeants yelled for the members of A Coy to start boarding the trams that had assembled on the tracks outside. As the stragglers from B Coy eventually climbed on board, a sweaty, red-faced sergeant sent Titch, me and a few of the others on our way when he yelled impatiently: 'ALRIGHT YOU BASTARDS FROM C COMPANY – GET ONTO THE BLOODY TRAMS!'

The talk of whether we'd be having Christmas at home was replaced by speculation about where we were headed.

Funnily enough, one of the blokes who'd been willing to bet we'd be spending 25 December at our family's dining table, tucking into our mothers' prized plum puddings, was now adamant we *had* to be headed to Ingleburn because it was only 'logical'. He was wrong, and I quickly learnt not to take too much notice whenever this bloke made a comment about anything because he had a terrible habit of putting two and two together and getting 33.

When our tram pulled out of Marrickville it didn't even cross my mind to take a lingering look at the landmarks that had formed the landscape of my youth because there was too much happening around me to be sentimental. Something that helped make my leaving home a bit easier was that I'd left on the best of terms with Betty. She'd made her peace with the reason for my reluctance to get married, although she didn't pretend to completely agree with it. However, we both knew we loved one another deeply, and that was all that mattered. Nevertheless, I was grateful that the mood of what would be our last evening together for a few months had been light and bright. Memories of that evening, which was spent talking about our future, strengthened me during some challenging times during basic training.

As we left Marrickville behind, Titch and I started to get to know some of the men we'd serve alongside in C Coy: Pee Wee Corr, Bluey, Dick Kayess, Ray and James 'Davo' Davison. Upon our arrival at Central train station, some uniformed soldiers directed us to the country train plat-forms. There we were greeted by a herd of sergeants who stood outside each carriage, and they bellowed at us to

climb on board as if we were dumb cattle. It was something of a mystery tour, because even when we were in the
middle of red-dirt country, well beyond the fabled Black
Stump, the officers and sergeants refused to tell us where
we were headed. It was a long trip made even longer by
the times the train had to pull over on a siding of the single
line we were travelling along to allow the trains carting
troops bound for North Queensland to pass by. While these
were called 'express trains' they were snail-slow and up to
a quarter of a mile long, which meant they took forever
to pass. It wasn't until our train came to its final stop that we
found out where we were: Dubbo, 400 kilometres west of
Sydney. It was the furthest I'd ever been away from home.

After a seven-kilometre march from the train station
to the base (the Western Plains Zoo now stands on what
was the old army camp) we learnt that the few hundred
of us who'd been sent there would learn to operate either
Vickers machine guns or to fire mortars, because neither
were available at the camp where we'd eventually do most
of our training. Of course, the army didn't tell us where
that was to be either – it was another of their closely
guarded secrets!

It became obvious during our few days at Dubbo that
the army wasn't the well-oiled machine we'd expected.
The quartermaster had no uniforms for us; he said we'd
have to drill and train in the clothes we'd brought from
home. While this was disappointing, nothing stunned
Titch and I quite like going to the armoury expecting to
be issued with our Lee–Enfield .303 bolt-action rifle, the
standard weapon of all the British Empire's armies, only

to be handed a broomstick. A *broomstick*! Adding to the farcical nature of the moment was that the fellow handing them out did so in a way that suggested there was nothing at all strange about it. When I asked if he was having a laugh at our expense because we were the new kids on the block, the armourer shook his head and explained matter-of-factly that there hadn't been any rifles set aside for the 2/55th. For the better part of two months, we pretended those broomsticks were our rifles.

My third surprise came the following morning when I went to the shower block at sunrise. I expected to find piles of freshly laundered towels in the block, but there was nothing there except the sound of dripping showerheads and taps. When I told a lieutenant about my dilemma he advised me to run to the canteen and find out whether I could buy a towel from there. The canteen was well decked out; you could buy almost anything there, except, it turned out, a towel! When I returned ten minutes later I was armed with a tea towel, and that was what I used to dry myself during my first few months as a soldier. Surprisingly enough, none of the recruitment posters I'd seen before I enlisted mentioned anything about joining an army with no uniforms, no guns and . . . no towels!

Titch, my new mate Bluey and I trained together as a Vickers machine gun crew. The Vickers was an incredible weapon, able to provide sustained fire for hours at a time due to its unique water cooling system. While this system was little more than a container that held a gallon of water, it proved effective in not allowing the weapon to overheat. Manning the Vickers was only a two-person job, but the reason there were three of us was sobering. The no. 1 fired the gun; the no. 2 fed the belt of bullets into it, and the third bloke was a reserve. His job was to wait in the wings in case one of the pair was killed. It was his job to move the body aside and replace the dead man.

Up until that stage of my life I'd never seen or heard anything like the Vickers. It chewed up .303 bullets and spat them out at the astonishing rate of 500 rounds per minute! I thought it was marvellous, and I don't mind admitting how exciting it felt to sit behind the beast and blaze away at the targets set up hundreds of yards away. Something I remember about that experience was the sound the weapon made as it was fired. It was a distinctive hacking noise that I figured would've been terrifying to hear on the battlefield. It was as though the Vickers was warning anyone who stood on the wrong side of its barrel that its purpose was to inflict as much death and misery as possible. Of course, Titch, Bluey and I would discover the Japanese had weapons whose calling cards were equally terrifying, especially the Type 92 heavy machine gun. The Americans and Australians dubbed it 'the Woodpecker', and take it from me, the Woodpecker was a cur of a thing . . .

On what I'm 99 per cent certain was Christmas Day, we were given what I suppose was the army's version of a present when they lent C Coy some tin helmets and .303 rifles to fire at the range. It was an eye-opener. You see, whenever I'd gone rabbiting with Mr Fleming, we'd used a .22 rifle. It was effective at short range, and because it didn't have much recoil when you fired it, it was ideal for a boy of my size to use. But while it was effective in stopping an unsuspecting rabbit dead in its unfortunate tracks, it was a peashooter when compared to a .303. I realised this the first time I fired the .303 because the kick it gave after I pulled the trigger threatened to knock my shoulder out of its socket! The butt of the rifle – complete with the brass plate that covered it – recoiled a few times and the result was some decent bruising. One of the older instructors took me aside and showed me how to use the rifle properly, and it saved me from serious injury. After I fired a few rounds the correct way he was impressed by what he called my 'good eye'.

That experience on the rifle range must've been the highlight of my Christmas Day in Dubbo, because apart from that, I can't remember much else about my first festive season as a soldier. In the early hours of Boxing Day, we were packed back onto a train for another long, slow trip of a couple of hundred kilometres to an army camp near the small country town of Greta in the Hunter Valley. It was at this camp that C Coy and the other men of the 2/55th would be drilled into a fighting force.

11

Dust Storms and Smallpox

*We referred to them as 'chocos' and all that sort of thing.
I was as bad as anybody else, but when I was in New
Guinea and I saw these kids I changed my mind . . . They
were kids 18 [or] 19-years-old and I saw them in action
and coming out of action. I still call them 'chocos', but it's
not derogatory any more. It's with a huge amount of love.*
Frank Rowell, 2/4th Australian Infantry Battalion

When Titch, Bluey and I arrived with the other members
of C Coy's Vickers machine gun crews and mortar platoons
at our camp at Greta, situated 40 kilometres north-west
of Newcastle, Mother Nature provided a memorable
welcome. The heat was stifling at 30-plus degrees, but it
was the region's dancing dust that surprised us. Indeed,
it forced us to sprint to safety! As we walked through the
base a 'whirly-whirly' – a 30-metre-high whirlwind of
dust – homed in on us at a rapid pace. As it raced across the
plain, one of the old hands who'd been at Greta for a couple
of weeks shouted at us to take cover . . . AND QUICKLY!

It didn't take long to realise he'd done us a huge favour. The whirly-whirly barrelled through the camp, and while it didn't have enough force to knock a man over or to cause damage to any of the base's buildings, we would most certainly have choked on the dust because it was so thick in the air. On the few occasions I was trapped in one, it wrapped around my face like a suffocating cloak. Oh, it was a dreadful sensation, and as I remember, also a painful one because my body was not only blasted by billions of dirt particles, but it was also whacked by the sticks and stones caught in the whirly-whirly.

Greta had become one of the largest army bases on the Australian mainland when the military acquired just under 3000 acres of farmland in November 1939. The construction crews had gone straight to work establishing a training base for the AIF's 'originals', the 6th Division, before they travelled to North Africa to terrorise Mussolini's forces. Over 60,000 men trained there between 1939 and 1945, but the arrival of the 2/55th Battalion in early January 1942 was a significant milestone in Australia's military history. This was because we were the army's first 'mixed' battalion, meaning that besides having a company's worth of AIF volunteers, our ranks also consisted of Militia volunteers (of which I was one) and political conscripts that the government had 'called up' (including my best mate Titch). The conscripts were known colloquially to some as Forced Into Action, and their critics pointed out that – even in name – these blokes were the reverse of the AIF. I've since read that some of the 2/55th's conscripts looked 'bewildered' as they adjusted to the rigours of military life. I don't know about that, but it's certainly true we were all thrown into a world we didn't ever expect to be in – and, in many cases, didn't want to be in. While the overwhelming majority of the conscripted men I served with developed into fine soldiers with a keen sense of duty, there were also those who were angry about their lot. I was friendly with one such bloke, and while he drilled, marched and fired his weapon at the rifle range with more than enough diligence to satisfy even the hardest-nosed sergeant, he devoted all of his free time to plotting ways to be issued with a discharge so he could resume his life as a civilian.

As I have already touched on, there was an attitude at the time that the Militia were 'second-rate' compared to the more glamorous all-volunteer AIF force. In my experience it was the ignorant people in pubs, offices and even churches who expressed such views; I didn't ever hear anything like this from any of the AIF members I served alongside. Those civilians with a negative opinion of our conscripted mates insinuated that any man ordered by the government to pick up a rifle to fight would lack the warrior's heart, and the stomach, of a volunteer. Even though conscripted soldiers made up only one part of the Militia, we all copped a pummelling. They called us 'Chocos', from 'chocolate soldiers', because they expected us to melt in the heat of battle; others branded us 'Rainbows' because we'd supposedly wait until the storm passed before we came out, while we were compared by some to 'koalas' – a 'protected species' like the much-loved bush creature, which the government had wisely banned hunters from shooting in the 1930s. It was all bullshit, but nonetheless these ideas about the Militia were widely held.

One of the reasons these opinions persisted was because whenever someone joined the AIF, they did so in the knowledge the army could send them to fight anywhere in the world. The Militia's detractors pointed out that the government's legislation didn't permit conscripts to serve outside Australian territory at a time when Britain was facing its darkest hour. However, in those days Papua New Guinea was considered a part of our territory, and this classification ultimately condemned thousands of conscripts to fight on what became one of the world's deadliest battlefields. Something else critics of the Militia conveniently overlooked was that among us were volunteers like me who were too young to join the AIF, or, at the other end of the scale, were too old. One such person in my mob was 'Poppa' West, a veteran of World War I. None of us was interested in politics; we just wanted to do our bit. Ultimately we had too many other things to worry about than the rubbish people said about us.

The celebrated author Thomas Keneally, who wrote such literary classics as *Schindler's Ark* and *The Chant of Jimmie Blacksmith*, recalled during a 2004 interview that his father and an older cousin wound him up to run onto the veranda of the family house in the New South Wales country town of Kempsey and yell 'CHOCO!' as members of the Militia walked by. These men were camped at the local showground, waiting to be deployed. Keneally said that his father grew to feel ashamed of what he'd made his son do, because he later realised some of those 'Chocos' had died while fighting on the Kokoda Trail.

All I'll say on the matter is this: it didn't matter to us if a bloke was a member of the AIF, if he was a Militia volunteer, or a political conscript. We all wore the same uniform, and our blood was the same colour. Besides that, regardless of how we'd ended up there, we all endured the same hell. Whenever a conscript from my company died – and it happened with sickening frequency – no-one ever said: 'Oh, you do know he was a conscript, don't you?' Who cares about such things when you look at a dead man? No-one. He was no different from any other poor bastard who sacrificed his life fighting against a barbaric enemy. *Chocos?* What a terrible joke. Each of them was a hero – especially those who gave all they could despite not even wanting to be there in the first place.

After being greeted by a sergeant, we were directed to a pile of body-sized hessian sacks and advised that they'd be our beds for the two-and-a-half months we'd be at the camp. The sergeant then advised us to stuff them with enough straw so the bag felt as though it would split at the seams. He warned that if we didn't do that, the straw would flatten under our body weight and we'd wake in the morning feeling as though we'd slept on the floorboards. The sacks proved to be extremely comfortable, and there were times in the jungle when I would've given anything to have had mine, plus the three blankets the army issued us. I slept on the ground, under the open sky, for most of the time I was in New Guinea.

After finding our 'possies' in the barracks, I explored our base with Bluey and Titch. It was divided into two sides, and our half was known as 'Chocolate City' on account of the brown-coloured wooden buildings we lived in. While our barracks had tin roofs, they were surprisingly cool. The base's other half was known as 'Silver City' because it contained dozens upon dozens of Nissen huts with corrugated-iron roofs and walls. On a sunny day, the light that bounced off those metal sheets was blinding. The materials used in the construction of the huts created a terrible living environment for the men accommodated in them. When you consider that the daytime temperature in Greta hovered around 33 degrees during summer, you'll understand why I likened the heat in those tin huts to Harry Fleming's oven at the Dundee Cake Shop.

We received one warning from the sergeant before lights out that night. He said any man who wasn't ready for drill by 5 am would have to run to the top of Mount Molly Morgan, which was adjacent to the camp, as punishment. The trip to the top took well over half an hour, and even though it was exhausting, the sleepy-headed and jelly-legged soldier would then be told to run back down to the bottom. Once there, he was immediately sent to do drill with his mates. With an elevation of 78 metres, 'Molly' was the veritable 'heartbreak hill', and very steep. When the army had done a test of the capabilities of a Bren Gun carrier, it couldn't go any further than halfway up. The boys were safe from enduring such a fate, however, thanks to my years of waking early to work my shift for Mr Fleming. It meant my body clock was set to wake me long before the sergeant had lifted his head from his pillow.

The following day, still dressed in our sandshoes and civilian clothes, we started training as 'footsloggers'.

The sergeants ordered us to get into formation, and we began our first session of the day, which was physical culture. Our instructor was a fellow from Marrickville named Sydney Yum, who was of Chinese heritage. Syd was a well-known baseball player for Marrickville, and his body rippled with muscles. Unlike most other instructors he didn't just stand at the front of the class and bark out orders, he walked up and down the lines and ensured everyone was doing the exercises correctly. He was tough, but Syd Yum helped bash us into shape. After that we marched for one-and-a-half kilometres. I thought it was strange that the sergeant dismissed us after such a short walk because I'd expected that we'd be made to march until our feet bled. The next morning C Coy walked two kilometres; the following day the distance increased a little more, and again the day after that. It became obvious the instructors were allowing us to build up our condition and stamina.

Before we became too settled at the camp, we received orders to line up on parade for our smallpox vaccinations. There were doctors waiting for us, but when one of the bigger men in our battalion saw them brandishing needles, he fainted. He landed with a thud, a bit like the sound a sack of spuds makes after falling off the back of a lorry. It turned out the poor bloke was more terrified of needles than of the prospect of coming under heavy Japanese fire. We watched on in disbelief as one of the doctors walked over to our mate who was out cold and sprawled in the dirt. Once he reached him the doctor casually administered the vaccination. 'I don't think he even felt that,' said the doc with a grin after he'd finished.

The doctors only used one needle to jab all the men in those days because the medical profession wasn't aware that sharing needles could spread any number of infectious diseases. We all received the vaccinations on the left shoulder, and were given the next four days to rest and recover. And it was just as well, because I felt bloody terrible! When I was in New Guinea I'd suffer some shocking illnesses – diseases that could quite easily have killed me. However, I felt rotten for those four days after my vaccination! I couldn't get off my back, and the area of my shoulder that had received the shot stung like hell. I also had a massive headache and high fever; my body ached, and the scab that formed over the injection site festered. We were told that was 'normal'.

The only person out of the entire company who didn't suffer any adverse effects was Titch. He was meant to get the full course of three shots, but once the doctors saw how well he tolerated the vaccine they told him he wouldn't need the final dose. However, Titch didn't get a holiday because another side effect of the inoculation was that we all had insatiable thirsts. My poor old mate was kept busy as our hut's 'water boy' for all four days. That meant he had to keep checking everyone's water bottle, and once they were empty he had to run out and refill them. I started to feel much better by the end of the fourth day, and it was just as well, because within a few weeks I'd be in the thick of a one-man war with a high-ranking officer.

12

The Cake Maker of Greta

Who called the cook a bastard?
Who called the bastard a cook?
World War I catchcry about army cooks

Titch was standing in front of me in the breakfast queue at the Greta Army Camp one morning when, without warning, he turned suddenly and yelled: 'Here you go, Chard, catch this!' He tossed me something that looked like a rock. It was as heavy as a lump of lead, and it didn't look as though it belonged to any of the food groups I was familiar with. I said to no-one in particular, 'What on earth is this?' One of the men who I presumed was a cook overheard me, and he was clearly unimpressed because he growled in my direction: '*It's a fucking scone!*' Not surprisingly, my next sentence won me no favour among the crew who worked hard to prepare meals for over a thousand men. After examining their handiwork, I joked to Titch that the army's idea of a scone would make a decent hand grenade . . . if we could only find some gunpowder! It didn't take long before three 'cooks' crowded around Titch and me, each sporting a ferocious look on their face. When one of them called me a 'smart-arse' it struck me that not only did these men look like the toughest soldiers in the Australian Army, they didn't look too worried about bruising their knuckles if a situation ever warranted it.

As he sized me up, the fellow – nicknamed 'Trigger' because he was missing what would've been his trigger finger – snarled: 'If you can do any better, *mate*, let's see you do it.' That was the opening Titch had been waiting for, and he didn't miss. He was well aware of the time I'd spent working at the Dundee Cake Shop, so he taunted Trigger by holding the scone under his nose and sneering: 'Oh, Chard can do much better than *this*!'

If ever a look could kill a man stone dead, I would've dropped when Trigger glared at me. 'Alright, smart-arse,' he said menacingly. 'After you finish drilling today, why don't you come up and show me, Nugget and Bula what you can do?' Even a blind man would've seen the smirks that creased Nugget and Bula's faces when I accepted Trigger's challenge.

After a tough day of drilling, Titch and I were bone-tired, but we took ourselves to the cookhouse where Bula Hayes, Nugget Cummins and Trigger Wilson greeted us with icy stares. Trigger's voice broke the uneasy silence when he said: 'So, *mate*, what can you cook?' When I replied: 'Whatever you want', he didn't even draw breath before he demanded chocolate eclairs. At first I thought Trigger had set what he considered to be the toughest culinary challenge possible in that army kitchen. After delivering his order he gave Bula and Nugget a not-so-subtle wink as if to say he'd 'got' me.

Well, I didn't even blink, and when I asked Trigger whether he had all the ingredients to make them, the notion that he was a chef of some note immediately crumbled. 'How the fuck would I know what goes in them, mate? I'm no cook!' With that, the cookhouse erupted into laughter, and in that instant Titch and I made three loyal mates who'd stick by us through thick and thin. And he *had* 'got' me. He'd winked at Nugget and Bula because he loved chocolate eclairs, and he couldn't believe his luck that the army had sent a recruit who could make them!

After a quick scout around the kitchen, I was surprised to find that an army that didn't have rifles or uniforms or boots for its troops had all the provisions needed to make pastries, including lashings of fresh cream. Then, when I looked at the Greta camp's oven, I could've hugged it like an old friend because it was similar to the model I used to fire up at the start of my shifts for Mr Fleming.

I suppose I was still an apprentice pastry chef at heart, because when I served up those eclairs, it was satisfying to see that the boys didn't leave a single crumb on their plates. As we yarned, the men seemed impressed to hear about my apprenticeship with Harry, but Bula made me think of Betty and Mr Fleming when he asked why I hadn't waited until I'd finished my final six months before joining the army? Like them, he figured a trade would be invaluable for a young bloke once the war ended.

Trigger, Bula and Nugget weren't cooks, but they did kitchen duties because they were friendly with the chefs. I thought it spoke volumes about their character that they defended their mates whenever a digger made a snide comment about their meals, including the one I'd made about a scone that could've stopped a German *Panzer*!

As a sign that we were now a part of their circle, Trigger said I was welcome to use the oven after hours if I wanted. The reason I started baking every night after that was because it not only gave me something to do of an evening, but because I realised I still had a passion for the craft. It also pleased me to know how much the 120 men of C Coy enjoyed eating the goods I baked. In the nights that followed, I whiled away what would otherwise have been hours of lying idly around in the barracks by whipping up madeira cakes, cream sponge cakes, rock cakes and plain cakes for the blokes I'd befriended, and for the others who I'd fight alongside.

Joining the army introduced me to a group of incredible men who, before enlisting, had worked as butchers, clerks, solicitors, bricklayers, brickmakers, pawn brokers, shop assistants and storemen. We even had one who'd studied for three years to become a priest, and he had the foulest tongue of any of the crew! My mate Bluey had a more interesting background than most. He came from Glebe, the inner-city suburb that was a haven for Sydney's criminal element back in the day. The boys and I had found out within three minutes of meeting Bluey that he didn't live life on the straight and narrow, but in all my years, I'm still to meet someone who is as honest about *who* and *what* they are as Bluey. Indeed, the cheery-faced 18-year-old with a shock of red hair – and the nimble fingers of a pianist – captured our undivided attention the moment he opened his mouth. 'Let me tell ya, fellas,' he said boldly, 'I'm not boasting when

I say this, but there's not a safe in Sydney I can't crack.' Once I recovered from my shock, I asked if he'd just told us he was a safecracker? 'My bloody oath, mate!' was his reply, putting any confusion to rest. While our newest mate was a thief, I thought if anyone could be so upfront about themselves, they *had* to be trustworthy. And for what it's worth, Bluey proved to be among the best of the men during the jungle campaign's most bitter fighting. What I'll say of his character is this: I didn't have any issue in trusting Bluey with my life on the battlefield or asking him to safeguard my personal effects when Titch, me and other members of our group went out on patrol. He was both a loyal mate and a courageous soldier.

At the other end of the legal spectrum was a solicitor from Ashfield named Spencer Barter. At 27, 'Spence' was a corporal, and he was one of the oldest men in our platoon, which was a sub-unit of a Coy and consisted of 14 men. He joined the battalion with our lieutenant, Bill Ryan, the colour sergeant, Dave Swaney, and the other sergeants and junior officers who'd recently completed their training courses at Bathurst. Bluey and Spencer remain as perfect examples of how the army is a great equaliser, because in civilian life they could well have found themselves sitting on opposite sides of the Newtown Court House with one arguing points of law and the other doing what he could to stay out of Long Bay prison. As soldiers, however, they became the best of mates who'd depend upon one another to survive the war.

We also had a professional boxer in our ranks, a handy lightweight who I'll call 'The Pugilist'. He was a political conscript, and from the first day he joined us he made it clear he was angry that the government had forced him to join the military. He said if he'd wanted to be a soldier he'd have volunteered. I didn't doubt it when he promised that come hell or high water, he wouldn't be going to the war, and made no secret of the fact that the only fighting he intended to do was in the boxing ring. He was also fuming about the income he was missing out on, because the money he'd made as a prize fighter in the main preliminary bout to events featuring the likes of my all-time favourite fighter, Vic Patrick, the world-rated Aboriginal boxer Ron Richards, and the former American world lightweight champion Tod Morgan, far outweighed the few shillings a day the government paid him to risk life and limb in the infantry.

When he joined us, The Pugilist boasted an impressive record of 17 wins, five losses, one draw and one 'no contest' from the 24 bouts he'd fought since making his professional debut at Leichhardt Stadium in late 1939. While he was definitely likeable, easily the fittest man in our battalion, and told cracking stories about the fight game, some members of our group thought The Pugilist spent too much of his time plotting how to get out of the army rather than buckling down to the business of soldiering. I never judged The Pugilist; he just didn't want to be a soldier. If anything, I admired that he was committed to correcting what he considered an injustice. Plus, despite his reluctance to be in the army, he couldn't ever be accused of shirking his duties and I liked that he was prepared to help out when needed.

Another athlete in our group was the champion still-water swimmer Geoffrey Valentin, from Ramsgate in Sydney's St George district. Unlike The Pugilist, he was committed to doing his bit to defend Australia. While he was extremely popular, Geoff made one major mistake during his early days with us; he made it clear that he didn't appreciate his nickname. When one of the lads saw Geoff's surname they christened him 'Miss Valentine'. However, rather than run with it, the swimmer decried it as 'bloody ridiculous', insisting his name was pronounced '*Val-en-tin*, not *Valentine*.' However, the more noise he made, the more pleasure the boys derived from calling him 'Miss'. It wasn't spiteful, it's just that like a fish, he'd taken the bait, and no-one was prepared to let him off the hook because we all found his reaction amusing. However, 'Miss Valentine' enjoyed our utmost respect because as a man and a soldier, he was outstanding. It was obvious from the first few days after he joined us that Geoff possessed all the traits of a natural leader. As for his courage, the day would come when he'd single-handedly save the lives of quite a few members of C Coy – including mine – when he'd swim across what was believed to be a crocodile-infested river with a long rope tied to his waist. At the time we were being pursued by a larger Japanese patrol, and when he tied the rope to a tree after reaching the other side, it gave me and all of the other non-swimmers a chance to escape the enemy by using the rope to pull ourselves across the river.

Norman Wolfson, who arrived with the AIF men from Bathurst, was an extremely quiet and shy man who was content to simply sit on the edge of the group, listen to our stories and laugh along with our shenanigans. He came from a well-to-do family who lived within earshot of the roar of the waves at the beachside suburb of Coogee, and he worked in the pawn shop his grandfather had opened in Kings Cross not long after he migrated to Australia from Odessa, Ukraine, in the late 1800s. If poor Norm received a penny every time someone joked that they'd be visiting his family's business when the war ended, he'd have had enough money to buy two houses in no time at all! Something else I remember about Norm was that on one of the rare occasions he initiated a conversation with the group, he proudly told us that his older brother, Harold, planned to join the Royal Australian Air Force.

Bill Mackie was another member of our crowd whose family ran a successful business, the landmark Mackie's Department Store in Hunter Street, Newcastle. I have no idea what Bill's mother fed him when he was a pup, but by the time he joined the army he'd developed the formidable frame of a middleweight boxer; he was naturally thickset and muscular. However, while he may have looked like a brawler, he was good-humoured and easygoing. The reason I would one day look back on Bill and Norm and admire them for not flaunting their good fortune in the barracks – for choosing to just be two of the boys – was because later on in life I'd watch how money changed another bloke who was a good friend. I have no doubt it would've helped my former friend to have learnt from Norm and Bill that a man's bank balance isn't a measure of his worth as a person.

One of the most interesting men in C Coy was Ken Horne, and that was because he worked as a 'layer-outer'.

'Horny' had a physique that wouldn't have been out of place on the professional wrestling circuit grappling with the likes of Chief Little Wolf at Sydney Stadium. Once he explained what a layer-outer was, I was fascinated. He told me that when someone passes away, their body bends from the middle until they finish at an angle that makes it impossible for the people at the funeral parlour to either bury them, or to display the corpse for mourners to view. I presume the bend is the result of rigor mortis – Latin for the 'stiffness of death'. As Ken put it, whenever the Grim Reaper came knocking, the funeral director contacted him to do his 'restoration' work. He'd roll up his sleeves and strain his muscles as he fought what he called incredible levels of resistance to straighten out the deceased's body. It was obviously a tough workout, and it explained why Ken had massive biceps and a bull-like neck. Fortunately, he was a gentle and patient giant, because I peppered him with questions about the most unusual occupation of all time.

Dick Kayess was similar to me in that he was an 18-year-old who was deeply in love with his childhood sweetheart, Isabelle. Whenever he spoke to the group about her, I heard the same tenderness in his voice as was in mine whenever I mentioned Betty. Like me, Dick was also an early riser, because his family ran a poultry farm at Ingleburn and he was awake by the time the roosters started crowing at sunrise. His family's farm wasn't too far from where Mr Fleming and I went rabbiting. Another interesting point about Dick was that he was a twin, and when he wasn't speaking about Isabelle, he'd tell us all about his brother Stewart, who was a member of the 2/14th Field Ambulance.

We had another lovestruck member in our group, Bill Elvy, who was involved in the production of bricks at the old St Peters kilns before the war. He was so desperate to spend as much time with his girlfriend as possible, he once jumped the fence and went Absent Without Leave. When the military police finally apprehended him, he ended up in the brig for five days and was fined one pound. He must have been a born romantic – or maybe something other than his head ruled his brain – because when he was asked if visiting his girl was worth all the trouble he said it was. Indeed, it must've been, because I seem to remember that before we were shipped out he went missing again after taking some more unauthorised leave to be in the arms of his lover!

My tiny friend Pee Wee Corr – whose heavy boots had helped him meet the weight requirements during our medical – was a popular member of the group, and one who punched well above his height and weight. Another member of our mob was English-born James Davison, who I was amazed to discover actually lived in my street! He and his family resided in the flat above the milk bar 300 metres from my front door. I had occasionally visited the shop as a young boy to buy a one-penny milk ice block on the rare occasions we had spare coins in the household. Davo was my age, and we invariably had mutual acquaintances from the neighbourhood, so I was surprised we'd never crossed paths. Another 'neighbour' who I didn't meet until we joined the army was Ray from Marrickville. He had enlisted under his mother's Anglo name because his father's surname was of German origin. Ray was easy to like, because he loved a chat and knew the value of a good laugh to gee the men up.

If that wasn't enough variety, we also had 'The Pianist'. He boasted slender fingers that weren't designed to curl around a .303's trigger. However, he gave up tinkling the ivories at one of the top Sydney nightclubs to become a soldier.

These were some of the 120 C Coy men who I baked cakes for of a night. However, every time I mixed the ingredients for the latest offerings, I had a feeling of dread that sat like a stone in the pit of my stomach. I was worried that if a certain senior officer, who I'll call 'The Officer', found out about my culinary skills, he might decide I'd be of better service to the army in the catering corps – and *that* wasn't in my plans. This man had a reputation for having a penchant for the finer things in life, and although I was only a kid I realised the skills I'd acquired as Harry's apprentice would appeal to him. I thought the game was up after about a week when our lieutenant, Bill Ryan, walked into the kitchen sniffing the air. 'Something smells lovely,' he said. 'What's going on?' When the boys replied, 'Oh, it's just Reg cooking cakes,' Bill asked: 'Reg who?' After introducing myself, I handed the lieutenant some samples and urged him to tell no-one about my nocturnal baking sessions because I didn't want to run the risk of being transferred out of the infantry by a senior officer who thought cooking was of far greater importance than combat. Lieutenant Ryan grinned and assured me he wouldn't breathe a word. However, to make my baking 'official', he assigned me to 'KP' – Kitchen Picket – every night until further notice.

I went merrily about the business of baking cakes for the blokes until a king-sized problem emerged in the form of The Officer, who despite my best efforts had indeed heard there was a private under his command who baked a mean batch of cupcakes, cream buns, and lamingtons . . .

The news I'd dreaded arrived one night when Lieutenant Ryan appeared in the kitchen with a concerned look on his face. He told me The Officer wanted to see me the following morning, and I felt sick to the stomach when he speculated that The Officer may have plans to make me his personal chef. I was mortified; that was the one posting I didn't want. Something I liked about Lieutenant Ryan from the outset was that I sensed he was a 'man's man'. I didn't know him before the war, but I was certainly well aware of his sporting prowess. He was a hard-running centre in the Newtown rugby league team, where he played alongside his brother Bruce, who was the New South Wales amateur sprint champion, Frank Hyde, who'd become a famous radio commentator later on in life, and the feared beat copper, Frank 'Bumper' Farrell, who was happy to use his meaty fists to lay down law and order in the name of the New South Wales police force. Only a few months before he became my 'lieut', Bill had played in the City representative team that thrashed Country 44–21. The boys who knew more about the game than me were adamant that had it not been for the war, Bill would have been well on track to represent Australia.

It was because Bill struck me as such a genuine bloke that I asked for his advice about how I could stop The Officer from forcing me to slave for him over a stove. I had my reasons for not holding much of an opinion about the bloke, who I'd describe as 'pompous'. First of all, we never saw him, and that was interpreted by us, the Militia, as a sign that he didn't think too highly of us. Secondly, rather than show empathy to the family men who needed a break, he enforced bloody-minded army discipline. There were occasions when police officers were sent to the camp to inform a soldier about a problem at home. For instance, a man's wife might've fallen ill and gone to hospital and the kids were sent to stay with a family member or neighbour. To most men, their overriding priority was to get home and ensure their family was safe. While they'd have needed no more than 24 hours – 48 at the most – The Officer rarely issued any of them with a compassionate leave pass. When the request for permission to return home was inevitably knocked back, everyone knew these men would be so desperate to do the right thing as husbands and fathers that they'd climb the wire. The Officer knew this too, and when the poor bastards were eventually rounded up by the military police they were locked up in the brig, *plus* they were hit with a heavy fine. That only added salt to their wounds, and it angered us because all that happened when a poorly paid private was fined one or two pounds was that his family suffered even more hardship. I felt this was terribly unjust. These were simply men who were trying to sort out family dramas and they deserved a break. My view remains this: they were husbands and fathers before they were soldiers, and that responsibility didn't end just because they'd put on a uniform. So, while The Officer had done nothing to me personally, his lack of empathy for men who needed it during times of stress was the reason I didn't hold him in high esteem. He was like the dictator who, when asked by his people to give them a loaf of bread, gave them a rock. In the few minutes that I spoke to Bill, I let him know how little I thought of the bloke.

Bill listened to me, but after I finished speaking he shook his head and warned me that I didn't have the right attitude. He'd been in the army for six months – which was much longer than me – so that meant he possessed a much better understanding of military diplomacy. He advised me to treat The Officer like he was 'a king' in order to get what I wanted. He said I had two choices: one, I could be nasty to The Officer and end up being hammered, or two, I could be respectful before requesting that we speak 'soldier to soldier, man to man'. Bill explained that if The Officer agreed to my request we'd stand on common ground and I could speak freely. He added that if I spoke civilly, I could do so without any fear of retribution. It turned out Bill was a fountain of useful knowledge, because he revealed there were two jobs the army couldn't force a soldier to do: the first was to cook, and the second was to serve as an offi- cer's batman – which is a personal servant. When I told Bill I understood what he was saying, he volunteered to accom- pany me to my appointment with The Officer to act as my witness. That, he explained, would ensure The Officer respected our agreement that we were speaking soldier to soldier, and not private to superior. If The Officer didn't respect the terms of our understanding – and there wasn't a witness to keep him honest – Bill said I'd run the risk of being charged with insubordination.

The following morning, I stood to attention in The Officer's office with Lieutenant Ryan beside me. I can only imagine he anticipated fireworks because Ryan had brought George Wearne, the company's level-headed adjutant, and the salt of the earth, to act as my second witness. The Officer must have wondered why his office was so crowded, but he told me to 'stand easy' and began to speak. 'Chard,' he said while clearing his throat, 'I believe you can cook, so I'd like you to cook for me.' When he finished I asked quite calmly if we could speak 'soldier to soldier, man to man'. The moment he invited me to do so, the temper I'd inherited from Dad exploded and I let rip. I told him I had no intention of cooking for him because I'd joined the army to fight and not serve as a chef for an officer. Of course, I overstepped the mark because then I told him the reasons *why* I'd never cook for him and cited the same complaints I'd expressed to Bill the previous night. Not surprisingly, The Officer was livid to think a mere private would dare to question his actions. His face turned crimson, and while I can't remember what he said, I do recall that when he leant over his desk to fire a salvo back at me his spittle flew wildly! I also remember responding to one of his tirades by saying I'd be stuffed if I'd even boil an egg for a man such as him! By the end of it Bill's face was ashen while George Wearne's contained a look of disbelief. For his part, The Officer continued to talk to me soldier to soldier alright, because his parting words went something along the lines of: 'Get the fuck out of here!'

'Well, I guess I won't be cooking for him,' I said triumphantly to Bill and George as we walked away from the scene of what, in normal circumstances, would have been a military crime. However, Bill appeared far more shaken by the commanding officer's outburst than I felt, while poor George couldn't stop shaking his head. He'd never seen anything like it. Bill offered what proved to be sage advice when he told me not to celebrate the 'victory' too early. He warned there'd certainly be reprisals, adding he feared all of C Coy would cop the brunt of The Officer's vengeance. George, who was a thorough gentleman, supported my lieutenant's verdict in no uncertain terms when he looked at me and said with a shrug of his shoulders: 'You're stuffed, Reg.' Nevertheless, I was happy. I had done what I needed to do to remain with my mates and fight with the infantry. However, they were right; The Officer was swift in singling out me and my mates for punishment.

The following morning members of my section and I began the first of our 'special duties' when we stood knee-deep in the Greta camp's sewage treatment to break up the lumps of human faeces that were flushed from the camp's countless rows of latrines. And yes, it was as terrible an experience as it sounds. I have no doubt The Officer ordered a sergeant to round up a group from my platoon, because the 'sarge' made a point of asking whether Chard was among our number. Once I confirmed I was, he pointed with his thick forefinger and said: 'Right, you, you, you, you and *you, Chard*, come with me.' We climbed aboard a horse-drawn dray, and when we arrived at the treatment plant each of us was handed sets of the all-in-one braces and boots anglers wear when they go fly fishing. We were then handed long sticks and told to step into a channel where our job was to break up the turds as they floated past us. After an hour, the bloke who ran the plant yelled out: 'Hey, fellas, would you like a drink of milk?' It was an offer we unanimously declined because there's no way we could've kept it down.

The army used the waste to make fertiliser, and what surprised me is that by the time it had gone through the treatment process it was so pure you could've rubbed your face in it without the slightest knowledge of its origins. We were forced to do this unpleasant work for the better part of a week, and whenever some of the other men laughed about the predicament me and my fellow members of the sewage squad were in, it's to their credit that my mates put on a united front as I replied: 'While you jokers are marching, we're up there drinking milk and doing hardly anything!' Of course, the reality was a completely different story, but they didn't know any better. While my mates never complained in front of the others, they did let me have it from time to time: 'Good on you, Reg! Why don't you just cook for the prick and get us out of this shithole!' However, I couldn't do that. Regardless of whatever punishments The Officer had in store for me, I'd joined the army to fight for my country, not cook filet mignon for an overbearing silvertail who couldn't handle the truth.

13

The Saint of Kokoda and Simple Jack

There were quite a number who really shouldn't have been there. They were just very slow ... They should have been a cook's off-sider. They should never have been at the front line.

Don Daniels, 39th Australian Infantry Battalion

The army sent thousands of men to fight on the frontline even though they weren't suited for the job. We had a man in C Coy who the recruiting officer should've sent straight home to his family. He was a political conscript who had legitimate grounds to refuse to serve in a combat role because he was a conscientious objector due to his belief in God. However, 'The Believer', as I'll call him, did what he thought was the right thing and followed the government's instructions to report for duty. For his trouble, the military sent this man to the infantry. He turned up at Greta and marched alongside us without complaint, and he did each drill as thoroughly as anyone else. While I never asked him about it, I suppose The Believer accepted his lot as

'God's will'. However, what I do know about him is he was a 29-year-old working-class man from Sydney's western suburbs; his wife and three daughters were undoubtedly the loves of his life; his faith in God was unwavering, and he didn't have a malicious bone in his body. Due to his age and his naturally warm nature, we younger blokes gravitated towards him as though he were our uncle. It was thanks to The Believer's moral compass that we 18- and 19-year-olds didn't stray too far from the 'good' path, although he disagreed with what I said was my God-given gift to 'obtain' a variety of items from the army stores. These treasures not only helped to make life a little bit more comfortable for all of us but they earnt me the nickname 'Scrounger'.

The story behind The Believer joining the 2/55th serves as an example that when the army stuffs something – or someone's life – up, they do it on a grander scale than any other organisation. While I was only a mere kid of 18, it was obvious to me after I'd witnessed The Believer's efforts on the rifle range, and then heard his story, that the military did the wrong thing by him. He was far too gentle a soul to serve in a unit whose primary function was to kill, kill and then kill even more of the enemy.

On the day The Officer dismissed us from our sewage plant detail, we were sent straight to the rifle range as the 'markers' for C Coy's shooting session. It wasn't as dangerous a job as it may sound; indeed, the markers operated from what was the safest place in the entire camp because we worked below ground level, and once the men started firing we took refuge in one of the tunnels that allowed us to walk back towards where the men were positioned.

We took shelter there as we waited for the 'all clear' signal to sound. At Greta we used targets made from large sheets of canvas with the traditional bullseye printed on them. The instructors had spaced them out at intervals ranging from 100 yards for the novices to 10,000 yards for eagle-eyed snipers to finetune their long-range 'kill' shots. The first job markers did was to fit and clip the canvas sheets into their frames, and you then raised them so the men could take aim and open fire. After receiving the 'all clear' we'd use the marker – a five-litre circular tin painted bright yellow and fastened by screws to the top of a stick that was three times as long as a household broomstick – to cover the holes left in the canvas targets by the rounds when they passed through them so the instructor could see how good the recruit's aim was. The majority of C Coy's men shot well enough, but on this particular day it appeared as though there was a blind man in our ranks because one of our blokes couldn't hit the target for love or money. Each time he finished his allocated number of rounds I'd signal 'wipe out' (meaning complete miss), which was achieved by quickly waving the marker from side to side. Obviously, I couldn't stick my head over the parapet to see who the unfortunate fellow was, but after his fourth turn without any success, I turned to Bluey and said: 'Whoever's shooting up there is bloody shocking!'

The following day when I was back behind my .303, I kept an eye out to see who the lousy shot was, and it shouldn't have surprised me to learn it was The Believer. What's more, I realised he wasn't even aiming his rifle at the target – he was missing the bloody thing on purpose! While I was deeply intrigued, I waited until we returned to our hut before I broached the subject with him. If The Believer had a problem with shooting, I figured it was better to know now instead of when we were out on the battlefield.

'Is something wrong with your eyes?' I said with all the bluntness of an army mess hall's butter knife. 'I'm only asking because your shooting is no good.' The Believer's response was to grimace before he slowly shook his head. He then explained that due to his religious beliefs he was a conscientious objector. *A conscientious objector!* Well, I was dumbstruck, and asked why on earth he was in the bloody infantry, a place where he risked breaking the sixth of the Ten Commandments: *Thou shalt not kill.* The Believer said he'd asked that the recruiting officer assign him to the stretcher bearers or any non-combatant's role. He reasoned that if he *had* to go to war, he wanted to save lives rather than take them. As a conscientious objector based on religious grounds, Australian law actually forbade the army from putting a rifle in his hands, but unfortunately the army ignored a reasonable enough plea because they were throwing everyone they possibly could into the infantry. I had seen with my own eyes that our army was making all number of compromises in order to recruit more men when they relaxed the medical standards that had ruled out hundreds, if not thousands, of men from joining up in 1939.

The Believer confessed that he'd missed the targets on purpose because he was horrified by the vision that appeared in his mind every time he lined up his rifle. He didn't see just a sheet of canvas in front of him, he saw human beings. He believed even the simple act of imagining he was killing someone, even a Japanese soldier whose goal was to murder as many Australians as possible, would offend God. I didn't share his faith; nevertheless, I'd be lying if I said The Believer's sincerity and his belief in the being he called 'the Almighty' didn't move me. His was a complex situation, but I appreciated that he'd explained himself to me because it allowed me to have an understanding of what he was going through.

The Believer would later prove on countless occasions to be the 'Saint of Kokoda', because in the true spirit of Christianity, he put everyone else before himself. Sometimes, knowing the turmoil he was going through on the Kokoda Trail meant I looked at him with a sense of pity that I know he wouldn't have welcomed. However, I couldn't help but wonder how my friend would survive the war as an infanteer if he didn't have it within him to kill another person. Eighty years on from my conversation with him, there are still days when I wish I'd spoken to Bill Ryan about The Believer's unfortunate situation.

Towards the end of January 1942, there was an unmistakeable urgency in the voices of our sergeants as they continued to put us through our paces. We'd finally received our boots, slouch hats and rifles (still no uniforms, though), and that seemed to be the signal for them to get even more kilometres into our legs. The distances we marched through the Hunter Valley became longer, and so much harder. It quickly became a case of us men marching for breakfast, for lunch and for dinner. Any hope we may have had of getting a full night's sleep was long gone because the sergeants would burst into the barracks at all hours of the night, screaming for us to get up and dress in full kit.

Minutes later we'd start a 40-kilometre route march – one that's via roads and tracks – in the darkness. There were also times when we'd return to our barracks after a tough day of drilling, and before even removing our boots, the three-stripers would charge in and yell: 'EVERYBODY OUT! AND TAKE ALL OF YOUR GEAR!' And with that order ringing in our ears, we took the first steps of what could be another 20- or 30-kilometre march into the darkness. The Pugilist (who was always in very deep thought during these route marches because he was busy plotting his escape) was far from impressed by the change in his circumstances.

Napoleon may have said the French army marched on its stomach, but Lieutenant Ryan and his sergeants made it clear the Australian Army lived – or died – by the state of its soldiers' feet. They drummed into us that it was crucial we made sure we looked after our 'plates of meat'. And we appreciated their wisdom when we were in the jungle because a soldier was all but useless if he couldn't fight because his feet were in poor condition. The army's insistence that our feet were weapons of war was the reason we had dozens of galvanised iron tubs waiting for us whenever we returned from a route march. We'd rip off our boots and a group of eight men would sit around the tub and place their feet into the hot water that contained a healthy splash of Condy's Crystals. A team of chiropodists would then get to work, and we kept them busy as they cut away corns, treated blisters and tended to anyone with an ingrown toenail – hands-down the most painful thing of all when you marched! By now, it seemed like a lifetime ago that I'd attended the Addison Road Drill Hall for my medical.

My concerns about my flat feet being a hindrance to my soldiering had amounted to nothing. After six weeks of soaking my feet every day in the Condy's Crystals, they became as hard as granite. Indeed, that was one of the best things the army did for me, because at 98 years of age, I've never had any problems with my feet. I wish I could say the same about most other parts of my body!

There was an obvious reason for the escalation in our training. Towards the end of January 1942, the Japanese advance throughout South-East Asia and the Pacific had gained a frightening momentum. The American defences in the Philippines were on the brink of capitulating; the Japanese were swarming across the Dutch East Indies (now Indonesia) and Dutch Borneo to Australia's north, and had marched into Burma; the Commonwealth force in Malaya was on the run; the garrison in Singapore was crumbling, and a Japanese task force consisting of two aircraft carriers, seven cruisers, 14 destroyers, a number of smaller vessels and 5000 highly trained members of the Imperial Japanese Army's 144th Infantry Battalion were preparing to steam towards the 1300 Australians based at Rabaul and the 130 poor souls on New Ireland. The Australians there didn't stand a chance against such an overwhelming force and its terrifying firepower. When the Japanese annihilated the defenders to establish a foothold on Australia's doorstep, the army responded to the threat by toughening us up. Ready or not, we were about to enter the fight to defend our nation and loved ones in a place I'd never heard of: Papua New Guinea.

It was at this point we had a new member join our group. 'Simple' Jack, a potato picker from a small township near Newcastle, had joined the battalion when the AIF boys arrived from Bathurst with Lieutenant Ryan and the other NCOs and sergeants. He was a harmless soul who smoked a little pipe to relax when he was off duty. He was a loner, and I hate to think what his childhood was like because he told us he became an orphan at a young age and was brought up in the 'state's care'. He didn't have a skerrick of confidence about him, which many of the boys found odd. However, even though he'd quite often march out of step to the rest of us on and off the parade ground, he became our mate.

Before finding us, Jack had been in the unfortunate situation of being the victim of a weak bastard of a senior officer (a different individual from the one who wanted me to cook for him) who delighted in bullying him. The officer singled Jack out because he was quiet and vulnerable, and, to a coward, those traits made him an irresistible punching bag on which to take out his frustrations. Even after Jack joined our mob and gained a measure of protection, the officer still belittled him by saying such things to us as: 'You know Jack is *different* from you men, don't you?' We would've loved to have cut loose on this 'officer' — and I use that term in name only — but all we could do to express our displeasure was to say absolutely nothing. Our response was to look straight through the bloke as though he wasn't there. The uncomfortable silence that followed his snide remarks guaranteed he'd quickly turn tail and skulk off back to his hole. This fellow didn't need to be a mind-reader to realise that none of us respected him.

Nevertheless, whenever Jack made his inevitable mistake on parade, or during a drill, the officer always seemed to be on hand to see it. He never missed an opportunity to humiliate Jack in front of the entire company. He'd scream at him for making his comrades look bad, and then he'd tell everyone we could 'thank Jack' for the extra drills we had to do as punishment. It was the act of a mongrel. Once we'd finished the extra drilling, blokes who weren't part of our group would front us to complain about our troubled mate. They'd start their whinge with three words: 'Bloody Simple Jack . . .' but that was as far as they ever got before someone – and it could've been any one of us, Bluey, Titch, Nugget, Bula, big Ken Horne, Bill Mackie, Trigger, myself, even shy Normie Wolfson – shut them down by saying something like: 'Hang on, sport, we all know Jack's a bit different from you and me, but he's *our* mate, so you'd better bloody well leave him alone!'

And they did.

Having found a group of mates who'd accepted him for who he was went a long way to helping Jack develop a sense of self-worth, and gave him a 'family'. One of the greatest days during our time at Greta was when Jack finally stood up to the officer who'd been terrorising him. Believe me, we were just as shocked as the bully when Jack finally snapped. Our mate clenched his fists, squared his shoulders, stepped forward and stared directly into his antagonist's eyes before offering a chilling warning through gritted teeth. Jack growled that if ever we were in a battle, the officer had better not make the mistake of standing in front of Jack when he was holding a gun. It was a death threat, and the officer's jaw dropped in disbelief. And, just to ensure he'd heard correctly, Jack repeated his warning. The officer then looked at us, and when he saw us smiling and nodding in approval, he swivelled smartly on his heel and beat it back to his quarters at a quicker than normal pace.

That should've been the end of it, but the officer's abuse of Jack only intensified because he'd been embarrassed. I suppose he wanted to save face by proving he wasn't scared of Jack's threat. Sadly his renewed attacks had a detrimental impact on our friend's mental health. We saw that Jack was close to breaking, and at risk of doing something rash. The group met – without Jack – and it was decided that when we went on our next bivouac (an overnight camp) we'd give the officer a message that let him know *we* weren't prepared to watch him bully a defenceless man. When the time came, four of us, and I was one of them, poured four gallons of petrol over the bully's tent and then one of our number struck a match and threw it. Well, the tent and all of its contents were destroyed by a fireball. It was a beautiful sight, and the bastard finally took the hint because he never dared to pick on Jack again.

If I'm proud about anything from my time as a soldier, it's that the blokes who I befriended looked out for one another at the battlefront, and at home.

14

The Other Enemy

There is no way you can convince me those bastards ever came anywhere near the front . . . They were a bunch of no-hopers and a complete waste of rations . . .

World War I digger's thoughts on MPs

The military police (MPs) who patrolled Sydney's Central Station had a terrible reputation for thuggery. They hunted in packs and thought nothing of ganging up on a soldier for no good reason. There were cowards and bullies among them who believed the red armband they wore to identify their role as the army's upholders of law and order was a free pass to throw their weight around without the threat of reprisal.

Not long after I joined up, word leaked out of Holsworthy – the army camp in south-western Sydney where the main military prison was based – about the treatment the MPs dished out to the prisoners. These revelations shone a light upon their cruelty and ensured that everyone in uniform despised them. Most of the men at Holsworthy were imprisoned for typical wartime behaviour including going AWOL, backchatting an officer, or playing up while drunk. However, besides their sentence and fines, they were also subjected to the unofficial punishments meted out by the MPs. One of the worst was when the men were told they had to scrub the floors of their prison cell. It was never the guards' intention for them to actually clean the floors. Instead, once the prisoners were on their hands and knees, the MPs would lay into them with their steel-capped boots. The injuries they inflicted were terrible. Indeed, the Provosts were so bad it's fair to say that by the middle of 1942, Australian soldiers had five enemies: the Nazis, the Italians, the Vichy French, the Japanese, and our own military police. The cold war between them and the enlisted men reached boiling point at Greta the night one of our reinforcements was towelled up by a group of the miserable so-and-sos at Central Station.

I don't recall the soldier's name, but what I do remember is that, like me, he was only young. When he was walking towards the country platform to return to Greta after his 48 hours' leave, the MPs challenged him to show his pass. Among this group was a giant who, before hostilities, was a famous professional wrestling champion. He had a distinguished fight record which included bouts in the United States, Europe, New Zealand and anywhere else in the world that had a ring, a promoter and an audience who liked the theatre of pro wrestling. The wrestler's aggressiveness flustered the reinforcement and he couldn't find his leave pass straight away. As the MPs screamed at him, he frantically patted at his shirt and shorts pockets as he pleaded for them to just give him a second to find it. They didn't. He was frogmarched from the public's view so the MPs could administer a brutal hiding. Considering that the heavyweight wrestler had a weight advantage of at least seven stone, you can imagine the damage he alone inflicted upon the helpless target. However, the three other MPs didn't miss him either, and he returned to camp in a shocking state. He had tears in his blackened eyes, frightful swelling disfigured his face, while ugly bruises tattooed his skinny frame. The poor kid said over and over he didn't know what he'd done wrong, and he complained it felt as though he'd been hit by a tram.

We were outraged, and a few of our crew said they'd like the chance to get square with the so-and-sos who'd done it. Oh, we were seething. The reinforcement had done nothing wrong because he had the pass; the MPs had lacked the patience to let him find it. Also, this wasn't the first time such a thing had happened, and we felt frustrated that the senior commanders didn't appear overly concerned about bringing the MPs to account. In saying that, I have no doubt that had our Lieutenant Ryan seen the 'red caps' gang up on an individual, he would've taken matters into his own hands because that's the man he was. Bula and Nugget were undoubtedly cut from the same cloth because I'd noticed that their eyes blazed with a terrible rage as they examined the young bloke's injuries. It was a genuine look of hatred, and I sensed they had a plan. As the kid was taken to the base hospital for treatment, the pair sought out two other kindred spirits, tough nuts from the 'Silver City' side of the camp. When Bula and Nugget told us they'd 'sort it out', they asked for us to cover for them by doing their duties throughout the following day. If we did that, they figured no-one would be wise to the fact they were missing. They departed for the train station that night armed with pick handles and a vengeful intent.

Funnily enough, when we assembled for our physical culture class the next morning, Lieutenant Ryan was waiting on the parade ground for us. He was obviously unaware that we'd already made our arrangements with Bula and Nugget. Bill assigned our small group to do their duties before telling us to keep it on the lowdown that they weren't about. We'd later find out Lieutenant Ryan had crossed paths with Bula, Nugget and their associates after they left the camp. When Bill heard what they'd planned to do with their clubs, he offered two sound pieces of advice. Firstly, he told them to make a good fist of it, but secondly he warned them to not get arrested because they'd never get out of Holsworthy alive. By not stopping them, our 'lieut' was an accessory to grievous assault, and we loved him for it because it further proved he was a unique officer. As I've suggested, Bill Ryan was a 'man's man' with no time for bullies, especially cowards who hid behind the protection of their MP's band or officer's pips.

When the time came, Greta's war party didn't miss their opportunity to strike. When they tracked down the wrestler and his cohort, they used their pick handles to execute swift and brutal justice, smashing the MPs in their legs, knees, ribs, arms and hips. While I never read anything in the newspapers about what happened in the shadows of the railway station, what I do know is that the wrestler and his three cronies required a lengthy spell in hospital to lick their wounds. While none of us ever breathed a word about the retaliation mission through fear our mates would end up in a military prison, we considered Bula, Nugget and the other pair as the enlisted man's unsung heroes. I'm sure that 80 years after the event, none of them would mind that I've spilt the beans on a closely guarded secret.

Not long after the MPs were battered, I faced my own moral dilemma when my values were challenged with the promise of a reward that was the equivalent of a king's ransom. On this particular day, one of the soldiers on guard duty sent another bloke to inform me there was a civilian visitor waiting for me at the gate. Those words made my blood chill because most times when someone made the long trip from Sydney to Greta it was to share unwelcome news from home. Naturally I feared the worst, wondering if something had happened to Jack in North Africa, or Mum? My father? *Betty!* However, as soon as I saw who the visitor was I breathed easy. It was Harry Fleming's arch rival, Len Storey – the bloke who spent far too much of his time wondering why the Scotsman's pies were more popular than his own fare. I guessed it was my mother who'd told Len I was at Greta, but our conversation didn't last long enough for me to ask such trivialities. Len didn't beat around the bush. He said he had one hundred pounds in his pocket and he'd give it to me in exchange for Harry's recipes. It was the most money anyone had ever offered me, and, to put it into perspective, the army was paying me five shillings a day and half of that went to my mother. However, there was no way I'd dirty my hands by touching Len's cash. Rather than feel angry that Storey thought I'd betray Harry, I was shocked to think he could be so brazen. After he'd put his grubby cards on the table, I advised Len that if he headed straight back to the station there might still be enough time for him to catch the early train home.

When I returned to Dulwich Hill a few days later for my 48 hours' leave, I saw no point in telling Mr Fleming about Storey's attempt to sway me to betray him. That would only have made Harry angry, and I was afraid that such was his loathing for his adversary he'd do something he was likely to regret.

I felt sorry for my quiet friend Jack, because as an orphan he had nowhere and no-one to go to for leave, so I invited him to stay with me and my family. I just couldn't leave him to stay at the camp on his own. Something I've never forgotten was how excited Jack was to climb on board the Sydney-bound steam train.

It proved to be an exciting trip for me, too, because it allowed me to briefly meet one of my heroes. The train always stopped at Brooklyn station near the Hawkesbury River to take on extra water so it could build up the steam required to chug its way up the steep gradient that led to Sydney. We stopped at the station for quite a while, and the people who worked on the oyster beds in the area had gathered on the platform to sell bottles of freshly shucked oysters for a shilling, which was great value. My parents loved oysters, so I always took a bottle home with me. However, with 400 men on a troop train you needed to move quickly to buy one, and that's why I jumped off the train as soon as it had slowed down enough. However, I was surprised to see that a mob of soldiers had surrounded one of the oyster sellers. They were shaking his hand and slapping him on the back. I wondered if it was a war hero because the crowd was genuinely happy to see him. As I drew closer, I understood the reason for the buzz . . . it was the great Australian lightweight boxing champion, Vic Patrick! He was on the platform helping to sell the latest offerings from his father's nearby oyster lease. He was a rangy, bony southpaw whose fighting style ensured he won a series of impressive victories at the Sydney Stadium. While Vic wasn't a soldier the day I saw him, he'd prove that he possessed a different outlook about an individual's duty to his nation than The Pugilist. Vic volunteered for the AIF in October 1942, and he insisted on being placed in a frontline role. However, his manager Ern McQuillan Snr obviously didn't want to lose the star of his stable. He worked his connections in the government and they convinced some ministers Vic was too important for public morale to risk him being killed on the battlefield. Vic was instead assigned to a transport unit based at Chippendale in Sydney's inner west, which, as 'luck' had it, was within jogging distance of McQuillan's gym in Newtown.

Vic was obviously a generous man because I've since learnt one of his first acts as a member of the AIF was to buy each of the men he served alongside a brand new bed. Apparently, he had no intention of sleeping on the military's regulation hessian sack stuffed with straw, but he couldn't bunk down in a bed while the others slept on the floor!

Vic Patrick was my favourite fighter, and 'the champ' made a great impression on me and the others that day at the Brooklyn train station because he was happy to speak to anyone who wanted to say hello. I'm not sure if the two men with him were his brothers, cousins, or just friends, but they did all the work of selling the oysters while Vic was mobbed by us. According to boxing aficionados, had it not been for the unholy trinity of Hitler, Mussolini and Hirohito, Vic would've become the world's lightweight champion. In its own small way, his missed opportunity is an example of how the war crushed millions of dreams and aspirations . . .

It was only when we arrived in Marrickville and I saw Betty again that I appreciated why I kept myself busy in Greta by baking cakes, scrounging for items that made life more bearable for me and my mates, throwing myself into whatever was going on around me, listening to my mates' stories about their home and lives, and constantly asking questions about how the army's array of machinery and weapons worked. It was because it helped to keep my mind off how much I missed her. Oh, there were many times when I felt numb because I hated being apart from her. However, I realised that pining to be with Betty would only make our absence even more painful. Keeping myself busy became the coping mechanism that allowed me to function. That day, it was only when I threw my arms around Betty that I knew I *really* was home. It was obvious she felt the same because I felt her tremble in our embrace. I could so easily have married Betty during that 48 hours we were together, but my father's advice about not ruining her life rang like a constant warning bell in my ears.

Betty had started work at a factory in Addison Road, Marrickville, not long after I left for basic training. She'd turned up at the jewellery store one morning to start her shift and found an official from the Manpower Department waiting for her. He advised her she'd been assigned to help the war effort by working in a factory which made tiny valves for radios. She worked long hours to meet the demand, but Betty didn't mind because it meant she worked closer to home and was paid better money. She could also ride her bike to work instead of catching a crowded tram, and rather than having to dress up to the nines as she did at the jewellers, she dressed less formally to work at the factory – although I can assure you that up until her death Betty loved nothing more than getting 'glammed' up in her best outfits whenever we went out!

I think Jack enjoyed the break too. He was, of course, encouraged by Mum to make himself feel at home, and while I could see he appreciated it, he was painfully shy and awkward. He didn't know how to relax around Mum and Betty, but he was polite and respectful. We didn't see much of my father, because even though it was the weekend, there was plenty of work around. Besides that, whenever the old man downed tools, he divided his time between Claude Fay's Hotel, the ANZAC Club, and drinking too many bottles of beers with his mates at their homes. I didn't mind too much because his not being about gave me more time to talk to Mum without his brooding presence.

That Saturday night, Betty, Jack and I went out to the Tivoli in Castlereagh Street. Apart from its world-class vaudeville acts, it was also famous for the Tivoli 'Tappers' – the glamourous dancers. Well, when Jack saw them in their skimpy costumes his head just about exploded! He'd never experienced anything quite like it, and he took in the whole experience with what I'd describe as childlike wonder. A few weeks later, as we melted in the humidity of Port Moresby, Jack's eyes became distant and he'd smile whenever he mentioned 'those dancers' and the great night out we'd had.

While Betty was happy that I'd brought Jack home with me, she couldn't help but wonder why. I explained that Jack was on his own because he had no family, and that when you're in the army there's nothing worse than having no-one to go home to. I told her it's a terrible lone-liness. Once Betty had digested what I'd said, her response said a lot about the beautiful person my future wife was because she asked who sent Jack letters. When I said Jack didn't receive mail because he had nobody to write to him, Betty said she'd drop him an occasional line to say hello. Her letters were nothing more than a matter of *Hope you're doing well*, or *It's been raining for a week*, or, *I hope you and Reg are keeping out of trouble*, but he thought it was marvellous someone had thought to write to him.

Over the course of the next few weeks, everyone in the 2/55th would have plenty to write home about. The step up in our training made it clear we were about to start earning our pay. We were being prepared to head to the front, and it now seems crazy to think that the thought of fighting the Japanese genuinely excited me.

15

Heading North

We were travelling on this stinking hot day, and the car-riages had more fellows than they had seats. Some fellows climbed up onto those wire racks. But it was terribly hot and there was far too many people on the train, but I suppose that's the way it was.

Sergeant Joe Dawson, 39th Australian Infantry Battalion

We'd barely found our feet back at Greta before we received orders to kit up and get ready for another march. Our com-manders planned to bring us back to earth with a thud after spending 48 hours sleeping in our own beds, eating home-cooked meals, spending time with our loved ones, and, in Jack's case, having his mind blown by the sight of the 'Tivoli Tappers' strutting their stuff.

We marched 90 kilometres from Greta to Port Stephens where we manned the coastal defences for a week. Military intelligence had pinpointed the 113-kilometre shoreline between Newcastle and Port Stephens as one of the points on the map where the Japanese were likely to launch an invasion of Australia. The area would have been suitable because it had long beaches and low sandhills, and it granted access to the network of roads that stretched to Sydney, Newcastle and beyond. When some of the boys realised where we were headed they joked that our time by the surf could be an opportunity to enjoy hours of sunbathing and swimming. However, we would find out soon enough that spending time at 'Port' was anything but a holiday.

Our stint at what's now a popular tourist area was, up until then, the most wretched time any of us had spent in the army. For the entire week the 55th – as we were known – was camped there we were hit by unseasonal high winds and stung by the sand they whipped up. We weren't issued with the goggles the soldiers in the Middle East had, and one of my memories of that week is of constantly having to shield my eyes, or turn my back, to the trillions of particles that felt like sandpaper rubbing up against my face! In all honesty, we weren't really needed to protect that strip of coastline, because that dreadful wind would've been enough to drive any Japanese force back to Tokyo!

Our only respite from Mother Nature was to sleep in the gun turrets that were half-buried in the beach. They had a commanding view of the district, and whenever you opened the steel slots you could see right across Port Stephens, but no-one dared open them during a sandstorm because that gave the swirling cloud of grit an entry point – and the damn stuff got into your food, your eyes, *everything*. When we were dismissed of an evening there was a frantic race between those men not stuck on overnight sentry duty to get a spot inside the turrets. It was the prized location because sleep was all but impossible for anyone who had to bunk in the open and withstand the sandstorms and the cold. All in all, it was a miserable week, and when it finally ended the jokers who'd thought they would get a tan and spend time in the surf couldn't wait to leg it back to Greta.

However, we barely had enough time to wash the Port Stephens sand out of our hair and ears before Lieutenant Ryan ordered us to dress in our full battle kit again. This time, we only needed to take a short 'stroll' to Stockton Beach, a 'mere' 58 kilometres away. To make it more challenging, we were permitted only one bottle of water despite the fact we would be marching under a blazing sun! We filled the bottles which had our names written on them as we left, and the same team of sergeants and corporals waited to collect them from us when we reached Stockton Beach. Believe me, it took a lot of restraint not to quench your thirst by guzzling the water in great gulps. Those who couldn't resist relied on the kindness of their mates for a few sips to keep them going.

As you might imagine, this march was as physically draining as it was mentally tough. While we were dehydrated, we somehow managed to reach the beach in one piece. However, Stockton and the other places we stopped at during our month-long coastal defence duty were so bloody rotten they made windswept Port Stephens seem like paradise! When we weren't running up and down the beach weighed down by our packs and rifles, we were buffeted by westerly winds which literally buried the men guarding the beach under mounds of sand. The wind then looped around to return as southerly busters which pushed the sand away from the pillboxes that dotted the beach.

Once exposed it was possible to see them from miles away. Interestingly enough, one link in that defensive chain that was designed to halt the Japanese invasion remains intact to this day – the Stockton Beach tank traps. They're 1.5-metre pyramid-shaped blocks of reinforced concrete which were lined up a few feet apart from one another. At the top was a crown of metal spikes which measured 10–20 centimetres long. In 2020 a long row of the traps reappeared when high tides washed away the tonnes of sand that covered them. And they're still dangerous, because in 2018 a surfer reported that he was badly stuck in the leg by one of the spikes that protruded from the sand.

After Stockton we moved on to Raymond Terrace. I vividly remember that the next hardship we endured was the region's vicious mosquitoes. These mongrels are known as 'Hexham Greys', and if they aren't as big as a blowfly they're close enough to it. They were massive, and, as we made our way towards their domain, one of C Coy's wiser heads offered Pee Wee Corr some sage advice.

'Hey, Pee Wee!' he called out to our jockey-sized mate in a voice which was loud enough to command everyone's attention.

'Yes, cobber, what do you want?' replied Pee Wee.

'When we get to our next stop, you'd better keep your boots on – even when you go to sleep.'

'Why's that?'

'I'll tell ya why. The Hexham Greys are so bloody big – and bad – they'll carry a little fella like you away with 'em!'

We all roared with laughter for the next three kilometres, but we certainly weren't laughing at dusk when the Hexham

Greys attacked us. We were sitting ducks because apart from the palms of our hands we had nothing to fight back with. Some of the men used dried cow dung as fuel for our fires because they thought the smoke would repel them – but apart from filling our lungs with what I was certain were toxic fumes, it had no effect. Something we learnt about those primeval bloodsuckers was this: they're fearless and relentless. Their sting as they fed on us was painful, but one saving grace was that unlike their cousins in Papua New Guinea they didn't spread diseases such as malaria. Fortunately, Pee Wee survived our time there without being kidnapped by a marauding gang of Hexham Greys!

When we completed our exercise and marched back through the gates at Greta, the sergeants screamed for the entire battalion to 'line up, line up!' on the parade ground. As we stood at attention, I heard the distinctive *clip, clop, clip, clop* of a horse's hooves striking the road. When it came closer to us I heard it snort, and not long after that the camp's doctor appeared. He was sitting on top of his steed, looking as resplendent as an ancient English king survey-ing his army. He looked down on each man and sized him up in what I could only imagine was a form of inspec-tion. However, it wasn't much of one, as it lasted for no more than ten seconds. Also, from where the good doctor sat high in his saddle, there was no way he could've noticed if a soldier had acne, let alone a serious medical complaint. When he'd finished observing the men we heard him say: 'Yes, Colonel, all of the men are fit for overseas service.'

Well, within seconds of the words 'overseas service' leaving the doctor's lips, Titch whispered with an unmistakeable urgency for me to take a look at The Pugilist . . . and when I did, it was impossible for me to shift my eyes from what was one of the most incredible scenes I saw as a soldier. The Pugilist had realised this was his last chance to get out of the army, and like a fighter in need of a KO to win a title fight in the dying seconds of the final round, he threw every punch he could muster. My goodness, that man didn't do things by half measures! While he remained standing The Pugilist shook and shivered, made clucking sounds, his eyes rolled uncontrollably, and his head wobbled like a bowl of jelly. It was an impressive final roll of the dice by our man, but none of us in C Coy could help ourselves — we were all in hysterics. We laughed so hard at his performance it hurt our stomachs and sides. It was the best comedy act any of us had seen since Charlie Chaplin. However, after a few minutes it looked as though The Pugilist's body was actually spasming. I had to hand it to him, because he'd gone past the point of no return and gave no indication that he heard us laughing at him. The colonel gasped in horror, and the doctor appeared to have either frozen or he realised he was being conned, because he didn't swing into action until the colonel screamed for him to get off his 'bloody horse' and check on that soldier before he died of a fit! Oh, it was hilarious alright, and the last we all saw of The Pugilist — the fittest man in the entire battalion — was his being assisted to the camp's hospital by two men.

What added to the humour as he continued to gargle and shake was the reaction of his escorts. They were laughing harder than any of us! I still have no idea how he did it, but The Pugilist achieved what he'd set his mind to, and was discharged from the army. I was happy enough for him, and while I dipped my slouch hat to him for his pluck, I do note that he made a full 'recovery' from his mysterious ailment. His fight record notes he returned to the ring on 2 July 1942, which was around the same time his old friends from C Coy were sent to a disease-ridden place in south-eastern Papua New Guinea called Milne Bay.

After the laughter which accompanied The Pugilist's departure from the armed service subsided, the colonel said we had been granted 14 days' leave. While he didn't spell it out, we realised this would be our final leave before being sent to the front. There were half-hearted attempts by some officers to shoot down that notion, but we knew what was in store for us. When we took our leave, I was placed on the second of two trains bound for Sydney. Everyone was excited and looking forward to the chance to spend time with our loved ones. While no-one spoke about it because we were too busy laughing and joking with one another, all of us knew the fortunes of war meant this might be the last time some of us would see our families again.

When our train pulled into Maitland we disembarked to buy fresh fruit from the farmers to take home with us. What we didn't realise as we yarned to them about the weather and their crops was that the front engine had been unhooked and was replaced at the other end of the train by another engine. We only realised what'd happened after we were ordered to get back on board in 'double time'. With a sudden jolt, the train headed back towards Greta, and our confusion quickly turned into frustration. I wanted to see Betty; Dick Kayess wanted to spend time with Isabelle, and

Bill Elvy, the brickmaker from St Peters, was frothing at the mouth to see the lady he'd done stints in the brig for! It's fair to say none of the hundreds of men cooped up in the carriages was impressed. However, considering we were kept in the dark for quite a while, I don't remember too many of the men whining and carrying on. I could only imagine it would've been even harder for the men on the first train because when they arrived at Sydney a ring of MPs was waiting for them. They barked at them to get back onto the train. The ones who were fast enough to evade the cordon were rounded up quickly enough and they eventually followed us north. That could only have been tough, especially for those who were as little as a 20-minute tram ride from home.

What none of us knew then was that 'impregnable' Singapore had fallen. The AIF's 8th Division, or 15,000 men, no longer existed as a fighting force. They were among the 80,000 British and Indian troops who were captured when the British Army's General, Arthur Percival, negotiated what his Prime Minister, Winston Churchill, decried as 'the worst disaster and largest capitulation in British history'. The outlook was bleak for Australia. Our best troops were in North Africa; after the Singapore shambles we couldn't expect any support whatsoever from Mother Britain, and our most powerful ally, the United States of America, was still mobilising its own forces. Undermanned and virtually undefended, Australia needed every available soldier it had to be sent north to brace for an imminent attack – and that included the 55th. However, in our ignorance, as our train carried us in the direction of New Guinea's soon-to-be horrific battlefields, we thought the fact we'd bought enough fruit to keep us going during the overnight train ride was important.

Titch was fortunate because he was among the blokes who slept all the way to south-east Queensland in the deep luggage racks that hung like a balcony over the seats below them. Others slept in between the kit that lay strewn across the carriage's aisle, or snoozed on the seats. Considering everything that was happening around them, most of the men had very little trouble drifting off to sleep. When we made it to the Queensland border we changed trains because the Sunshine State's rail gauge was smaller than that of New South Wales. When we saw how tiny the Queensland Rail carriages were everyone laughed loudly and one of the boys described them as 'toys'. Nevertheless, we made it to Brisbane and received permission to take a look around the city as we waited for the boys who were turned around at Sydney to meet up with us.

I followed my mates as they made a beeline to a pub not far from Roma Street Station and ordered 'pots' of the local brew, Fourex. The born and bred Queensland troops who were perched at the bar drank the stuff as though it was going out of business. They called the beer 'barbed wire' because the brand – XXXX – was said to have resembled the fencing that could be found around the properties of boundaries in the state's vast outback. A few of the Queenslanders we met offered to shout me what they heard would have been my first beer, but I abstained. I still had no intention of drinking alcohol because I saw the hand it had played in my father's life. I'd had opportunities to have a drink before, but I couldn't ever bring myself to even taste it. Every Christmas, the Brumby's Flour Mill gave the bakers who used their products a little hamper, and there was always a bottle of pink champagne in it. During my first year as his apprentice Mr Fleming urged me to try the stuff, but when I refused, explaining that I planned to never touch a drop of alcohol, he took a long swig of the sickly looking liquid and spat it into the sink. 'Just as well you didn't drink it, son,' he gasped before rinsing his mouth out with water. 'The bloody stuff tastes like vinegar!' And vinegar became the taste I'd associate with all forms of alcohol. None of my army mates ever tried to pressure me into drinking, and it was the same that day as we sat in the pub on the outskirts of Brisbane's city centre. The round for the seven of us never changed throughout the entire afternoon: six pots of beer and one lemonade!

Wartime regulations stated that because our battalion was being sent to the front we had to travel at night in what was an attempt to conceal our movements. The following night we left Brisbane for the 1300-kilometre journey to Townsville, and believe me, it was a long, slow hike. We were always hungry, and on the one occasion we stopped at a town that was a mere speck on the map of Queensland, the boys noticed what appeared to be a large dairy canteen full of milk standing on the platform. Perhaps a train was meant to collect it and drop it off at another town further along the track. We didn't know, and we didn't really care, as one of the men jumped off the train, dashed to the milk can, put a handful of coins down to compensate the owner for his loss, and raced back onto the train. Well, our plan for a drink of fresh, country milk turned sour when we discovered it was cream! With only seconds before the train left, our man jumped back onto the platform, returned the can to its original spot, gathered all the coins, and just made it back into our carriage in the nick of time as the train pulled out of the sleepy hollow. He was lucky he did, because I don't think he would ever have lived down the 'shame' of being charged AWOL for a drink of milk!

16

Damien Parer

I didn't enjoy the voyage to Port Moresby. I spent my time watching bloody flying fish all the time. No, I didn't like it but the [Aquitania] was a good ship and I thought it was a shame to see the blokes carving their names or initials into the ornate railings and polished timber when they decided to try out their jack knives.

Private Cecil Driscoll, 39th Australian Infantry Battalion

Despite the train lurching and jolting all the way to Townsville, the majority of us still managed to write long letters as we headed to our 'staging' point. Most of our collective scribble explained to our sweethearts and families in plain soldier's language why we couldn't see them to say our final goodbyes before being sent overseas, or as the military preferred to call it, 'Away On Active Service'. If the other men wrote letters that were anything like mine to Betty, there would've been references to love and 'looking forward to the promise of the bright future' that awaited us when the war ended. And I meant each and every word. However, each outpouring of raw emotion seemed destined for the rubbish bin because when we arrived at what was still a big, sleepy country town it was 11 pm, and the city's post office had shut hours earlier. There wasn't even one stamp to be had between C Coy's 120 men, so we had no way of mailing our letters. It was the final, cruel twist to our unsettlingly rushed departure from Australia. After being denied the opportunity to say our farewells in person to those we cared for, we were now frustrated to think we couldn't do something as simple as send a letter to let our people know we'd left the country, and that we'd miss them terribly!

Just as all appeared lost, Townsville's harbourmaster, a jovial person named Hardy, arrived on the scene. He struck me as a cheerful soul because as he bounded up and down the lines of men, he carried with him an old sugar sack. He shouted above the noise of our marching feet: 'Mail, mail, who's got mail!' as if it was a joyful song. Whenever he took an envelope from a grateful soldier he'd simply say with a nod and big wink: 'No worries, digger – I'll make sure she gets home for ya!' He was a champion. I suppose he had realised after the first lot of soldiers passed through his city – the 39th, the 49th and 53rd battalions – at a similar witching hour, that unless *he* took action, the men's letters wouldn't reach their intended destinations. Hardy, who would have paid for the postage out of his own pocket, couldn't have had any idea of what his kindness meant to each man, and to our loved ones. Indeed, his actions helped make going away a little bit easier, because thanks to him we'd at least managed to say our goodbyes.

The harbourmaster also made sure our mob didn't leave Australia under a cloak of secrecy and darkness. I understand it was he and his wife who were responsible for telling half of Townsville to be at the quay at an ungodly hour to farewell yet another load of men who were leaving via their city's port to fight the Japanese. He risked being charged with breaching the wartime secrecy act by doing that, but when I'd meet Hardy at a much later date, I learnt he'd realised the importance of our duty. He was well aware that the Japanese were 'just over there', and that there were men among us who'd never see Australia again. Needless to say, we were amazed by the huge crowd that gathered to farewell us. They waved with such enthusiasm, while men, women and even the children shouted such messages as 'GOOD ON YA, MATE!' 'DO AUSTRALIA PROUD!' and 'STOP THE JAPS!' While it wasn't the same as a loving hug and farewell kiss from Betty, it was a lovely gesture all the same. That outpouring of warmth in Townsville also helped each of us to appreciate we were fighting to defend more than our own little patch of turf – we had the job of sparing the entire nation from the horrors the Japanese had inflicted everywhere they'd invaded. I clearly remember that as I climbed aboard the SS *Taroona* I was determined to do whatever was necessary to defeat what we called at the time 'those fucking Jap bastards'. We said things like that because hatred is a crucial, necessary weapon when fighting a war. And I make no apology for my thoughts, because the Japanese would prove over the next few months that theirs was an empire that *had* to be stopped regardless of the costs.

There were too many men for the entire 55th Battalion to leave Australia on the one ship. However, when C Coy and other companies boarded the SS *Taroona*, no-one among the ranks had the foggiest idea where we were heading. Nevertheless, the same old, ill-informed debates occupied far too many minds. On this occasion some of the boys thought we were bound for India, but others insisted we ought to expect the *Taroona* to drop anchor in Burma. As usual, I kept an open mind because if I'd learnt anything from my previous experiences it was that the men had absolutely no idea of where we were going until we arrived.

For 80 years the radio has reminded me of something the *Taroona*'s skipper did in the early hours of that morning as we steamed out of Townsville Harbour. Even though we could still hear the distant cheers and last cries of 'COOEE!' from the throng, the captain played two songs over the ship's loudspeakers: 'Red Sails in the Sunset' and 'Harbour Lights'. He played them because it was still safe to do so while we were in the harbour, but once we hit the open water he and his crew maintained silence – radio and otherwise – due to the genuine fear of being sunk by a Japanese submarine. Those two songs are embedded in my memory because they were the last pieces of music from home I heard for the entire time I was in Papua New Guinea. Besides one time when The Pianist played 'Nola' on a dilapidated piano in a bombed-out structure, there was nothing, not even a gramophone, in Port Moresby, for anyone to play music on. I'm now at the stage of my life where those tunes tug way too heavily on my heartstrings whenever I hear them played. The memories they stir up overwhelm me, and the reason I can't help crying when I hear them is because of the images that appear in my mind. I see the men, especially the other 18-year-olds who, like me, left on the *Taroona* full of hope and belief in the cause they were fighting for. However, so many never returned. And even the ones who didn't die in the jungle aren't around now. At the time of my writing this book, I'm among the last of the 55th still standing, and while I do count my blessings, it also hurts to know that.

Later that morning, the officers told us to cut one another's hair on the main deck. While our company consisted of men from a variety of occupations, there wasn't a single barber among us – and if there was, he kept quiet! By the time we'd finished with the clippers there were some extremely rough-looking heads on parade, and mine was among the worst of them. However, regardless of my new hairstyle, for the few days we were on the *Taroona*, I found it relaxing to lose myself by staring out at the great expanse of the ocean. Funnily enough, even though I couldn't swim a stroke to save myself, I wasn't ever concerned by the prospect of the ship sinking. I suppose the fact I thought like that reinforced that I was a typical 18-year-old in an army uniform, who foolishly believed he was bulletproof. Thankfully, it didn't take all that long for me to find my sea legs, and I was grateful to be among the more fortunate members of the 55th who didn't suffer from seasickness. It must've been a terrible business for those affected by it because the poor blokes genuinely feared the boat trip was going to kill them long before we'd encountered the Japanese!

One sight that never failed to fascinate me as we cut through the sea was the thousands of flying fish that leapt in and out of the water. They resembled tiny, silver torpedoes as they hurtled along in their bid to flee what must've been for them the terrifying sound of the *Taroona*'s engines. While watching them one day, I happened to look down towards the other end of the ship and saw men hurling things over the side into the water. Within seconds word reached us that the officers had ordered the men to toss their cameras overboard. The edict had come from Military Intelligence: they didn't want the cameras to fall into the hands of the Japanese as they feared the photos could provide the enemy with information about the state of our troops, the numbers of men we had, our weapons, and all manner of things. It made good sense, but unfortunately for the army, two items I'd brought along that I had no intention of parting company with were the waterproof watch my parents had presented to me as a gift when I enlisted, and my prized camera – a 120 Folding Kodak. It was only eight inches long, three inches high and an inch thick, but it took great snaps while we trained in Dubbo and Greta. I planned to document my time at the front, because even though I was only a teenager, I thought that one day Betty's and my kids and grandkids would be interested to see what I'd done during the war.

It wasn't too long before Lieutenant Ryan was standing in front of me and asked whether I had a camera on me. I replied 'No,' which technically wasn't a fib because it wasn't *on* me. If Bill had asked whether I had a camera under my slouch hat I *might* have felt compelled to come clean.

After our lieutenant moved on, I was surprised to hear someone I didn't know pipe up from behind me: 'When we get wherever it is we're going, I'll be happy to look after your films.' Well, I wheeled around and saw the speaker was a bloke I'd noticed earlier in the day leaning up against the ship's bulkhead and gazing out at the ocean. Of course, he was only being friendly, but I was on the defensive because he'd seen that I'd hidden my camera. When I finally replied to him, it was probably with more aggression than was required given that he had, in fact, made an extremely kind offer.

'Well,' I said through gritted teeth, 'who are *you*?' My blunt response didn't seem to faze this man in the slightest because he simply grinned and stuck out his hand. 'I'm Damien, Damien Parer.' I shook his hand and soon learnt he was a war correspondent who'd covered the AIF in North Africa, Greece, Crete and Syria. He was obviously keen to join us on our mystery cruise because he'd driven a military car from Adelaide to Sydney, and then thousands more kilometres to Townsville, in order to get the accreditation all correspondents needed to cover the war. That took weeks to be rubber stamped, so I couldn't help but admire this Parer fellow's dedication to his job. I also liked his attitude, which was that he was looking forward to getting among it when we fought the Japanese. He explained that the war photographer's job was to record the experience of being in a battle to capture what the soldiers go through. He struck me as a genuine bloke, and even though it didn't appear to bother him, I regretted my initial reaction to what was actually a generous offer.

At a much later date I'd learn of the reputation Parer had forged as a result of his willingness to face the same dangers as the men he was covering while a member of the Australian Photographic Unit throughout the Mediterranean. He'd shot iconic photographs during his time there, including the aftermath of the Battle of Tobruk when, in the absence of an Australian flag, a digger named Russell 'Rusty' McWilliam from the New South Wales bush raised a slouch hat on the flagpole just minutes after the Italians surrendered. He also cared for the men, and there's an account of Parer rushing to assist an Aussie soldier who hit the ground after a mortar attack in Syria. After dragging the man to safety, Parer, a devout Catholic, was relieved to discover the digger was alive. He'd simply been KO'd by one of the rocks that had kicked up after the blast. Even though he took a camera and not a rifle into battle, Parer was a soldier – and he was a smart one. There is an account of him enlightening the commander of the AIF in Syria, General Lavarack, as to the Australian and Vichy French positions. When Damien had finished his summation the general thanked him, saying he was glad *someone* knew what was going on because despite being in charge of the operation he had no idea.

So, Damien Parer had both an eye for, and a good understanding of, warfare, and he'd use that in the mountains of Papua New Guinea, a campaign which he identified before so many others as the battle to save Australia. Before we disembarked, Damien handed me a small tin crammed with tea leaves. He explained the tea would protect my film from what was its natural enemy in the tropics – moisture.

He repeated his kind offer to send whatever films I used in his Official War Correspondents pouch to Sydney Riley's photographic studio, which was a place I knew quite well because it was situated slap-bang in the middle of Marrickville. When Damien began to explain to me where Marrickville was, I just laughed and told him not to bother! Damien shook his head in disbelief and said it was a small world when I explained that apart from being not too far from the cake shop I'd worked at, I'd also had my portrait taken in my uniform at Riley's studio for Betty and Mum.

During the months that followed our conversation I'd see enough of Damien to say we were on quite friendly terms with one another. We shook hands and wished one another well before disembarking at Port Moresby, a place I'd never heard of. My first impressions of the town weren't good. The military vehicles kicked up enough dust to make you cough, and the heat and humidity were so severe I figured not even hell could be as hot as the infernal place we'd arrived at.

17

Port Moresby

The town was not a big town. There was two hotels . . . and we were actually able to go into milk bars and buy milk shakes served by native girls.
Sergeant Keith Irwin, 53rd Australian Infantry Battalion

I suppose the Japs will try to capture Port Moresby, because it would give them a marvellous striking base for air blows against the Australian mainland. If it becomes necessary we must be prepared to make Port Moresby the Tobruk of the Pacific.
Major-General Basil Morris after the fall of Singapore

As we clambered down the *Taroona's* gangplank one of our blokes yelled to a deeply suntanned soldier who was labouring on the port's solitary T-Jetty: 'Where are we, mate?' When he answered, 'Port fucking Moresby, cobber!' another member of my company spoke on behalf of me, and I imagine many others, when he shouted back: 'Where the fuck is that?' I didn't have the slightest idea where Port

Moresby was, or, for that matter, many places outside of the area where I grew up. Even when he said we were in New Guinea I was still clueless. That was due as much to my poor schooling as it was to the fact that before I joined the army the furthest I'd been away from home was when my family made the 80-odd kilometre trek to Gosford in Dad's jalopy. However, it took no time at all to realise the military had shipped us to a place where the humidity made it hard to breathe. We must have looked like a school of foolish goldfish that had jumped out of their aquarium as we gasped for air while making our way to the assembly point on the wharf. I'm not exaggerating when I say that during the first couple of hours we were in Papua New Guinea it felt as though the heat had sucked the oxygen from my lungs.

Once we assembled on the wharves our officers told us we wouldn't have to do anything during the next three days except acclimatise – although, they added, that would be *after* we marched three kilometres in full kit to our base at a place called Simpsons Gap. We walked there in our heavy boots because there weren't any trucks available to transport us. We'd trained hard during our time at Greta, but nothing we did in the Hunter Valley prepared us for that day's effort. The heat was debilitating, and towards the end – even though it was a relatively short distance – it became a mighty effort just to put one foot in front of the other. We hadn't experienced conditions like it, and in the end everyone in C Coy just did their best to shuffle towards what we thought would be the comfort of our barracks, a shower and a bed. As it turned out, *that* was wishful thinking.

Port Moresby was a small town of only a handful of streets in 1942. There was a cinema, a post office that had been left in ruins by the Japanese bombers, and a relatively impressive-looking building that was called the European Hospital. The hospital was built on the side of the hill and while its bright red roof made it a prime target for the Japanese, for some reason they kept missing it! Apart from taking note of its few landmarks, my other initial observation of Port Moresby as we walked through the place was that there weren't any white women. I'd find out later on that in early 1942, our government had accepted that it was only a matter of time before the Japanese invaded New Guinea and some bureaucrats took the initiative to evacuate the European women and children to get them out of harm's way. The only females who remained were the civilian nurses and missionaries, and they were brave women. Some of them stayed in the territories to do their jobs for God and the Papuans even after the Japanese landed.

As we sauntered towards 'The Gap' I think most of us experienced for the first time what's termed as 'culture shock'. While my group of mates and I didn't react to the sight of the bare-breasted Papuan women in their grass skirts – in my mind I reasoned to myself, *It's their country, their way of life, so show respect* – there were some men who couldn't contain their surprise. I put that down to the fact they were young, and, like me, it was probably the first time they'd ever seen a woman without a top on. More often than not the 'Marys', as the local women were called in the New Guinea Pidgin language, walked behind their husbands, who usually carried a spear with them, and they were in turn followed by their children and the family's pet dog. As for those blokes who were excited by the sight of the semi-naked women walking openly about, I don't believe any of them acted on any 'urges' they may have had. Firstly, we'd had it drummed into us that any illicit affair was fraught with danger on so many fronts. Apart from the adulterer running the risk of having the husband's stone axe embedded in his brain, they also risked damaging the entire Australian Army's relationship with the locals. It was sound advice because, apart from the morality issue, the relationship we Australian soldiers enjoyed with the Papuan porters – who'd become affectionately known as 'Fuzzy Wuzzy Angels' – would ultimately provide us with an important edge over our foe. Besides hauling tonnes of supplies over the Owen Stanley Range, these amazing men also saved countless Australian lives by carrying the wounded or dangerously ill on makeshift stretchers over sheer mountains and down deep ravines for anywhere up to 14 backbreaking days. It was the sweat and the endurance of the 'Fuzzy Wuzzies' that allowed many of us, including me, the chance to receive lifesaving medical care. The Japanese, who, according to witnesses, wantonly raped Papuan women of all ages, didn't enjoy the same level of support at Kokoda, although I do note that in some parts of the country there were Papuans who sided with them because they wanted to see an end to Australia's colonial rule over their nation. However, I'm sure in the wash-up of their defeats at Kokoda, Buna, Gona and Sanananda, the Japanese military would have to have acknowledged that their troops' collective disregard for the locals played a significant role in their failed campaign.

When the 55th entered our 'base' at Simpsons Gap on that first day, it was terrible to see that it was nothing more than a bare, rock-strewn paddock in the middle of nowhere. There weren't any tents, mosquito nets, or even the most basic of amenities that were essential to accommodate an army. Unlike the 39th and 53rd battalions, who were forced to live under the stars because their tents were buried beneath tonnes of cargo in the cavernous hull of the *Aquitania* (no-one had had the foresight to realise they'd be the most immediate items the men would need), the 55th was sent to Papua New Guinea in such a rush that there wasn't time to pack 'comforts' at all. To give you an understanding of how little our intelligence people knew about the place they'd sent us to, we were told not to worry about taking our groundsheets because they'd be 'too hot'. I can assure those boffins the sheets would've come in very handy when we were exposed to the elements and rendered helpless against the clouds of malaria-carrying mosquitoes that rolled in at dusk. Living rough also made us vulnerable to any number of wicked diseases that thrived in the tropical heat and humidity, including malaria, dysentery, tropical dermatitis and the many other ailments that filled our hospital's wards.

Once our three days of 'acclimatising' finished, C Coy spent its time walking to and from the harbour helping to unload ships during the day shift. It was a risky business because the Japanese regularly bombed the town with their planes that were based in Rabaul, and the hull of a ship could easily become a death trap if a bomb landed in it. Until the RAAF's No. 75 squadrons arrived with their

P-40 Kittyhawks, the men from Nippon ruled the skies, meaning those of us stuck on the ground or in the ships were at their mercy. It was miserable. We had anti-aircraft units based on a big hill, but they wasted their time and ammunition trying to shoot down the Japanese aeroplanes. This was because when the Japanese pilots realised our guns had a range of 19,000 feet, their pilots toyed with the gunners by remaining out of harm's way at 23,000 feet. And didn't the bastards give us curry? You never knew the bombs were headed towards you until they started to whistle, and then you'd race to take cover. Sometimes that meant you'd wedge yourself in between the rocks and try to bury your face in the dirt as deeply as possible. Funnily enough, even when the ground was trembling and dirt and rocks kicked up with a dangerous force, I never thought I'd die in a raid. Of course, I was scared – everyone was – but I always thought another poor soul would 'buy it' before me.

My loathing for the former Prime Minister Robert Menzies only increased after one raid, and I would have throttled him if he'd stood within range of my outstretched hands. When I was scouting around after the Japanese bombers returned to Rabaul, I found a lump of shrapnel which had stamped across it the words *PROPERTY OF NSW GOVERNMENT RAILWAY.* It was still warm from the explosion, and I was angry because it was obviously a chunk of the scrap metal 'Pig Iron' Menzies had sold to the Japanese: the very metal his advisors had warned him against selling to them during their war with China. Their warnings that it'd one day be used to bomb Australian troops had become a dreadful reality. I took a photograph of it to document our former leader's mistake, and over the years I've shown it to people as a cautionary tale about the dire consequences that can come from ignoring sound advice.

One raid I clearly recall occurred on the morning of 18 June 1942, when at least 18 bombers and their escorts came in from all directions to attack the 4408-tonne Burns, Philp & Co. coastal motorship, SS *Macdhui*. The enemy had returned with a vengeance after targeting the ship the previous day. However, to 66-year-old Captain James Campbell's enduring credit, as skipper of the *Macdhui*, he made them fight hard for their 'kill'. I'd seen the *Macdhui* when it docked at Moresby's Harbour three days earlier after ferrying 154 soldiers from Sydney via Townsville. However, it had taken the men days to unload the aviation fuel and petrol the ship had transported in dozens of 44-gallon drums. I'd missed the previous day's attack, but Titch and Dick Kayess filled me in on the details with a blow-by-blow account. At 6 am on 17 June, Campbell moved his ship from the harbour's only wharf to allow another ship to have its cargo unloaded. He dropped anchor in the harbour and he stayed put as the fuel was loaded onto barges and taken ashore. While there, the city's air-raid siren sounded its familiar warning when six Japanese Zero fighter planes appeared over the horizon. Surprisingly, they showed no interest in the *Macdhui* and Campbell returned to the wharf to allow the troops who'd been put to work as labourers an opportunity to remove the ship's cargo. In anticipation of more raids, the skipper wisely released the minimum amount of anchor chain so he could make a quick getaway in case he needed to scarper.

At 9.45 am the siren sounded to warn of what would be the city's 61st air raid, and Campbell weighed anchor at 10.07 am and headed at speed towards the Paga Hill battery which was based at the south-eastern entrance to the harbour. According to Dick and Titch, Captain Campbell did an amazing job of evading the bombs, with one of them saying it was as if he'd made the ship dance on the water. Unfortunately, the last bomb the Japanese dropped that day struck the bridge from where Campbell had staged his desperate battle, and it sliced through three steel decks and exploded in the saloon. Tragically, the ship's surgeon, Charles Tunstall, who like Campbell was 66, died along with a young soldier and two stewards who, I believe, were both aged over 50. The ship's purser, Benjamin Allen from Sydney, gave an insight into how horrifying it must have been on board when he revealed that shrapnel from the Japanese bomb cut the legs off the dining tables in the saloon. It also pierced holes in the sides of the ship as fires broke out. Fortunately, they were contained when Campbell's teenaged nephew, Donald, joined the other crew members who extinguished the blaze in the no. 3 cargo hold.

Undeterred by the experience, Campbell again docked at the wharf to unload the dead and wounded, and he also allowed the troops to try to unload the last of the cargo he carried. His expert seamanship – and the hopeless performance by the swarms of Japanese planes against a merchant ship armed with six light machine guns and a four-inch naval gun from World War I – was the talk of Moresby. Campbell and his crew enjoyed hero status, and it's important to realise that while most people think it was young men who paid the supreme price in New Guinea, members of Campbell's crew were men aged in their late 40s, 50s and 60s.

As gutsy as the crew of the *Macdhui* were, everyone knew the Japanese would return for another go the following day. In scenes that must've been reminiscent of ancient Rome when the Emperor pitted Christians against the lions, I joined the scores of men who sat on one of the hills overlooking the harbour as the 18 bombers and their escort returned at 10.05 am on 18 June to finish the job. We watched on helplessly as they attacked from four different directions, and this time four of the 68 bombs they dropped scored fatal hits on the mighty *Macdhui*. One of the bombs wiped out the five-man gun crew that was fighting so valiantly. While grief-stricken by the loss of his men, the wily Captain Campbell admitted the near misses were just as frightening as the direct hits because they 'lifted the ship out of the water' as though a giant hand had picked it up and slammed it down. The last bomb of the attack hit the bridge, and the blast sent Captain Campbell crashing to the deck below. Although wounded in the face, torso, and arm, Campbell insisted on being the last to leave his ship. It was a noble act, and one which highlighted that Campbell was a true captain of the high seas. However, his ship was alight and everyone knew she was done for. The fires on board burnt until the following night, and after it lurched towards a reef near the village of Hanuabada, the ship capsized onto its port side. While the hull is all that remains visible these days, it serves as a memorial to the bravery of the captain and all who served on her.

One little-known fact about Campbell's decision to get his ship away from the wharf underscores his status as a hero. When the Japanese attacked, he was well aware that had the vessel been at the wharf when it sunk, it would've prevented other ships from docking and that would've denied the men who fought in the ensuing battles on the Kokoda Trail – and beyond – from receiving much-needed supplies. The *Macdhui's* stand was without doubt a heroic action, but, as I'd see with my own eyes, it was far from the last of them. Other men would make similar stands against incredible odds, and they would also pay the ultimate price.

18

The Expendables: Milne Bay

Coming into Milne Bay there is a little island before you get there — Samarai — we thought 'oh this looks good.' We came into this big harbour and saw these coconut trees right down to the beach . . . it looked lovely until you got in there.

Sergeant Errol Jorgenson,
2/25th Australian Infantry Battalion

After weeks of working in the stifling hulls of the ships that we helped to unload, C Coy received word that we were bound for a place called Milne Bay. It was situated on the furthest point of the island's south-eastern corner, 360 kilometres east of Port Moresby, and it was a deep-water harbour. We received these orders at a time when the rumour mill suggested the Japanese were preparing to invade somewhere in Papua New Guinea. Indeed, some officers warned there was the possibility that the enemy could even be lying in wait for us at our isolated outpost. Take it from me, I wasn't the only soldier who stood on the wharf on the day of our embarkation feeling as though we'd been marked as 'expendable' by our military's High Command. Our officer in charge was told that we'd be on our own if the Japanese invaded because there were no men, ships, or planes available to assist us. The 55th's orders were to hold the Japanese for as long as possible before making our way back to Port Moresby via the coast. If we survived the first few weeks after arriving at Milne Bay – or 'Fall River' as the military called it in an effort to confuse the Japanese – American engineers would be sent to build aerodromes.

Apart from C Coy, the 55th was providing men from A Coy and a detachment of machine gunners from E Coy to 'man the fort'. I think it's safe to say we were considered by the generals as easy a sacrifice as the rust bucket that was assigned to transport C Coy to Milne Bay: the Dutch coastal ship, SS *Bontekoe*. While we had a naval escort for our journey, the reality is that unlike a naval frigate or destroyer, no-one would have missed this merchant vessel if it was sent to the bottom of the sea. After getting the impression that those in command weren't overly concerned about our fate, what happened next could be described as either the most macabre sight, or, at best, the army's idea of black comedy.

You see, minutes after being told we'd be on our own, all of the religious ministers who were attached to the army in Port Moresby suddenly rushed towards us. They offered their respective flocks – the Roman Catholics, Anglicans and Methodists – God's glory and peace. They did that by either splashing soldiers with holy water, making the sign of the cross towards them, providing communion, or mut-tering a multitude of blessings. It was quite the revelation because until that day I'm quite certain not many of us knew there were any religious ministers in Port Moresby!

None of this inspired confidence in us that we'd return from Milne Bay in one piece. The only religious man I recall doing anything which passed as 'practical' that day was the Salvation Army's captain, who I'm sure was Albert Moore. He climbed down from 'the pulpit' – the higher ground – where his peers stood to walk among the men. Besides offering us his best wishes and prayers, Moore handed each of us two pieces of cardboard while he broke up a pile of pencils so we could write Christmas messages to our loved ones back home. The reason that surprised us was because it was only 25 June! In normal times I would've asked why it was going to take so long for the mail to reach home, however, on this occasion I thought probably I didn't want to know. The cardboard squares only con-tained enough room to write a short message, which in my case went something like: *Dear Mum and Dad, hope everyone has a Merry Christmas and Happy New Year. Write later.* Once finished we either crossed or circled a symbol that was printed on the back of the card which signified whether we wanted it sent home in the event of our death. While some of my mates crossed theirs to ensure it was destroyed if they died, I circled mine because I wanted Betty and Mum to know that they were on my mind before I received what the diggers of the Great War called a 'dead meat ticket'.

As we boarded the ship the religious ministers promised to personally ensure we received our mail while we were stationed at Milne Bay. 'We know you'll be wanting some comfort from home,' said one, with an annoying pious tone in his voice. While most other soldiers thanked them for their concern for their fellow man, many of the holy men were taken aback when Bula growled that they'd better make good on their promise otherwise he'd come back, hunt them down one by one, and 'break their bloody necks'. Bula was ticked off because in all the time the 55th had been in Port Moresby, none of us had heard even a peep from home. It felt very unlikely that these religious men could follow through on their promise. The reaction from the Catholic priest to Bula's threat was hilarious. The poor coot was so startled, he grasped at the crucifix hanging around his neck as though he was about to ward off a vampire or an evil demon! All we could do was trust that they'd forward our mail as they prayed for our souls and waved us off to God only knew what.

Once our journey began, it wasn't long before we understood why the authorities weren't overly worried about the prospect of losing the *Bontekoe* to a Japanese submarine's torpedo. She was slow, clunky and cumbersome. Indeed, if it was possible to walk on water, we would easily have beaten her to Milne Bay without breaking a sweat! While we laughed and told jokes during the trip, I could feel the trepidation grow among the men of C Coy as we slowly but surely approached our destination. The Believer, Pee Wee, Jack, Miss Valentine, Dick Kayess, The Pianist, Normie, Bula, Nugget, Bluey and me were braced for the possibility of a 'hot' reception from the already entrenched Japanese. One of the few thoughts I took comfort from was knowing

My mum, Annie, and dad, Herb, at the ANZAC Club, Marrickville, in the late 1940s. They're attending the annual ball, which, incredibly, was the only night of the year when women were allowed through the doors.

A quiet family moment for the Chards in our backyard at Francis Street. TOP LEFT TO RIGHT: Herb Jnr, Mum, and me. BOTTOM LEFT TO RIGHT: Ray, Ken and Jean.

My dad was one of the men who laboured on the wharves of the Hungry Mile during the Great Depression. It was tough, but he was strong as an ox.

Betty and I didn't realise we were in the same class in 1929 until we saw this photo. She's on the right of the girl holding the '1A' sign, I'm on the far right hand side of the third row – wishing I was anywhere else but school.

Looking like the man about town when I was a 17-year-old in 1941. A few short months after this photo was taken I swapped my snappy sports coat for a khaki army tunic.

LEFT TO RIGHT: My great mate Thomas Claude Whitney, aka 'Titch', me and another C Coy mate take time out from our basic training at Greta. My time at Greta is remembered for my personal war with a senior officer who wanted me to become his personal chef.

LEFT TO RIGHT: Me, Titch, Mum, my sister Myra and niece Pam. Titch joined my family on an outing in Sydney before we left for Port Moresby in 1942.

We had no idea of where the army had sent us when our ship dropped anchor in Port Moresby's harbour. Our first impressions of Papua New Guinea weren't great because the humidity was oppressive, many of the buildings were damaged by Japanese bombs, and we marched to a camp that had no tents, barracks or even showers. I spent some of my free time taking photos, including this shot of the harbour during a rare break from the Japanese air raids.

At our camp in Simpsons Gap, near Port Moresby, 1942. I'm in the front row – second from the right – brandishing the ill-fated watch my parents gave me as a gift when I enlisted.

ABOVE LEFT: Most of our time in Port Moresby was spent unloading ships and working as labourers, however, we did do some infantry training. I'm second from the right, looking armed and dangerous with my trusty Lee–Enfield .303 bolt-action rifle – it almost broke my shoulder the first time I fired it!
ABOVE RIGHT: Over the top with fixed bayonets, near Simpsons Gap.

I'm inspecting the damage the Japanese pilots inflicted on a Flying Fortress they caught napping on the runway of Port Moresby's Seven Mile Drome.

C Coy, playing like the kids we were, in the wreckage of an American Airacobra that was shot down near Port Moresby.

The Japanese shrapnel at my feet was still warm from its bomb's explosion, and I was infuriated to see *PROPERTY OF NSW GOVERNMENT RAILWAY* stamped across one particular chunk of metal. It was some of the scrap metal our Prime Minister Bob 'Pig Iron' Menzies had unwisely sold to the militant Japanese.

Water was scarce in Port Moresby, and my having a bath in a 44 gallon drum that was sliced in half was a luxury.

When you found a comb in the army, you'd use it. I'm on the right with not a hair out of place!

One of the saddest aspects about the war in Paupa New Guinea was, through no fault of their own, the Papuans suffered terrible hardships. Their tranquil way of life (ABOVE LEFT) of dance and song, and (ABOVE RIGHT) being at one with nature on the shores of Milne Bay, was shattered by such scenes as houses and buildings being flattened by bombs of foreign armies (BELOW).

This portrait of Sister Ruth Campbell hangs in my house, and I look upon it as though she's a saint. She saved my life, and the lives of hundreds of other diggers, through her devotion to duty. She's as much of a hero – if not more – as any soldier who faced the enemy. One of her toughest duties was having to become 'Mum' to those poor men who used their dying breath to cry for their mothers in the early hours of the morning.

Titch and I celebrating Christmas Day, 1944, in Coolangatta, Queensland. At this stage my war had all but ended because of the toll malaria had taken on me.

The first time I saw Betty ride by our house I told my mother, 'I'm going to marry that girl,' while Mum told me to stop talking rubbish! At 5 pm on Saturday, 6 October 1945, Betty and I became husband and wife, surrounded by family and friends. It was the happiest day of my life.

My beautiful Betty. She looked radiant the day she walked down the aisle of St Clement's in Marrickville.

My brother Jack and I on ANZAC Day, 1946. Unfortunately, the horror of war took a terrible mental and physical toll on Jack, and he was never the same. Even my mother said the army should never have taken him because he had too soft a nature for military life. It was the first – and last time – I marched.

Taken in 1946, like so many other returned servicemen I still wore my uniform after being discharged because I didn't have many civilian clothes at home.

On 25 February 1958, Betty, our 10-year-old son Robert, and two-year-old son Garry, dressed in our Sunday best as we waited for Queen Elizabeth The Queen Mother to visit our home. During her trip to Australia, Her Majesty visited some veterans to see how we were adapting to life after the war.

ABOVE: When The Queen Mother asked Garry why he was crying, he immediately turned off the tears. Her Majesty made a wonderful impression on Betty and me.

Betty was the only queen in our house, but she was proud to be complimented by The Queen Mother for how beautiful she'd made our home. She even asked Betty about our towels because she loved how bright they were.

Betty and I walking up the gangplank to go on a cruise around the Gold Coast in July, 2007. While we loved our trips up north when I retired from work, Sydney was always our home.

While I was fighting in the jungle I was determined to do whatever I could to protect Betty, my family and all Australians from the horrors the Japanese inflicted upon the people they conquered throughout South-East Asia. Sometimes when I attend family celebrations, such as my beautiful granddaughter Renee's 21st birthday dinner, I know the hardships and horrors we endured on the Kokoda Trail and at Sanananda were worth it. As terrible as it was, I'd do it all over again, if needed, to protect them. LEFT TO RIGHT: my daughter-in-law's parents Ken and Mary Robertson, Renee, my daughter-in-law Elaine, my son Robert, me and Betty.

Whenever I'm invited to speak to schoolchildren, I can't help but to think Australia's future is in good hands. I've found that even the so-called 'problem kids' are moved by the stories I tell them about the wartime sacrifices of boys who weren't much older than them.

The Kokoda Track Memorial Walkway at Concord is the closest thing I have to a church, and whenever I go there I'm overcome by a deep sense of peacefulness. I'm serious when I tell people finding this place helped save my life after I lost Betty.

At 98, I often ask myself why I survived such things as the snipers at Sanananda, when poor Dick Kayess was killed just minutes after asking me to be the best man at his wedding. I put it down to not being in the wrong place at the wrong time – and blind luck. These days, as I show people the Kokoda Track Memorial Walkway, I consider it my duty to honour all my comrades, especially those who didn't return. I consider them to be 'Australia's greatest heroes'.

Titch wasn't with us. My mate had fallen ill with malaria just before we left, and I thought it was a small mercy that he'd require a long recovery in hospital before rejoining us.

From afar, Milne Bay looked like a tropical paradise such as Robert Louis Stevenson might have imagined. The bay was surrounded by three jungle-covered mountains which climbed 3500 feet into the sky. For those who were inclined to do such things, it would've been possible to jump from the side of the mountains into the sparkling Coral Sea. As I looked from the deck I was impressed by the tall coconut trees that stood along the shoreline like Mother Nature's sentries. The sight of an old lugger ploughing through the water with its sails billowing was impressive, and it inspired me to think we were in a special part of God's earth. Naturally enough, there wasn't a wharf there big enough for all of the men to use because it was a remote and undeveloped place. That meant some soldiers made their way to shore by negotiating the coral reefs in small dinghies. While that added to their sense of being on an adventure, there was the danger that these flimsy craft would either sink or capsize under the weight of the men and equipment they ferried.

Once we reached the safety of the shore, all of us who'd commented on the beauty of the place realised we'd over-estimated the appeal of Milne Bay. It looked good from afar, but far from good up close. If it rains in hell, then it more than qualified as a stinking hellhole. Indeed, it turned out it rained like billyo in Milne Bay, and we'd soon learn that the water that gushed down the mountains had a destructive force. It flooded the land, and the trails the Papuans used as trade routes between neighbouring villages doubled as mud-churned disease traps because mosquitoes bred in the water. The mangrove swamps were another breeding ground for an uncountable number of malaria-ridden *Anopheles* mosquitoes, while we faced another unexpected danger – falling coconuts! An officer had his collarbone broken when he was bombed by a coconut from a great height, and after that we were ordered to wear our steel helmets at all times. Added to all of this was the fact that most of us lived rough. There was a limited number of two-man tents, and while some men built Papuan-style huts to gain some protection, I joined the majority of troops who slept beneath the cover of the jungle's thick, dark canopy. Unfortunately, that consigned us to falling asleep to the lullaby of the ceaseless hum from the mosquitoes that feasted on us. The wretches bit us to high heaven.

Apart from the coconut plantation the British-owned company Lever Brothers had established long before the war, there was absolutely nothing at Milne Bay. Lever Brothers harvested copra: the oil that's extracted from the kernel of the coconut and used in such things as soap, shampoo, detergent and even margarine. The manager who ran the plantation was the only European in the district, but what I found interesting was that soon after we arrived, the locals – and all of the water buffalo – headed into the jungle to get away from us. Perhaps both man and beast sensed our arrival was a threat to their peaceful – albeit tough – existence. Later on, Papuan labour proved invaluable as they were employed to carry the ballast that was used to build the jetty.

Our officers explained that the reason we were in such a godforsaken, malarial cesspool was because the Allies and the Japanese had identified Milne Bay as being a place of strategic importance. Whoever held it dominated the vital eastern sea lanes between Australia and New Guinea. If the Japanese seized it from us, it would give them a place from which to continue their push south as well as harass Allied ships. The American commander and supreme commander of all Allied forces in the South-West Pacific, General Douglas MacArthur, wanted airstrips built there to not only provide Papua New Guinea with a steel-like curtain of air defence, but also to launch raids on Japanese-held territory and shipping.

After we'd established our camp and the authorities realised the Japanese hadn't overrun us, the US Army's 46th Engineering Battalion joined us. It was their job to build two steel-matted airstrips, while ours was to defend them as they set about their work. We had that duty even though the heaviest weapons at our disposal were a couple of Lewis guns. There's no doubt about it, we were like the men of Rabaul, New Ireland and Ambon in that we were considered sacrificial lambs. The brass wanted to appear as though they'd done their job by at least identifying hotspots; it didn't matter to them that they hadn't deployed enough men to hold the ground.

Adding to our problems was the fact that Milne Bay wasn't the easiest place to defend. It's 35 kilometres long and 15 kilometres wide, which made it big enough for a Japanese fleet to enter and cause mayhem. We'd heard enough about the trials and tribulations of the inadequately armed and equipped Allied defenders at Rabaul, New Ireland, Ambon, Timor and anywhere else the Japanese had conquered to realise we needed to have an escape plan in the event of us being swamped by thousands of enemy troops. You didn't need to be a boy scout to realise it'd be murderous to trek across the terrain towards Port Moresby, so my group formed what we thought was a solid plan. In the event of the place going to rack and ruin, we intended to commandeer the Lever Brothers' old lugger and sail it back to Port Moresby. It didn't matter that none of us had ever sailed before, and that no-one knew how to do such things as set the sails; it was a plan, our plan, and that allowed us to sleep as soundly as possible of a night.

My platoon was based at Gili Gili, which was on the north-west coast of Milne Bay, situated between Swinger Bay to the east and Ladava to the west. It was the site for one of the aerodromes the Americans would construct. Up until their arrival we unloaded the *Bontekoe*, which made midnight runs in order to avoid detection by Japanese fighters and bombers. While it was indeed a rust bucket, the captain and his crew were tremendous. After we'd unloaded its cargo of steel mesh and 44-gallon drums filled with fuel bound for the 'dromes', the ship left at 3 am to steam 40 miles out to sea where it was beyond the range of the Japanese aircraft. We found the quickest and most convenient way to unload the fuel once the *Bontekoe* dropped its anchor was simply to roll eight drums at a time over the side and into the water. The men who could swim, blokes such as Geoff Valentin, worked with the incoming tide to push the drums towards the shore. There, a second group of men, which included me, dragged the drums across the sand and into the jungle, where we established a storage depot under the dense foliage. It was crucial that this work was completed well before daybreak and before the first of the Japanese patrols flew overhead.

Outside of labouring, digging defensive positions, and our other duties, there wasn't anything to do. Boredom quickly set in, and I noticed the impact it had on Bula. As each day passed without us receiving the mail the religious ministers had promised to forward, his plans for those men once he returned to Port Moresby became even more graphic and violent. They were in for a thrashing! Other men grumbled about having no tobacco, and one of our fellows was so desperate for a puff he went to the extreme of trying to smoke dried water buffalo dung. He used the white paper from our 'dog biscuits', packed it with dung and quickly tossed it to the ground, saying it tasted like crap! Which, I guess, is what it really was. The 'dog biscuits' weren't much better. Men cracked their teeth on these biscuits because they were so hard. Some troops soaked them in water overnight and ate the mush the following morning as if it was porridge.

The food situation was deplorable, and it reached the stage where men would be sent to throw grenades into the water to collect the stunned fish that rose to the surface. We were so desperate for some variety in our boring diet that a sergeant, Reg Wilkinson, shot an eagle from the sky. A creature of such incredible beauty and majesty would normally have been spared such a fate, however, we needed a break from fish. The poor thing tasted stringy, and while I wouldn't eat it these days, we hooked into that particular night's dinner because a change was as good as a holiday. I remember how some blokes did absolutely crazy things for entertainment. While I'm not sure if it happened at Milne Bay or Port Moresby's Bootless Bay, I remember seeing one of our blokes hit a crocodile on the snout with a hard whack from the butt of his rifle as he wielded it like a baseball bat. I thought to myself, *What's going on here?* When the man-eater opened its jaws to display rows of sharp teeth, the man's mate lobbed a grenade straight into its mouth, and they ran back before the creature exploded into a million pieces. I didn't condone such things because they were cruel, but I did understand why they happened. The endless boredom of being stuck in the middle of nowhere could really get to you. However, we should've counted our blessings during the 'calm', because things soon heated up when the Americans started to construct the aerodromes. The Japanese pilots were on to them, and they wasted no time at all in making their unwelcome presence felt.

19

The 'Can Do' Men

Butchers of Milne Bay . . .

**Japanese propagandist Tokyo Rose's description of the
Australian troops who triumphed at Milne Bay**

After a few days of flying under the Japanese radar as we did
the groundwork to develop Milne Bay into a fully operational military base, the Zeroes finally arrived, and boy, they
made their presence felt. Their pilots machine-gunned the
tripe out of us at all hours of the day. However, they didn't
drop any bombs during these attacks, and eventually we
realised that was because the Japanese command didn't want
to damage the airstrips the Americans were constructing.
They obviously thought they would eventually walk in and
take them over wholesale, so their engineers (or prisoners
of war) would be spared months of backbreaking work.
Nevertheless, these air raids were a terrifying experience
because I found that at Milne Bay, unlike Moresby where
the aeroplanes unleashed hell from 22,000 feet above the
earth, the Zeroes screamed down at 580 kilometres per

hour with guns blazing until they were almost level with us on the ground. They flew so low it's not a complete exaggeration to suggest it would've been possible for the braver members of C Coy to reach out and touch the aircraft as they rocketed by! We hadn't dug any trenches because they'd only have filled with water, so that meant whenever the Japanese strafed us we either dropped everything and bolted to the relative safety of the jungle, or simply dropped face first to the ground and hoped their bullets would miss us. Unfortunately, some men couldn't move quickly enough – or just didn't have luck on their side – and they're remembered as the first casualties of Milne Bay.

The Japanese flew so low we could sometimes make out the expressions on the pilots' faces as they went about their destructive business. Sometimes, when I speak to the young ones who visit the Kokoda Track Memorial Walkway for a school excursion, a child – and it's normally one who's been reared on video games which allow kids with sharp reflexes and anticipation to single-handedly defeat an army of digital warriors – asks why we didn't just fire our rifles at the planes. It's a fair question and, as I explain, it wasn't as though we didn't try during the first few attacks. However, what we discovered was that the Zeroes travelled at such a great speed that it was a waste of time – and bullets – taking pot shots at the pilots. You'd blink and they'd be long gone. Instead we made it our priority to find a safe spot to sit out what I describe as 'lead hailstorms'. I'm not being flippant when I say this, but as time went by the men who garrisoned Milne Bay learnt to live with these air attacks just as we'd accepted that our lot in life included the mosquitoes, our monotonous diet, the mud, the rain, the occasional wayward coconut, and the hours upon hours we spent biding time.

What none of us imagined was that the Japanese plans to invade Milne Bay were at an advanced stage, and besides trying to blow us away in their air raids, the pilots were also photographing the place. Their intelligence officers used the photos to glean as much information as possible, including the number of Australian troops stationed there, the progress that'd been made on the aerodromes, and whether there were any fortifications or heavy weaponry (of which there were none, at least while I was there). They used this information to calculate the number of men who'd be needed to ensure yet another Japanese victory. It was thanks to some Aussie ingenuity by the 7th Division's Major-General, Cyril Clowes, when he arrived with the AIF troops later on, that the Japanese underestimated out strength. However, until that fateful night in August when the enemy landed in the mangrove swamps, the strafing continued for as long as the American engineers worked on the 'dromes'.

While plenty of Australians would criticise the American troops' combat nous in their first few battles of the New Guinea campaign, I was one who admired their 'can do' approach towards what were a number of tough engineering tasks at Milne Bay. A company of Yanks arrived on 29 June, four days after us, and they wasted no time at all in getting down to business. I watched in awe as they used the little bulldozer they'd brought with them to knock down row upon row of coconut trees so they could begin building the airstrip. I was fascinated by the sight of the driver ploughing through them as though they were nothing. I still have no idea how the Yanks managed to get the 'dozer' off the ship and transport it to Gili Gili via the muddy road that linked the village to the wharf, but it must have been one heck of an effort. This was at a time when our own logistics supply chain in Port Moresby struggled to send us a crate of bully beef or box of 'dog biscuits' – or even our mail, which was still driving Bula crazy. We Aussies watched on almost shamefaced as our allies built that airstrip in what was virgin jungle. Indeed, I became a part of the construction process the day one of the engineers asked Bill Ryan what it was exactly that we Australians were doing? At first we didn't know if he was having a crack at us by suggesting we were bludging. However, when Bill replied that it was our job to guard them, the American asked if we could instead help him and his mates so they could finish the job more quickly. It didn't strike Bill – or us – as an unreasonable request and I was among the group of C Coy men who worked alongside some African Americans as they unloaded supplies from their navy's ships. We helped to unload the fleet of modern US Army trucks, and I was also among the C Coy men who helped lay the steel mesh on the airstrip the RAAF's Kittyhawks would one day use. It was hard work, but it was a sure-fire way to beat the boredom.

The strips were the result of American innovation and known as a Marston Mat runway. They comprised planks that were 0.25 inches thick and pierced by dozens of circular holes. Laying the mesh was a simple enough process: you just clipped the long strips together as if it were a big Meccano set. When I wondered why the mesh had holes in it, an engineer asked me if I knew what it was like when a plane landed with a 'bang'. I replied that I'd never flown before, and he explained that if the mesh didn't have the holes to allow the mud underneath it to ooze through them, the pressure of the plane landing on them would rip the strips apart. That made sense to me. The sheets provided the Kittyhawks with a solid enough surface to land on despite Milne Bay's daily torrential rain.

Food remained a constant problem, and while I was at Milne Bay I utilised my scrounging skills for the good of the group. At this stage I'd also volunteered to help Bula and Nugget cook our dinner because it helped me ward off boredom and distracted me from my pining for Betty. However, the food I was helping to prepare was bland and barely satisfied the men's hunger. I was always on the lookout for something new to add to their diets, but more often than not it proved an impossible task.

One day an American Liberty ship – one of 2710 cargo ships that were mass produced in American shipyards between 1941 and 1945 – dropped anchor at Milne Bay. Although uninvited, I made my way on board to speak to the cook, an African American who had a brilliant, explosive-like laugh and a happy outlook on life. I'm certain we would've been great mates if we'd served together. I asked whether we could have some sugar, and he sized me up before asking: 'Don't you guys have your own supplies?' His suspicion was fair enough – he couldn't deplete his own stock to help just anyone out – and I explained our situation.

I told him we weren't getting anything from Port Moresby and we'd reached the stage where we were tossing hand grenades into the water to catch fish. He looked at me sympathetically as he listened, and said while he couldn't spare any sugar, he had plenty of rice and condensed milk that he could share. It was generous, and I thanked him because I was happy to think the boys would at least have something different to eat for their dinner that evening. After we shook hands, I thought I'd push my scrounger's luck by asking him whether he was sure there wasn't some sugar he could spare. He laughed loudly as he exclaimed: 'Boy, you're good!' He told me to wait, and after a few minutes he returned with half a sack of sugar. His actions were typical of the generosity of the Seabees, and I was grateful. When I returned to our camp with the bounty, Lieutenant Ryan sent some of the boys to find a 24-gallon drum so I could boil the rice. While I wasn't used to cooking the stuff, the meal tasted quite good. Indeed, it went down so well with all ranks that Bill asked whether I wanted to become C Coy's head cook. I reeled as though I'd taken a right hook to the chin when I heard his suggestion. He must have forgotten the fallout after my 'man-to-man, soldier-to-soldier' chat with The Officer at Greta who wanted me to become his personal chef. I just looked at Bill, shook my head violently, and replied: 'Not on your life!' I wasn't in the army to beat an egg, I was determined to defeat the Japanese with bullet and bayonet.

Indeed, it seemed we would get our chance to fight the Japanese sooner rather than later, because things around us had started to escalate. After we'd manned Milne Bay on our own for two months, AIF troops – groups of Queenslanders under the command of 'Silent' Cyril Clowes – were shipped in over a number of nights. They were battle-hardened men who'd forged fierce reputations during their service in the Middle East. Indeed, I feel no shame in admitting it was a mighty relief to be shaking their hands in welcome. These sun-bronzed diggers, with their easygoing manner and proud record against the German and Italian armies, inspired a belief that we'd at least give the enemy a tougher fight than they might have anticipated. As part of Clowes's plans, these troops remained hidden deep in the jungle, where, as they acclimatised to the pervasive humidity and enjoyed the many other 'delights' of Milne Bay, they were well out of sight of the Japanese pilots. For their part, the Japanese would have returned to their airfield after each patrol adamant we only had a few hundred men on hand to defend the bay from their soldiers. Unbeknown to them, when the time came, 5000 highly trained (and motivated) men were waiting for whatever Tokyo threw at them.

Besides the AIF, the RAAF's 75th and 76th squadrons, who were equipped with the American-built Kittyhawks, had also arrived at Milne Bay. The 75th wasted no time in forging a mighty reputation for itself over the skies of Papua New Guinea, despite having only one week's training. On the afternoon of their arrival from Australia to Port Moresby in March 1942, two of their pilots shot down a Japanese bomber; the following day they destroyed 14 enemy aircraft during an attack on Lae airfield. This must have been a wake-up call for the enemy, who'd experienced no resistance before their arrival. The pilots were all courageous men, and the toll their campaign took on the squadron is best reflected by the fact that after just six weeks of fighting – in which they hammered the Japanese – the 75th had only one serviceable Kittyhawk available for combat. They'd also lost 12 pilots, including Peter Turnbull who we'd found burnt to death in the cockpit of his aircraft. We became friendly with the pilots, and finding Turnbull in such a state was upsetting for all of us. No-one knew if he crashed or was shot down, but there was no disputing he'd come to a grisly end. The 76th Squadron was also sent from Queensland to Milne Bay, and while they've never been fully recognised for their efforts during the defence of our base – which included sinking and strafing Japanese barges that were loaded with hundreds of men on their way to attack the Aussies – their efforts to attack the advancing enemy went a long way to defeating the Japanese.

One of the pilots I met – and photographed with my Kodak camera – was Acting Squadron Leader Keith 'Bluey' Truscott, who was awarded the Distinguished Flying Cross for the courage he displayed flying a Spitfire while based in England. He enjoyed fame in Victoria as an Aussie Rules player who was a member of the Melbourne team that won the 1939 premiership. I knew nothing about his football feats, but I was in awe of the stories I'd heard about his dogfights with Hitler's *Luftwaffe*. After destroying at least 11 German aeroplanes, Truscott became one of the RAAF's best-known pilots. He struck me as a good bloke and he was happy to speak to the soldiers, but what stood out to me was that he was so broad around the girth I thought he must have needed to have a bigger cockpit than the other pilots. However, I admired all of the pilots from the 75th and 76th Squadrons, including John Jackson and his brother Les, Peter Turnbull, John Piper, and the rest. We often spoke to them about their exploits, and it didn't take long for us ground troops to count them among the bravest of the brave, and perhaps even the craziest of all. These men and their aircraft added starch to our defence, and on 4 August the RAAF made its first kills over Milne Bay when they shot down an Aichi Val dive bomber and two of the four Zeroes that had attacked the Gili Gili Strip. This show of force gave us a welcome respite from the Japanese air raids for a few days.

20

Mice of Moresby

Australian troops had, at Milne Bay, inflicted on the Japanese their first undoubted defeat on land. Some of us may forget that, of all the allies, it was the Australians who first broke the invincibility of the Japanese army . . .

**British Field Marshal William Slim,
13th Governor-General of Australia**

By August, C Coy's men were 'cooked'. All of us were rotting from the inside out as a result of living rough at Milne Bay. Our diet was substandard and lacked any nutritional value, and we lived in a cesspool of diseases which included dengue fever, dysentery and malaria. The malaria was so bad that by the time the AIF's 7th Division relieved us, 80 per cent of our number had the disease. When we gathered at the pontoon to board what I'm quite certain was the HMAS *Stuart* which was waiting to return us to Port Moresby, we met with the 55th's A Coy and the machine gunners from E Coy – and they were the mirror image of us: an army of scarecrows dressed in the tattered remains of their uniforms. Our clothing had all but disintegrated in the region's incessant wet weather and dripping humidity. While I was far from being anywhere near peak condition, I was one of the few men classified as 'fit' – only because I didn't have malaria. However, like most others described as 'fit', I was blissfully unaware that a shocking disease was brewing within my belly and bowels. I'd contracted dysentery, and when we returned to Port Moresby I'd need to spend time in hospital. When I reflect on the sick men at Milne Bay it still amazes me that regardless of how crook they were – and, mark my words, dozens of them could barely move – there was an understanding that every single man would pick up his rifle and fight the Japanese whenever they appeared.

On the wharf I found myself among an angry mob. The men were seething because the sailors had simply thrown the ropes over the side and showed no interest whatsoever in hauling us the 30-odd feet to the deck. It was outrageous to think men with barely enough energy to carry their packs should climb ropes. It appeared heartless, and I didn't hesitate to add my voice to the chorus of abuse that was shouted to the men on the deck. 'Come on, you lousy navy bastards,' I yelled. 'Where the hell are you?' No doubt the choice language used to emphasise our displeasure helped the sailors identify our nationality because we heard a voice call out from above the din to his mates on the deck: 'Oi, they're Aussies! Get over here and help the poor buggers up!' Suddenly sailors rushed from everywhere and leant over the side of the ship to assist. They hollered instructions to us: 'Grab hold of the rope, mate, and we'll drag you up!' 'Just hold on to the rope as tight as you can cobber, you'll be sweet.'

As it turned out, the sailors were a friendly bunch, and by way of apology they explained that the reason for simply dangling the ropes over the side was because they'd expected Yanks. When I asked why they treated our allies in such a manner, the sailors said it was only because they carried so much gear they weighed a tonne, and it was backbreaking work dragging them up. Some of the navy men added in their next breaths that we'd become 'famous' during our stay at Milne Bay because Tokyo Rose had mentioned us in her broadcast on numerous occasions. Tokyo Rose was the name given to the collection of American women of Japanese heritage who worked on Nippon's propaganda radio broadcasts. Their job was to smash our morale, and the only time I ever listened to one of their programs they said we were losing the war; Japan was destined to be the new rulers of South-East Asia and the Pacific; Port Moresby would run red with our blood, and thousands of Allied soldiers were being unnecessarily slaughtered on a daily basis. All of us laughed at the commentary because it sounded more like a comedy act than anything fair dinkum – and it was for that reason Tokyo Rose became popular. One bloke even said he imagined she'd be a 'good sort'. Nevertheless, the sailors were excited to be meeting the blokes who Tokyo Rose had mentioned. One of the more excitable of the young sailors told us the broadcaster had said that the Rats of Tobruk were our fathers, and so we were the Mice of Moresby. 'How good is that?' he exclaimed. So, we became the Mice of Moresby.

While it was clearly meant to be an insult, we followed the lead of the men of Tobruk in that we were proud to wear the moniker as a badge of honour.

From what I observed during my brief stay on the ship, the life of a sailor was quite good. They enjoyed three square meals a day, slept in their own bed, and were far away from the jungle's infernal mosquitoes and stinking mud. I asked one of them how I would go transferring between the services, and he reckoned it wouldn't be a problem because every ship needed more men. He even took me to the galley to meet an officer to talk about my plans, and I was surprised to learn that he was the ship's commander. I had no idea of the naval ranks and I was shocked because I'd figured I was talking to a petty officer! While I was surprised the skipper would take the time to talk to a potential recruit, the sailor was right in thinking the navy needed more crew members. I liked the idea of becoming a sailor, and before I disembarked the skipper handed me a sealed letter which requested the army grant me a transfer to the navy – and the quicker the better. When I handed it to the 55th's administration clerk I watched as he skimmed over the letter's contents. When he finished he looked at me, and then ripped up my ticket to what I thought was a better life and threw it into his wastepaper bin. He then cleared his throat for dramatic effect before saying: 'Request denied, Private Chard.' The clerk said that with everything that was on the line because of the Japanese landing at Gona and their blazing down the Kokoda Trail, the infantry's needs trumped those of the navy. And that was that; he'd condemned me to more months of mud, illness and hunger!

What amazed me most after being away from Port Moresby for a few months was seeing the transformation of the place into a genuine military base. *Our* planes now flew overhead; there was a glut of trucks transporting all sorts of supplies; the wharves were better organised with American labourers, who seemed to be more efficient than we were when we had the job, and there were noticeably more men dressed in either Aussie or Yank military uniforms. There was also a different vibe about the place. In the space of 12 weeks Port Moresby no longer felt like a town the enemy could take without working up a sweat. It's true that much of that confidence came from the volume of AIF troops who'd returned from the Middle East to defend their homeland, but the Americans deserve credit for improving Port Moresby's infrastructure. Apart from the equipment, supplies, and money that accompanied Uncle Sam's troops, they'd also brought that admirable 'can do' attitude that I'd seen turn a coconut grove at Gili Gili into a fully functioning airstrip.

Like the majority of the men who'd garrisoned Milne Bay, I ended up in hospital after dysentery ironed me out. It hit me as Australians continued to fight the Japanese on the Kokoda Trail. They'd been there since late July after the outnumbered, poorly equipped and inadequately trained 39th Infantry Battalion – all Militia men – met the first of the Japanese invasion force. They held them for as long as they could before performing a series of fighting withdrawals which prevented the Japanese from encircling them – as they had their enemy in other campaigns – and slaughtering them.

While the vicious battle raged less than a hundred miles away from Port Moresby, I went to a place the troops called 'Lux Lane' to recover. Lux was a scented soap which was popular back then, so naturally we used the name to describe the stench that emanated from the rows and rows of latrines – which smelled just about as pleasant as you'd expect! Medical orderlies, and not doctors or nurses, treated us, and they followed what I suppose was the textbook treatment for dysentery. Boy, I had the works! My colon felt like it was on fire; blood covered my stool; my stomach ached like nothing I'd felt before; a wicked fever racked my body; I was nauseous, terribly dehydrated, and I had the most shocking wind. At the worst of it, it felt as if I was going to poo my intestines out!

Upon my arrival I received a big aluminium cup of castor oil, and apart from the litres of water I drank to remain hydrated while I was there, that was it. I had nothing to eat on the second day, but on the third day I received some arrowroot – not arrowroot biscuits, but the raw stuff. Apart from its health benefits (it contains potassium, iron and vitamins) it was useful in the treatment of dysentery because it puts a lining on your stomach. If a patient showed further signs of improvement by the next day he received a mug which contained a concoction of hot water, marmite and pepper. By that stage you were so hungry you'd have paid anything for it. Then, if you showed further improvement, you'd drink a mug of jelly the day after that. All being well, you then received your Return to Unit (RTU) orders, and the 'meal' the hospital provided to give you sustenance until you rejoined your mates was one lousy slice of bread. I knew that the food I'd receive when I returned to C Coy would not be enough to satisfy my hunger either, so I decided that before I left, I would organise a feast for myself and the hundred or so blokes who were also recovering from having their guts ripped out through their backsides – even if I needed to scrounge it myself.

I borrowed a couple of cloth sacks the orderlies used to take the bedding to the laundry and hoofed it to the nearby road. There was no shortage of trucks, and in no time at all an American pulled up to offer me a ride. Like most Yanks I'd met, he was easygoing and eager to please.

'Where you goin', Aussie?'

'Mate, I need to get some food for the hospital, but I have no idea where to go.'

'Sounds like you need to get to a food supply dump. Do you want to go to one of ours or the Australian one?'

'Aussie, mate. The Aussie one would be great.'

So the driver took me to the Australian supply depot and I was relieved to find it poorly guarded. I walked into the place unchallenged because there was no sentry. Boy, I was amazed by what I found. There were boxes of every foodstuff you could imagine stacked high. There was so much that it crossed my mind to wonder why we hadn't seen any of this in Milne Bay. I have no doubt my expression must have been as excited as the British Egyptologist Howard Carter's was when he discovered Tutankhamun's tomb. I thought to myself, *Picnic*, and I quickly broke open a crate of tinned pineapple. I was loading up one of my sacks without a care in the world when someone yelled so loudly, my immediate reaction was to think it was a pistol shot: '*Oi, you, what the fuck do you think you're doing?*'

Thankfully, I hadn't been caught by a bullet-headed MP but by a fresh-faced lieutenant. He seemed nervous, and that made me realise I had half a chance of getting what I needed. When he started firing questions at me, I figured honesty was the best policy. I explained I was recuperating at Lux Lane, and because no-one had given us any food we were all starving. I then added that I was rejoining my unit the following day, and I wanted to return to my mates with food in my stomach. The lieutenant interrupted me to say the food I was 'thieving' was for the men at the front. I sniggered at that, and when he asked what I found so funny I set him straight. I told him that I'd just returned from Milne Bay where we hadn't seen any of this tucker. Indeed, I told him our food situation was so desperate I had begged for scraps from the Yanks because we were lobbing hand grenades into the ocean to catch fish. 'I can assure you of this,' I said. 'Hardly any of this food will go to the men at the front.' Judging by the questions he was asking, I was starting to get the impression this officer was actually a decent bloke. He then asked why I wasn't getting any food at Lux Lane, and when I told him about the hospital's rations, he asked me how many men were in the hospital. When I said a hundred-odd, he simply waved his hand as an invitation to help myself.

After he helped load me up with more than enough supplies, the lieutenant arranged for one of his men to drive me back to Lux Lane in one of the depot's trucks. The escapade proved to be well worth the effort when I saw the reaction of the boys in the ward to the food. You'd have thought Santa Claus was visiting an orphanage! They were all cheering and laughing and saying: 'Good on you, mate!' I remember that evening's feast as one of the best meals I ate during my time in Papua New Guinea – and it was just as well, because in a matter of days I was to learn what real misery looked, felt and tasted like at Kokoda and beyond.

Not long after the 55th left Milne Bay, the Japanese finally attacked. They landed a force of 2400 men along with two small tanks. Their commanders had fallen for General Clowes's bluff because they believed that would be more than enough to wipe out the few hundred Australian troops and American engineers stationed there. The RAAF struck the first of their decisive blows when they strafed seven Japanese barges moored off Goodenough Island, leaving those of the 350 Japanese troops who survived the raid stranded. Nevertheless, the main force arrived and the fighting was so bitter the Japanese threatened at one stage to overrun one of the airfields. From the Australian perspective it was a sometimes confused action because when Clowes had the invaders on the rack, General MacArthur advised him his intelligence suggested a strong Japanese force was preparing to attack him from behind and from the flanks. This was incorrect, and it not only delayed the victory, it may have saved the Japanese from total annihilation because, acting on MacArthur's advice, Clowes didn't send every man he had at his disposal to chase them. Between 4 and 7 September, 1318 Japanese evacuated. It's estimated 612 of their comrades lay dead around Milne Bay, while scores more perished trying to make the brutal overland trip back to the Japanese base at Buna. A total of 161 Australians and 14 Americans lost their lives and among them was John 'Jack' French, a corporal from the 2/9th Infantry Battalion. He's remembered for receiving the Victoria Cross after single-handedly wiping out two Japanese machine-gun nests before a salvo of bullets killed him as he silenced the third. The reality for all of us was that the brand of courage Corporal French displayed on that September afternoon was the kind needed to ensure Australia remained free of the Japanese.

21

Punchy Meets MacArthur

. . . by some act of God your brigade has been chosen for this job. The eyes of the Western world are upon you. I have every confidence in you and your men. Good luck, and don't stop.

General Douglas MacArthur, 3 October 1942

After I left Lux Lane, I joined the 55th Battalion at Owers' Corner late in the afternoon. Owers' Corner was the jumping off point for Australian troops as they went on the Kokoda Trail. It was late in the afternoon when we climbed from the trucks that had transported us the 30-odd kilometres from Port Moresby and Lieutenant Ryan decided we'd bunk down there. He saw no point in having us men trip over tree roots or stumble blindly in the pitch black of the jungle's night. 'We'll leave tomorrow,' he said before telling everyone to settle down for a quiet night. However, as we prepared to leave the following morning we were told to wait. After a few hours we observed three jeeps bouncing towards us along the muddy track that passed as a road. The circus had come to Owers' Corner! Each vehicle was driven by an American MP, and they guarded what the Japanese would have described as prized targets. In the first jeep, puffing away on his corncob pipe, was MacArthur; seated next to him was another American general, Robert Eichelberger, while Australian commander-in-chief General Thomas Blamey's ample backside filled the car's other seat. In the next jeep sat the two Aussie generals dressed in their Sunday best. But it was their companion, the Australian government's Minister for the Army – and Prime Minister Curtin's loyal deputy – Frank Forde, who was memorable that day. The Queensland politician sported an oversized pith helmet, wore semi-military gear that looked like a khaki-coloured potato sack, and had a pistol hanging awkwardly from his well-cushioned hip. We sniggered among ourselves because Forde's headwear gave him the appearance of an actor from the set of a B-grade comedy. I can't remember who was in the third jeep, it may have been four Yank MPs. But even if it had had been the Pope, the Archbishop of Canterbury and Don Bradman, their presence would've been overshadowed by the presence of our military's bigwigs.

As is the way in the army, some of the boys took their desire to have a laugh at Forde's expense a step too far. As he promised them the world and asked how he could make their lives a little easier, they revealed that the Japanese had a 'strange' way of fighting. They told him the enemy wore a suit of armour similar to Ned Kelly's under their uniforms and that it was near impossible to kill them! I understand Forde swallowed the gee-up hook, line and sinker. Indeed, the lads were so convincing apparently Forde reported what they had told him upon his return to Canberra. It was kept a closely guarded secret by the bureaucrats to save the Army Minister from looking like a boofhead.

As highly ranking as these figures were, I was unimpressed. I felt the entire event was a farce, and MacArthur's smile as fake as a crocodile's. After wishing us well, he commended the fighting qualities of the Australian soldier. It was hypocritical because the general had spent the previous months badgering our commanders for a quick victory in the most horrific of conditions. He'd wantonly sullied the reputation of our men by accusing them of lacking the will to fight and saying he needed Americans to save Australia. The reason for MacArthur's change of heart – and for his presence at Owers' Corner – was because a week earlier the 7th Division had commenced its counterattack against the retreating Japanese. This was after MacArthur had slammed them for withdrawing to Imita Ridge from Ioribaiwa because their commander believed the condensed front would allow him to have more men spare for strong patrols, and also to launch the counterattack. With the barbarians so close to the gates (at Ioribaiwa the Japanese were only 56 kilometres away from Port Moresby, meaning they could see the city's lights twinkling against the night sky), Tubby Allen drew a line in the sand. He said there'd be no further retreat, and the directive from his HQ was that every man would die before conceding another inch. Indeed, we learnt that the word that travelled along the line to the men was: 'If you die at Imita Ridge, that's where you die – don't let the bastards get past you because we have no-one left to fight in Australia . . .' And now, MacArthur was making his presence felt to provide the public with the impression he was in the thick of the fighting. It was a spectacular and carefully staged performance, and one which received extensive media coverage because, just as a garbage truck attracts blowflies, a horde of sycophantic American correspondents and photographers followed MacArthur everywhere.

As the morning progressed we men watched with disdain as the so-called saviour of Australia and its people played up to the camera. Indeed, he held one pose for so long – he stared over us and into the great unknown beyond the horizon while the photographers clicked away – I wondered if he'd become petrified!

For one of our number, a former middleweight boxer complete with a crooked nose and short temper named 'Punchy' McDonald, the chance visit by military leaders dressed in crisp, clean uniforms represented the perfect opportunity to create some mayhem. Oh, we'd all kept our eye on this particular fellow because if anyone could do something to upset MacArthur's 'courageous' visit to the frontline, it was him. We heard him say quite loudly to the soldiers around him: 'Just watch me – I'm going to get a fag off this fucking bloke!' A lot of the men hadn't had cigarettes for a long time, and the heaviest of the smokers were getting antsy for a puff. Despite that, I doubt any of them would have dared contemplate Punchy's brazen course of action. He broke the line and walked towards MacArthur, saying loudly enough for everyone to hear: 'Hey, General, how about a fag?' The American leader ignored him, which was the worst thing he could've done to a person with Punchy's disposition. He didn't care about rank, pomp, ceremony, or 'acceptable' behaviour if he felt slighted. Punchy was a soldier who respected those who respected him, and Lord help those who displayed indifference. After being snubbed a second time, he stormed towards the general, pointing his finger at him and shouting: 'HEY, YOU! I'M TALKING TO YOU! HOW ABOUT A CIGARETTE?' MacArthur chose to continue ignoring him, which only infuriated the former pug further. That was when two anxious-looking MPs stepped towards him with their firing hands clasped on the holsters of their sidearms. We saw the dangerous situation Punchy's temper – and pride – had put him in, and we took a step forward, brandishing the .303s that had, only minutes earlier, been presented in the commander's honour. I'm quite certain Bula was the soldier who clicked the bolt of his rifle to let the Yanks know there'd be dire consequences if they dared to touch Punchy. Fortunately, sanity prevailed, and Punchy returned to us, albeit as angry as all hell. Not long after that, the jeeps and their prized cargo left, racing away down the muddy road. I watched on, in awe of Punchy's pluck as he spat in the direction of the retreating vehicles. 'What a fuckwit,' he said of his supreme commander.

We were told to stay put, and I figured we were going to cop it because of Punchy's performance and the aggression we'd shown towards the Yank MPs. I don't know how long it was after that, perhaps an hour, maybe two, but someone said: 'Who's this fucking swagman?' I turned and saw a chubby bloke dressed in Bombay bloomers that were rolled up, boots without any socks, a ragged shirt unbuttoned to reveal his bulging belly, and a battered slouch hat. His greeting to us was to ask: 'Who are you blokes?' One of the men replied that we'd just been in Milne Bay, and the 'swagman' cut him short. 'I don't give a fuck where you've been, I want to know what you are.' He found out that we were infantry, and he gave a knowing grin as he used his arm to indicate an imaginary line which divided us into two halves. 'Righto,' he said. 'I'll take you lot; you can join one of my battalions.' I was one of the men in 'his' group, but upon seeing what was happening Bill Ryan stepped forward. He was having none of it and he quizzed the stranger with what was an authoritative tone.

'Excuse me, I'm the lieutenant in charge here – who are you and what do you think you're doing?' said Ryan.

'My name is Tubby, who are you?'

'I'm *Lieutenant* Bill Ryan of the 55th Infantry Battalion, and these are *my* men.'

'Well, *Lieutenant*, you can address *me* as *General* Allen . . . but you other blokes can just call me Tubby. They might be *your* men, Lieutenant, but *I'm* still taking this half with *me*.'

When Bill stood his ground and said he needed to know what was happening to the men who were under his command, the general's tone softened. There's every chance Tubby respected that Bill obviously cared for his troops, and he explained that the 2/33rd Infantry Battalion was down 50 per cent on its full strength and needed reinforcements for the coming battles. I'd later learn that whenever a battalion had been smashed up by the Japanese, the general or one of his offsiders would wait at Owers' Corner to see who came through. As Bill Ryan discovered, it didn't matter who you were, or who you belonged to, at Kokoda you marched wherever Tubby Allen commanded, to fill the holes in the line. And that was how I became a (temporary) member of the 7th Division's 2/33rd for a few months, along with Simple Jack, Titch, Bluey, The Believer, Normie, The Pianist, Punchy McDonald, Bula, Dick Kayess, Nugget and the other men who formed my 'mob'. As for the rest of the 55th I heard Tubby give Lieutenant Ryan a direct order that he was to take the boys along the Goldie River Valley and towards the east coast. He wanted Bill to make sure the Japanese weren't using that as an avenue to get behind the Australians. I listened as Tubby said if Bill Ryan and his men didn't come across the enemy it would be their duty to find their way back to the frontline. After saying our goodbyes those of us who were claimed by Tubby on behalf of the 2/33rd made our way towards the fighting.

Tubby was a great leader, although he was also under incredible pressure. He had two greater, and even more sinister, enemies than the Japanese. MacArthur and Blamey had their daggers drawn and had been stabbing the poor bloke in the back ever since he took command of operations in the middle of August. Nothing he did pleased that pair. It was a joke considering that MacArthur, apart from that one brief visit to Owers' Corner, spent the Kokoda campaign bunkered safely in his heavily guarded headquarters in Brisbane. He demanded quick results and quick victories, because that translated to even more public adulation for him as the man protecting Australia. It didn't seem to matter to him if his reputation was built on the bodies of thousands of dead young soldiers. MacArthur craved positive media and acknowledgement that he was a great military man. Allen, who had served in the bloodiest battles of the Great War, had a different outlook. Of course, he wanted victory – and the sooner the better – but he'd seen too much sacrifice as a captain during the 1914–18 war to needlessly throw his men's lives away. I liked him, and I also appreciated his common-sense approach to his job because it gave me half a chance to return to Betty. This common-sense approach extended to his shabby appearance, which I asked him about later in the campaign.

'You're a general,' I said. 'Why do you dress the way you do?'

Of course, he didn't have to answer me, he was a busy man trying to win a war. However, he took the time to ask *me* a question. 'If I came dressed in my braid and badges, Private, and asked you how things were going, what would you tell me?'

I replied, 'Probably nothing,' and he nodded his head.

'But if I asked you a question while dressed like this, what would you tell me?'

My one-word answer was, 'Everything.'

General Allen certainly understood Australian soldiers better than most.

I knew as much about the Kokoda Trail as I did about Papua New Guinea when we first landed in Port Moresby. Of course we knew about the battle that was raging there, but the names of the places where the 39th and the other

Australian Battalions that followed them had fought and died hadn't yet become legendary – places seldom do until long after the smoke clears from the battlefield and the historians get to work. However, while we were given warnings by older hands about the ferocity and the cruelty of the Japanese, no-one had told us about the physical toll just walking the trail would take on us all. To reach Imita Ridge – the first point after Owers' Corner – we needed to negotiate the infamous 'Golden Stairs', a crude jungle stairway the engineers had cut into the side of the mountain. The 2000 steps were nothing more than mud held together by a frame of rough logs. It was impossible not to slip and slide when we used them because the logs meant the surface of the steps trapped the afternoon rain. It took two steps to clear each one, and it was important to remain focused to avoid taking a tumble. However, it was much worse climbing down them than up because when you put your weight on your back foot as you made your way down to the next step you risked having your foot shoot forward, leaving you on your backside. It was a bastard of a climb, and one that sapped the energy from even the fittest of soldiers.

Once you reached the top of the Golden Stairs you left the Uberi Track only to find Imita Ridge was nature's roller-coaster, because it rose about 400 metres in the first two kilometres, then dipped by about 500 metres before rising 700 metres for the final two-and-a-half kilometres. While it wasn't the steepest, or even the highest, of the mountains we'd need to climb over the trail, Imita Ridge provided an unwelcome indication of the hardship that was to come over the next few months. It exhausted us, and whenever we had the opportunity we lay sprawled on the ground and gasping for oxygen. It was a frustrating climb because when it appeared as though you'd finished, there was another summit, and yet another after that. These false summits could be heartbreaking, and it sometimes felt as though we'd never reach the top of the ridge, let alone meet up with the 33rd who were waiting for us.

We pushed on, through the entangled thick vines, over sharp spurs, through even sharper kunai grass, over single log bridges that lay in swirling, swollen mountain streams, passing through deserted Papuan camps of which the gardens had been stripped bare by the retreating Japanese, and occasionally we'd stumble across the decaying corpse of a Japanese soldier of which the pungent stench could have been its lament of: 'My life was robbed!' Occasionally, in this forlorn place, there was the flash of colour from a brightly coloured butterfly that danced in the dappled daylight, or the glow of fungi in the highlands that we men used to comfort us in the terrifying darkness, as infants in their cots do night lights. Though, the rare beauty of this place was lost when the rains fell – bringing discomfort to Australians, Papuans and Japanese alike – in the form of gushing yellow streams that Mother Nature vomited over the mountains and canopy from midday until darkness fell. These streams crashed upon us, turning the ground into a foetid black mud that we wretched creatures slept in, ate in and fought in.

The trail really was wicked. There were parts where it was only 18 inches wide, with the mountainside on one

side and a sheer, dangerous drop of thousands of feet on the
other. When malaria or dysentery took hold of a soldier,
a split-second loss of balance – especially if he lagged at the
back of the line – could prove fatal. There were instances
where men who were struggling to keep up with the others
were assumed to have toppled over the side to their deaths.
There was nothing we could do to even try to rescue
them because we often had no idea of when – or where –
they'd gone over. Death was everywhere on the trail. If you
slipped over the side you were gone; malaria was killing
scores of men, plus we learnt of another potentially fatal
disease called scrub typhus, which came from tick bites –
and this was all quite apart from the four 'Bs' – bastard
Japanese, bullets, bombs and bayonets. We walked single file
all the time and the two most vulnerable men were the
fellow at the front of the line and the one at the rear. In
time we'd alternate our spots so everyone had a turn at
the head and back of the line. Taking either position was a
nerve-racking duty because the reality was that every step
could well be your last.

Finally, we 'chosen ones' reached the 33rd. I now had to
face the fact that I was about to fulfil every infantryman's
basic role in the army: to participate in combat and kill
the enemy. I'd later realise that my life could never be the
same again after I squeezed the trigger on that first shot at
a Japanese soldier.

22

The Business of War

Our knowledge of life is limited to death.
Erich Maria Remarque, All Quiet on the Western Front

There was no particular reason I picked out the first man I shot. He was among dozens of Japanese who surged like a king tide from out of the jungle to attack our line. He was the same as the others in that he was charging at us with a bayonet attached to his rifle and screaming at the top of his lungs. I can only imagine this doomed figure had shouted he was going to send me to hell along with my friends and the rest of the men. The reason I suppose that is what he was screaming is because that's exactly what some of the more experienced men alongside me yelled at him and his mates. Then, it was time for me to do what the army had trained me to do. I shot him . . . and I confess that I did so without any thought or the slightest hesitation. As he performed his duty and ran towards me, I did mine. I raised my .303; wedged its butt into my shoulder to absorb the recoil from the shot; sighted my 'target'; took a breath and squeezed – not pulled – the trigger. And that was it. Within a split second of hearing the *BANG* from my rifle I watched as the Japanese soldier collapsed to the ground in a crumpled heap. Dead.

The most honest thing I can say about what I'd done is that I felt nothing in that instant. If I'm asked for my thoughts about that enemy's death it is this: he was in the wrong place at the wrong time. That, I believe, is the same epitaph for anyone else who was killed – or maimed – in combat, regardless of which nation's uniform they wore. I could tell you that I vomited that day with disgust as a result of my actions, or that later on I felt an urge to write an ode to a fallen foe as an outlet to express my sorrow about taking his life . . . but that would be a lie. The truth is that when I first spotted him, my only thought was: *There's a Jap bastard!* and I accepted the responsibility that I was to become his executioner. And, when he fell, I immediately looked for another one to shoot. Once again, I did it without any hesitation. While I obviously didn't know that first man I shot, and he hadn't personally done anything wrong by me, I'll go to my own grave adamant I had a just cause to kill him and each of the others that came after. I maintain that view because of the threat he – all of them, really – posed to Australia, to my family, and to Betty.

I know the generations born after World War II will find my view hard to stomach. If I hadn't lived through it, I probably would too. However, it was a different time from the one they know. By 1942 the Japanese military had already spent years inculcating a culture of extreme brutality, emotional detachment and fanaticism in their troops.

The military had immense power in a Japanese society that was already inherently primed to conform. I suspect people would find the Japanese soldiers I faced in World War II unrecognisable from the people with whom Australia has formed strong relationships through trade and tourism over the last few decades. I've also met young Japanese people in recent years, and for all I know they might even have been the great-grandchildren of the men I fought. However, I found they were beautiful kids, very respectful and full of energy. It's my wish for them that they enjoy a long and happy life free from the stupidities of the past.

The Japanese I encountered 80 years ago were so very different. Their army committed terrible atrocities throughout South-East Asia and the South-West Pacific. The list of cruelties is long and ugly. For instance, in China two Japanese soldiers had a race to see who could chop off the heads of a hundred civilians the quickest; we know the treatment of the Allied prisoners of war was barbaric; Australian troops became murderous towards the Japanese when they discovered while mopping up the Milne Bay battlefields the remains of a digger who'd been tied to a long leash and made to run from his captors as they used him for bayonet training; in New Britain they left a sign next to a pile of mutilated Australian bodies proclaiming: 'It took them a long time to die.' The Japanese military of that era also used rape to dehumanise women and girls and socially stigmatise them in the populations they'd conquered or taken prisoner. When I heard about it after the war, I felt a renewed violent hatred towards them for their treatment of women which included the rape and murder of British nurses in Hong Kong. We've only recently learnt that a group of Australian nurses that included the heroic Vivian Bullwinkel were raped by Japanese troops before being machine-gunned to death in the surf off Bangka Island (near Sumatra, Indonesia). Australian troops in New Guinea discovered a Papuan woman who the Japanese had bound by her arms to a hut, and they were sickened to see that the ground around her was littered with 70 used condoms. After the war I'd learn from Australian nurses who were recuperating at Concord Hospital about their mistreatment during captivity. While their stories appalled me, I felt they justified my hatred and killing.

The Japanese who were guilty of those despicable crimes deserved death, in my opinion. Knowing what I knew about them – and what I feared they were capable of – while I was on the Kokoda Trail meant I considered it my duty to ensure they never made it anywhere near Betty, my mother, my sisters, or any Australian woman or young girl. Despite the ghastliness of the act of taking another human's life – and it *is* ghastly to think I have done such a terrible deed – I remain adamant that I killed for the right reason. That doesn't mean I enjoyed it or consider it a source of pride; only a madman could celebrate such a thing. However, I will say with my hand on my heart that I'd do it all over again if the same situation or circumstance ever arose. To my mind, I fought an evil that should *never* have been inflicted upon humanity.

★

I can't tell you where that first action occurred because I never knew where I was on the Kokoda Trail – there weren't any signposts. However, my memory of that first battle is vivid. Apart from the first man I killed, I can also clearly remember the Japanese officer who charged at us that day, waving his samurai sword in the air as he screamed his blood-curdling war cry. I figured if I shot him it might break down their attack. I took aim and curled my finger around the trigger . . . *BANG* . . . he fell. To this day I don't know whether mine was the bullet that killed him because as an officer he drew fire from many Australians. His death didn't stop the assault. Even though their leader was killed the Japanese continued throwing themselves at us. A mass of them targeted the centre of our line before two groups tried to break out and encircle us. That had been a tactic that had worked extremely well for them in the early stages of the Pacific campaign, but it was one they overplayed. Our officers knew what they planned to do, and they'd positioned men to cut them down. While Australian soldiers had the adaptability to change tactics, the Japanese were too rigid in this regard. I was in a position that the Japanese had hit with heavy attacks, and our main problem was that while we were killing plenty of men, there were so many of them that they just kept coming. Something I'll say for the Japanese is that even though they were retreating, whenever they decided to fight they really scrapped – and many of them were so pumped up they were suicidal in the way they charged into our line of fire.

That first combat experience represented a steep learning curve for me, and several things became clearly apparent. I quickly appreciated that I needed to trust the man next to me to do his job. During that firefight 'Simple' Jack was in close proximity to me, and from the moment the battle started he proved he had the perfect temperament for combat. He may have stuffed up drills on the parade ground which earned us 'extras' as punishment, but on the battlefield he was instinctive, a 'natural-born killer' who didn't need to be told twice to shoot our foe. I also realised that you needed to honour the trust of the man next to you by giving your all. What became obvious to me that day was that if someone didn't do their job, or ran while the others stood and fought, the Japanese would bore through the hole they'd made – and the battle was lost. Something else I discovered was that the longer the battle raged, the more I lost the ability to feel any pity for the enemy. Indeed, as the adrenaline raced through my veins at a rapid pace I became 'zombified'. I found myself in exactly the same mindset as when I'd tried to throw 'Hughie' McIntosh over the railway bridge that day when we were kids. I just lost all sense of reality and, I'm afraid, my humanity as well.

As unbelievable as it may sound, I almost welcomed fire-fights because they were a relief from the stress that came from the silence that enveloped the jungle. The Kokoda campaign was one time when birds proved they could sometimes be smarter than humankind because when the bombs started falling and the bullets firing, they flew far away, taking their songs with them. It left an unnerving silence which brought with it the dreadful anticipation that something was always about to happen. In addition, as we waited to move up to the front, we listened to the men who'd already faced the full fury of the Japanese, and they painted the enemy as something to fear. They were apparently better trained in jungle fighting than us; they could be standing two feet from a digger who'd have no idea he was there until they slit his throat from ear to ear with a sharp dagger; they didn't fear death; their massed attacks were terrifying, and they showed no mercy. That anticipation that the Japanese were about to explode from out of the shadows of the jungle's canopy without any notice was terrifying. It kept us in a mental state psychiatrists now call 'hypervigilance', and our inability to switch off took a terrible toll on our nerves. It was all so terribly draining.

However, something I noticed was that from the moment I clicked into survival mode while on the Kokoda Trail, my senses became the sharpest they'd ever been – and each worked in sync with the others. Whenever I scanned the foliage for even the slightest movement, or a shrub a Japanese could be hiding behind, I found myself also smelling the air for something that wasn't 'right' while listening acutely for any telltale sounds that suggested the Japanese might be nearby. Perhaps the greatest problem was that my imagination went into overdrive whenever I heard even the tiniest noise. It was all too easy to picture a squad of bloodthirsty Japanese infantry lying in wait behind the jungle's green screen. There were times when my imagination grew wild and the hairs on the back of my neck stood on end like little antennas receiving Morse code messages that danger was imminent. The waves of primal fear that followed – and they made your blood run cold whenever they washed over you – were terrible. I'm sure others would agree it took all of our discipline not to open fire when a shadow made us jump.

That disconcerting silence I speak of magnified the *BOOM* of the Japanese small mountain guns when they were fired at us. That noise was awful, and it crushed morale because it heralded the Angel of Death – in the form of white-hot shrapnel – which was inevitably hurtling towards some unlucky sods. The projectiles from those guns screamed through the trees, and the only course of action that was available to us was to drop flat onto the jungle floor and hope to high heaven that it missed. Only an idiot, or someone with a death wish, remained on their feet during a bombardment from those cursed guns, because we all knew the shells came in at four feet, and that meant they'd cut to pieces anything that stood in their way. However, as I'd later discover, the jungle of Papua New Guinea had hazards of its own that forced many diggers to endure up to a two-week trip across the mountains on the broad and sturdy shoulders of the Fuzzy Wuzzy Angels.

23

A Heart of Darkness

I thought I was dead and I remember saying to myself
'Fancy dying in a shit place like this . . .'
Jim Moir, 2/16th Australian Infantry Battalion

In spite of the extremely difficult circumstances on the trail, we had the Japanese on the run, and as we pushed forward there were some bloody skirmishes. Even though they were an army in retreat, they threw everything they had at us. I vividly recall one firefight when a group of Japanese soldiers charged fanatically into our guns on a jungle path that was only wide enough for men to walk in single file. Nevertheless, as they charged towards us yelling at the top of their lungs, we sat back and butchered them. Although it was obvious they had no chance of surviving – they were running over the corpses of their fallen mates – they continued bolting towards us, seemingly oblivious to their impending deaths. On their part, it was akin to mass suicide; on ours, it was little more than murder.

As an 18-year-old I couldn't fathom how anyone could throw their life away so recklessly, but I'd find out two things many years later. The first was that when people hit rock bottom, death seems a decent option. Secondly, in the case of those particular Japanese that we obliterated, I've read that besides almost being driven to insanity by starvation, some of those men were broken by their commander Tomitarō Horii's order to retreat. This was an enemy who had believed they were capable of taking Port Moresby from us. According to reports, many considered death a more attractive option than continuing to live with the dishonour of fleeing from us.

My heart raced whenever we 'mopped up' the killing fields after our engagements because of the unnerving quiet that followed the ear-splitting noise of a battlefield. I always experienced a bowel-loosening atmosphere of suspense immediately after a battle because of the constant dread that something bad was about to follow – such as 'dead' Japanese suddenly rising to their feet. Indeed, battle-hardened veterans had warned us never to assume that all of the Japanese troops who lay spread-eagled on the ground around us had met their maker. Those diggers had learnt the hard way that the Japanese had mastered the art of playing 'possum' or 'doggo' – old terms to describe pretending to be dead. In the early days of the campaign, when the Australians thought all was clear and they'd relax, one of the 'dead' would miraculously be 'resurrected', springing to their feet to kill the nearest unassuming Aussies with their gun, sword, bayonet or even a grenade. It was a bastard of an act, but at the same time it said volumes about their hatred, and their desire to kill as many of us as possible. I have no doubt the Japanese who did this realised that no matter how many of us they killed, we'd slaughter them for their treachery. To ensure they were 'done' after any skirmish or major battle, we'd walk among the dead and fire a bullet through the brain of every Japanese who lay on the ground. Despite The Believer's misgivings, our actions were justified on the odd occasion when, after copping a bullet through their skull, a 'corpse' kicked as though it had been blasted by a jolt of electricity. They'd been lying in wait and biding their time until they had a chance to strike.

There were other reasons to be wary of the dead Japanese soldiers. We'd often search the bodies of the slain to see what they were carrying, but it eventually reached the stage where we'd only examine those who we actually saw hit the ground after we'd shot them. This was because, after they realised Australians searched the dead for anything of interest – or value – the Japanese started rigging their men's corpses with booby traps. The diggers who didn't lose their lives when a grenade buried under a corpse exploded could still lose hands, arms, feet, or have their faces terribly disfigured by the shrapnel.

As our hatred for the enemy increased, we Australians became just as creative in finding ways to kill them. When it became known the Japanese were so desperate for food (they'd resorted to eating grass), our rations were used to lure them into 'kill zones'. As their hunger intensified, these men ignored the strict military discipline that was beaten into them from an early age and would rush for the tins of food that were scattered around clearings. Australians would sit still and wait among the tall grass to ambush them. We killed them so swiftly I doubt whether any of them knew what hit them. Few, if any, survived our bullets. While I wasn't involved in the initial withdrawal from Kokoda, I heard that the men of the 39th stuck their bayonets through tins of bully beef that needed to be dumped alongside the other supplies that weighed them down during their retreat and tossed them along the track. The Japanese dined on what was by then meat that had been contaminated by bacteria, and the illnesses that developed played havoc with their numbers. It's a bloody cruel game, war.

When we gunned down the Japanese on that narrow jungle path, I was deep in the throes of malaria. After months of being bitten by mosquitoes in Port Moresby, Milne Bay and the Kokoda Trail, my body could take no more and I began going downhill fast. I was burning from fever and my entire body shook with violent chills; my temperature would most certainly have hit close to 40 degrees. I had the most debilitating of headaches; dehydration had set in through constant diarrhoea and vomiting, while a deep-seated pain made my muscles hurt, making it hard for me to move. That's not to mention the pain I felt from my limbs becoming grotesquely swollen when the welts from the bites became infected.

However, like the others who battled the disease (one which, to this day, annually kills hundreds of thousands of people around the world, especially little kids) I was deemed fit enough to slog on and fight. Despite my poor state, I soldiered on and I can only recall glimpses of what happened because by that stage I was struggling just to stand up. I remember heading into a part of the mountains that was a place of ceaseless gloom. No sunlight broke through the canopy that enclosed the place; there was only mist and moss, and the stench of rotting vegetation.

As my illness consumed me, all I craved was somewhere comfortable and warm to rest, and on one of the nights we were there, I lay against something that felt soft against a tree. It was pitch black and I slept soundly for a few hours. However, when I woke I was horrified to find myself covered in thousands of *maggots*. The 'soft' object I'd used as a mattress was actually a corpse. My God, I was so horrified I dry-retched as I brushed the maggots off me. I only remember glimpses of what happened next: coming under withering fire from the Japanese as I followed the others across a creek via a thick log. The bullets whipped up the water as I sprinted ... or was it staggered? ... for my life. I recall seeing dead Aussies floating in the water. The machine-gun fire that raked the banks of the creek hit other men as they tried to get close enough to silence the Japanese. We were trying to make our way behind the enemy's positions when – just like that – my world suddenly went blank.

24

Angels and Demons

Lines of exhausted carriers were squatting . . . eating muddy
rice off muddy banana leaves, their woolly hair was plas-
tered with rain and muck. Their eyes rolling and bloodshot
with the strain of long carrying. Some of them were still
panting.

Osmar White, war correspondent and author

The malaria had finally taken too great a toll on my health.
After I joined the flanking movement to get behind the
Japanese positions, I collapsed. I imagine I resembled one of
Vic Patrick's opponents at the old Sydney Stadium because
I was down and out for the count. It will sound strange
to say this, but I never found out whether it was Titch,
The Believer, Ray, Dick Kayess or even Simple Jack who
carried me back to the staging post where the Fuzzy Wuzzy
Angels congregated to transport the wounded and ill.
These magnificent men worked in teams of eight, carting
men back to Port Moresby on their makeshift stretcher
of an army blanket folded in half, and two long carrying

poles held together by deep stitching. They preferred that to the army's canvas stretchers because the latter rotted too quickly in the tropics. After placing me on their stretcher they took a long piece of rope they'd braided from the blades of the kunai grass that grow eight to ten feet tall and used it to attach me to the stretcher so I wouldn't fall off. Once they'd decided I was secure enough, the Fuzzy Wuzzies took the first steps of what would be a two-week journey for me to reach the trucks that waited at Owers' Corner to cart the wounded to the hospital tent in Port Moresby for treatment. It was a trek during which relays of Papuan men used their broad and calloused bare feet to act as claws as they slipped and slid through mud and slime, carefully negotiated moss-covered rocks, crossed waist-deep rivers and running streams, and climbed sheer mountains to allow me to get the medical attention I needed.

They really were the closest beings to guardian angels in human form. When it rained they'd carefully place the stretcher on the ground while two of them held large sago leaves over my face as if they were umbrellas. In the more severe downpours these groups of eight men – who didn't even know me – huddled over my shivering body in an attempt to shield me from the rain. They were incredible, and their compassion for a stranger knew no bounds. In their attempt to keep me comfortable and dry, they built a shelter at night which provided me with cover. Whenever they slept these men formed a protective circle around me, keeping an ear out for the slightest hint of danger or any sound from me that might have suggested I needed their attention. It was humbling because they tended my every need without hesitation. They gave me water, fed me teaspoons of a powdered milk paste, and had no qualms at all about offering me portions of their own food. While it was an incredibly generous gesture, I lacked any appetite to accept it.

However, these angels without halos suffered terribly for helping Australian diggers in a war which had been inflicted upon them. They spent great lengths of time away from their homes and families, and with no lines of communication available to them they were unaware of whether their loved ones were even safe. Working for us exposed them to the many dangers of the battlefield as well as the hazards of the rain and cold in the highlands and the dust and dryness of the lowlands; they also went hungry, and lived with the heavy responsibility of knowing that every time they hoisted a stretcher onto their shoulders they were responsible for that man's life. As Christians, they took that duty to heart; and the grotesque sights of the bullet- and bomb-mangled men they carried scarred them. Of course, they placed their own bodies under incredible strain as they trekked countless times – and countless kilometres – over the Owen Stanley Range. These men saved hundreds of Australian lives, and as a nation we owe the Fuzzy Wuzzies, and indeed their grandchildren, who 80 years on live in squalor, an enormous debt of gratitude. I hope that it's repaid in full one day because I'm afraid that over the last 80 years we haven't been overly generous to them. While we believed it with all our hearts when we called them Fuzzy Wuzzy Angels because of their frizzy hair and their wonderful sense of humanity and devotion to duty, I'm terribly embarrassed to admit that I can't even tell you the names of any of the men – and from start to finish the total could have been well over 80 – who saved me.

Not all of the Papuan carriers wanted to do the job. There were those press-ganged into service – including old men – by the Australian Army for the occasional token payments of a single silver sixpence coin. While the overwhelming number of our troops adored them, it would be remiss of me not to note that there were also those in our ranks who didn't respect them or treat them in the manner they deserved. These Australians, although the minority, were shameful bastards, and their behaviour towards the Papuans was disgraceful. There were other ways in which the Fuzzy Wuzzies received shabby treatment from us – and it never should have happened. For instance, while they received sixpence coins for their labour, the agreement forged from the outset between the Australian Army and the Papuan porters was that their main source of payment would be food. However, despite the arrangement, scores of these men suffered from malnutrition under our watch because they worked hard for us but weren't properly fed. It was wrong, and it didn't reflect well on Australia. Indeed, there was never a truer word written during the war than the 21st Brigade report which noted of the Papuan porters: *The Fuzzy Wuzzies performed all tasks we asked of them; tasks that few white men could have stood up to.* While I was too ill to remember much about the experience, to this day I wish that I at least knew the names of the teams of men who carried me. They were among thousands of such angels who plucked an army of men who'd abandoned all hope from the gates of hell.

When we arrived at Owers' Corner, the Australian orderlies placed me on the back of a truck that took me to the 2/9th Australian General Hospital (AGH), which was known to the troops as the '17 Mile' because that's how far it was from Port Moresby. Once there, I became acquainted with some more angels: the three Australian nursing sisters, including the indomitable Sister Ruth Campbell. They refused to follow the order from the Australian government and its military leaders that all European (white) women were to leave Papua New Guinea when the Japanese invaded. If I remember correctly, they were the only white women in the country for a number of months, and during that time they were subjected to the same air raids and other deprivations that drove the men insane.

I remember this trio as being every bit as big-hearted and amazing as the Fuzzy Wuzzy Angels. They were tender and kind. As I recovered from the malaria, the care they provided the dying and wounded men moved me deeply. Night-time in the hospital was awful for everyone because there was always at least one death. On bad nights there could be three, and it was a dreadful thing to witness. The pitifulness of the men's voices, and what they spoke about, was hard to stomach because it was so sad. Sometimes you'd cover your ears in an attempt to block it out. What I quickly realised was that regardless of how old the soldier was – 18 or 48 – as they were passing from this life to the great unknown they'd cry out for their mother. Whenever this happened one of the nurses, and she might have worked a solid 12-hour shift during the day, became the dying man's 'mother'. She held his hand and offered the soothing words a mother would give her child. It was beautiful in its own way, but, at the same time, it was so damned tragic. While some patients had tears in their eyes as they heard the narrative, the nurses remained composed and focused on letting the dying digger know that his mother loved him, that she cared for him, and that she was proud of the man he'd become. I asked Sister Campbell – whose boldness would save my own life months later – why the men cried out for their mother just before they died. Sister Campbell told me that she and the other nursing sisters had spoken about it, and they'd agreed the patients' thoughts had returned to their childhoods and that made them think of their mother. You can only imagine how this affected the sisters. I understand there were nurses who didn't marry because they couldn't find inner peace due to their wartime experiences. All I can say is this: the demands that Sister Campbell and the other women had placed upon them meant they were much more mentally and emotionally strong than me or any other man who carried a rifle over his shoulder. Those women, and all of the nurses who served during the war for that matter, were my heroes.

There were so many patients in the tent used as a ward. I rested upon a stretcher that lay in the mud – yes, the mud – beneath a bed with a patient in it. It's only because I remember seeing a piece of paper during my time there with my name and 'EORA CREEK' scribbled on it pinned to my stretcher that I believe that's where I collapsed on the trail. Something else I recall about the tent is the heat. It was terrible, bad enough to make you boil. That's why the orderlies rolled the side flaps of the tent up during the day to allow the breeze to rush through, and it was quite cooling. They rolled the sides down before dusk to prevent the sick and wounded from attacks by the infernal mozzies. While our ward contained men who were recovering from battle wounds, there were also those who, like me, were sick with malaria. It was an epidemic and the officers needed troops at the front – not in hospital beds. They had realised the mosquitoes were a menace in the first six months of 1942 when the medical authorities noted 1184 cases of malaria among the 6500 diggers in Port Moresby.

One of our problems was that when the Japanese had captured the Dutch East Indies – Indonesia – they had seized the chinchona plantations on Java. At that time the bark of that tree was the source of the majority of the world's supplies of quinine. Australia secured 120 tonnes of it in January 1942 when Dr Neil Fairley, the consultant physician to the AIF, procured two shiploads of the stuff. However, when these supplies didn't arrive (presumedly due to sabotage) we had nothing at all with which to fight the disease. In time we received a synthetic form of quinine which was produced in American laboratories. It was known as Atebrin – and it tasted *terrible*! While it didn't cure malaria, it suppressed it for as long as you took it. However, the yellow tablets turned your skin the same colour as a banana, and among its other side effects were nausea, headaches and diarrhoea. There were also patients who'd suffered disturbing psychiatric symptoms while taking it, such as hallucinations, nightmares and panic attacks. Added to all of that, there was a rumour which suggested that prolonged use of the stuff made you infertile. Not surprisingly, that instilled enough fear in some men for them to refuse it.

While I was in hospital my thoughts invariably wandered to Betty, and I'd wonder how she was. I scribbled letters from my stretcher, but I didn't tell her much about what I'd been through. For instance, I didn't dare recall killing that first Japanese soldier, or any of the other deaths I was responsible for. Nor did my letters include the horrors from the jungle – including the time when I woke covered in maggots. I had enlisted so she'd never experience such things, so no, I had no desire at all to give her the blood and guts accounts others wrote to their loved ones at home.

Eventually, after fourteen days in hospital, I received my Return to Unit orders. I was to head back to my mates at the front, and I'd appreciate that nothing I'd witnessed in my first taste of warfare prepared me for the ugliness that waited.

25

The Massacre

*[A mate of ours was found] tied to a tree by the Japs with a
length of bamboo forced into his backside. He was alive but
died soon after. I went insane for a little while and when we
cornered some Japs later on, the things we did to them now
seem horrifying . . .*

Australian soldier VX66349

On 3 November 1942 there was an Australian flag–raising
ceremony at Kokoda village. Its purpose was symbolic: to let
the world know that the ground we'd lost to the Japanese
four months earlier was again under our control, and that
it was now our enemy who were on the run. Our troops
reoccupied the Kokoda area on 2 November when a patrol
from the 2/31st Battalion cautiously entered the Government
Station's compound. Instead of coming under murderous fire,
they were relieved to hear nothing but silence because the
Japanese had abandoned it two days earlier. By that evening's
sunset the 2/31st, and soldiers from other battalions (including the 2/33rd), had moved into the district.

While the pomp and pageantry took place, I joined The Believer, Ray, Bluey and Dick Kayess in the jungle as part of the defensive line. While we'd recaptured Kokoda without having to fire a bullet, the 7th Division's officers had learnt enough about the Japanese to not drop their guard. They established a strong perimeter, and for two full days we lay in wait for the surprise attack that never came. As we watched and waited, the main Japanese force was legging their way towards the beachheads on the north coast where they believed food and reinforcements awaited them. It would only be a matter of weeks before we'd find out that the Japanese had turned one place, Sanananda, into a fortress while they'd transformed the swamps that surrounded it into a killing zone, which is an area covered by direct and effective gun fire in which an enemy force is trapped and destroyed. That revelation – that the campaign was far from won – came a few weeks after we triumphantly raised the Australian flag over Kokoda.

One of the reasons we celebrated regaining Kokoda was because we were back in possession of the only airstrip between Port Moresby and the coast. That was significant because while it was nothing more than a flat, grass field, it provided us with a strategic advantage. We now had a place from where we could evacuate casualties to Moresby by air, and that would save lives. It also meant we could reinforce our lines with a steady stream of fresh troops as well as enough supplies to keep us fighting. However, when we took our first look at the airfield that would be an essential element in the upcoming Battle of the Beachheads, it was obvious we'd need to invest hard yakka – and time we didn't have – to make it operational again. During their 'tenure' the Japanese had allowed the grass to grow at least one metre high, and they'd attempted to delay our taking advantage of the strip by placing all number of obstacles on it. However, once cleared, our C–53 Dakotas became the 'packhorses of the sky' because they made frequent sorties carting men, weapons, ammunition, medical supplies, bully beef and 'dog biscuits' from Port Moresby. The trip took under an hour rather than weeks.

Although I was exhausted after the trek to meet up with the boys, my first thought upon my reunification with everyone was to feel grateful that we'd lost no-one from my platoon in battle. To help pass the time as we waited for our orders, I told my mates about the many changes that'd made Port Moresby a genuine military base; about my time in the hospital, and about my admiration for the wonderful job the three nursing sisters were doing in caring for the wounded and ill. I then told them I'd celebrated my 19th birthday on the trail by sharing a tin of bully beef with five other blokes, and told them of the occasions that I'd crossed paths with Damien Parer, the war photographer I'd befriended on the troopship that ferried us from Townsville to the battlefront. Parer was by now a legend among the troops because they saw he wasn't scared to suffer the same hardships we endured to capture our stories. Parer went just as hungry as any digger, and he had none of the creature comforts of home. Like us, he didn't have the opportunity to shower, shave or bathe, and his decision to tell as authentic a story as possible meant he risked his life (although I do note there were scenes in his documentary said to have been staged). Damien was behind his camera and filming the troops when I trudged towards him. By this stage he'd grown a heavy beard, and, like always, he didn't appear too fussed about using bad language. 'Hey, Chard,' he yelled from his vantage point when he spotted me. 'Why don't you give the nice people back home a big fucking smile, for fuck's sake!' It made me laugh, and I grinned widely while looking straight into the lens of his camera. By using those few frames in his documentary, *Kokoda Front Line*, Damien made me an extra in what became the first Australian film to win an Academy Award when Parer's work received the Oscar for Best Documentary in 1943. It was a fitting tribute both to his courage and the instinct that made him a great war correspondent. Thanks to Damien's handiwork I see my image whenever I play the copy of his documentary when schoolkids visit the Kokoda Track Memorial Walkway at Concord in Sydney. When I see myself in that iconic black and white footage, I can't help but weep because it shows how young we all were.

Back in the defensive line I was so tired that after yarning to our gang I fell asleep with my rifle still facing towards the jungle. The only reason I woke just before dawn the following morning was because the boys shouted abuse at a Papuan who emerged quietly from out of the bush and sneaked up on them. He was lucky not to have had his head blown off because he'd startled them. However, he seemed nonplussed by the abuse hurled at him, including the call that he was a 'lucky so-and-so' and a 'fucking drongo'. Even though I looked at him through sleep-filled eyes, it was obvious our visitor was a man on a mission because he appeared frantic. I can only suppose the reason he approached The Believer for help ahead of anyone else was because The Believer looked the oldest of our group. While the Fuzzy Wuzzy spoke broken English, his accent was so thick we couldn't decipher what he was saying. When that became obvious he resorted to sign language. Firstly, he pointed to his black skin and then The Believer's white skin. He then held his hands near his chest and used them to form the shape of a female's bosom. After doing that he pointed to the sun and held one digit up to signify ... something. He soon became as frustrated by our failure to understand him as we were. In the end, I'm certain it was Bluey the safecracker from Glebe who cracked the code: 'Oi, he's sayin' white women. One day's walk.' That didn't seem feasible because, as one of the boys noted, the government had evacuated the vast majority of the white women in New Guinea long before the Japanese invasion. Another was suspicious, and he warned that the Papuan could be a Japanese sympathiser (as some were) and he might be planning to lead us to a trap. However, another volunteered a suggestion that horrified us. He speculated that the women could be prisoners of the Japanese.

To a man, each of us said we'd want to rescue any woman from what was surely a wretched existence, but how could we be sure our informer wasn't setting us up for an ambush? The Believer, however, was insistent that as men we had no choice but to take the chance and investigate. 'I couldn't live with myself if he's telling the truth and we did nothing to help them,' he said. If The Believer was anything, he was a tremendous moral compass, and like the others I found myself nodding in agreement. After receiving an officer's permission to search for the women, we followed the Papuan man. However, he walked in front of us at all times – just in case. One thing I'll say for that bloke is that he was cucumber cool, because if he was nervous about having a gun trained on him as he guided us during that cursed journey it certainly didn't show.

My mind went into overdrive about the indignities the women had more than likely experienced. I couldn't help but think sickening thoughts because the Japanese had a reputation for raping and murdering women in the territories they'd occupied. Each twisted thought that filled my head made me even more determined – and desperate – to do whatever was necessary to rescue the women. The reason for that came back to Betty. I was fighting this war to spare her from the depravities the Japanese had subjected other women to, and while I remained committed to doing everything possible to save her from them, I also wanted to ensure no woman suffered at the hands of our enemy. While I had no idea of the number of Japanese troops we'd face during our patrol, I was up for the fight because I knew the Japanese wouldn't simply hand the women over.

It was late in the afternoon when the Papuan stopped suddenly and crouched on his haunches before pointing through the foliage at what appeared to be a jungle clearing. We then heard what sounded like a celebration; a Japanese man shouted something, and a raucous chorus of laughter followed. I feared that whatever they were laughing at didn't bode well for the women's welfare. We needed to know what was happening, and I'm quite certain it was Ray who crept forward to investigate. As he moved quietly towards the noises my stomach tightened and my heart started racing. We'd soon by fighting, and I knew it wouldn't be long before the adrenaline started to race through my veins. At that point I had no room in my senses for fear, although there was fear – there was always fear – but I tried my hardest to block it out by fixating on doing whatever was necessary to rescue the women. That was all that mattered.

Ray was gone a long time. We were all becoming impatient, and while it was silly for him to do so – because every sound was like a cannon blast – one of the boys behind us asked in a hoarse whisper: 'What the fuck is he doing?' Ray took so long I felt relieved when I saw him retrace his footsteps and return to us. When he reached us it was impossible not to read the look of absolute horror on his face. Whatever he'd seen had made the blood drain from him, and while his eyes appeared glassy – as if he wanted to burst out crying – they glowed with what I'd describe as a murderous fury. 'We're too late, fellas,' he said. 'The women ... all of them are dead. The Japs stripped them naked and fucking well killed all of them. They're still there, the mongrels. It looks like the bastards are having a piss-up, and I don't know about you blokes but I want to kill each and every one of the fucking c—ts!'

It's hard to explain how you react to hearing such news. My initial emotion was shock, but once I'd digested what'd happened I felt utter disgust towards the Japanese. I could still hear them laughing and shouting as we crept towards them. Once we reached Ray's vantage point, we laid eyes on their evil handiwork.

Before that particular day I'd fought in battles and I'd figured my experiences had made me 'hard-bitten'. However, nothing I'd seen or done in combat prepared me for what I looked upon. There were women's garments scattered about the ground, and near them was a series of clumps that littered the clearing. It took a few seconds for me to register what they were, and once I did ... well, Jesus wept. The bundles were the dismembered body parts of the women. The Japanese – all officers who stood only feet away from the mutilated bodies as they toasted themselves with bottles of rice wine – had stripped the women naked; lopped off the women's heads; hacked the limbs from each body, and then gutted them, cutting them from crutch to throat. If that weren't enough, I then saw that the Japanese had jammed glass bottles and tree branches into the women's front and back private parts.

I can hardly describe the feelings that built up in me, but one thing was clear: we were no longer an army patrol. We were a revenge party who would ensure that none of the Japanese officers who were drinking, laughing and shouting to the sky would see that day out. It was as if there had been an explosion in my head; the 11-year-old me who wanted to throw Hughie McIntosh from the bridge and onto the railway lines resurfaced.

Despite our shock and rage we somehow kept it together well enough to get into position to launch an attack on the 40-odd Japanese soldiers. The best barometer of our murderous intentions was when I looked at The Believer. It was clear that just like me, Ray, Bluey and the rest, he intended to make the bastards crawl through the fire of hell before stealing their last breaths. One thing I knew for certain when we prepared to charge was that no matter what happened, there'd be no prisoners.

The events of that terrible day have haunted me for 80 years, and while I remember it for so many things, one of them was that this was the only time I ever saw fear in the eyes of a Japanese soldier during the war. When we crashed through the jungle, screaming bloodcurdling cries like demons as we charged across the 20-odd metres needed to get at them, each Japanese officer knew his time was up. We shot those who reached for their sidearms at point-blank range, and by the time we finished with the others I had no doubt they would've wished for the 'clean' death their mates received.

The things we did in revenge's name were terrible. However, while we wanted those officers to suffer as much as the women they'd mutilated, I don't think we matched their cruelty. The Believer – who couldn't shoot at a target because he feared that even imagining he was shooting at a human would offend God – was at the forefront of the killing spree. I am certain that seeing the atrocities those officers perpetrated pushed him over the edge of sanity. His desire to avenge the defenceless women proved that every man has his breaking point, and just like us, he was caked in the blood and gore of the Japanese he'd slaughtered.

After we thought we'd killed them all we started to take whatever identification they had on them and destroyed all of it to ensure they'd remain nameless for eternity as further punishment for their crimes. They'd lost any claim to human names. What they had done made them unworthy of commemoration. We left them in the open to be a feast for the wild boars.

Revenge wasn't sweet, and we paid a high price for allowing our emotions to overcome us. In our angry state we forgot the first piece of advice the veterans gave us, and that was to shoot any Japanese corpse through the brain to ensure they were dead. The sudden crack of a pistol shot, followed by the instantaneous cry of The Believer, made each of us return to our senses. One of the officers had played 'doggo', and he'd killed the man who'd been an uncle to us all. He paid for his actions, but just as killing all of the officers didn't bring the women back, the brutality we inflicted upon that man didn't help The Believer. As I looked at his lifeless features I felt gutted, overcome by a deep sense of sorrow. It struck me that if a divine being had decided this wonderful man's fate was to die in the state of sin he'd tried so hard to avoid, well, what hope was there for the rest of us? It just wasn't fair. The Believer deserved a more peaceful ending than that. His death rattled me for a long time because he'd proved himself on countless occasions to be the Saint of Kokoda by selflessly doing his God's work. He had constantly put himself at risk to save others, and he was forever putting our needs ahead of his own. It seemed too cruel a twist that such a man – one who wanted to get through the war and home to his family without the blood of another human on his hands – had died with such rage in his heart. It's long been my hope that the God he worshipped with such faithfulness and love forgave The Believer for being human in his last minutes on earth.

Over the years I've replayed The Believer's death in my mind on so many occasions, and it always finishes with the same pang of regret and sorrow. If only each of us had put our emotions aside and followed the advice the veterans had given us, his wife wouldn't have lost a good husband, nor his three daughters a loving father. The years have done nothing to diminish the hurt I feel whenever I think about his fate.

The final cut to the heart that day was having no choice but to leave The Believer's body with the women. Outside of the day I lost Betty, tending to the women's remains is the toughest thing I've done in my life. We couldn't just leave them as they were, so we tried to 'reassemble' them in an attempt to allow them to resemble the people they had been. It might sound a strange thing, but at that moment each of us felt it was the only decent thing we could do for them. It turned out there were 25 bodies in all. We gently placed their limbs and heads – each with an unforgettable look of distress etched on her face – with the torsos we thought they belonged to. No-one spoke for the entirety of this ordeal, and once we finished we covered them with branches and leaves. Adding to our grief as we performed this grim duty was that we realised the Japanese had butchered them while they were still alive. We knew this because the ground was heavily stained by their now sticky blood, it was clear their blood had still been flowing when they had been dismembered. It was all so sickening, and what stung me was that even though Betty and I had been going together since we were 16, we were both still virgins. That day was the first time I saw a naked woman, and, try as

I might, the hideous images of what the enemy had done to defile them has never left my mind.

As the last surviving member of that patrol, I've refused to identify whether the women were nuns or nurses, Australian, Dutch, American, or German, because I don't want their family members to realise the terrible way in which they perished. My only wish is that we had reached them earlier than we did because I know we would've rescued them. On the flipside, though, I wonder what chance they would've had of a normal life after what I'm certain they were subjected to. I'd witness terrible sights before my war ended, the deaths of three of my best mates among them, but nothing I experienced in the jungle and swamps affected me quite like the fate of those women.

I became hardened after that and possessed not even an ounce of mercy whatsoever for the Japanese. My loathing for them intensified when it became common knowledge they'd resorted to cannibalising our dead when their supply chain broke down completely. A patrol found on the trail the corpse of a digger they knew with strips cut from the buttocks. His mates were distraught to find that the meat found inside small pots which belonged to the Japanese was his flesh. From that moment on, most Australians showed no quarter towards the Japanese. While very few of them ever surrendered to us, we did everything possible to ensure none of them survived the battles. In the end, our officers, and the Americans as well, offered the men bribes of such things as ice cream, beer and even leave passes in exchange for live prisoners. The brass needed the prisoners to interrogate for military intelligence, and they figured offering the men such luxuries would make them think twice before killing any captured Japanese.

When our patrol returned to our post we reported the death of The Believer and the discovery of the 25 women to an officer. He took the details of our friend being 'Killed In Action', but he had no interest in the fate of the women. Who knows why? The officer might have thought it was all too much trouble because they were dead and not his problem. On a deeper level, perhaps there was a sense of shame that the Japanese did what they did to 25 white women less than a day's march from our camp. What I do know is that I was too broken by what I saw to push it, and it soon became an unspoken secret – maybe because each of us regretted that we didn't reach them in time. I'll say this, though: I thought it was appalling to see how the Allies treated crimes the Japanese committed against women from Allied nations. For reasons I've never understood, the survivors who gave evidence at the War Crimes Trials received orders to tone down the suffering they endured. While I can't explain the reason for the army's disinterest in the 25 women the Japanese butchered that day, I've always believed we didn't do enough for the women who suffered at the hands of an enemy that proved itself time and again to be utterly barbaric.

Even though it's been 80 years since that terrible day, I've relived the entire ordeal every night since the war ended through the most terrible nightmares. It's so vivid it feels as though I'm back there, looking at the disembowelled bodies. It doesn't matter whether I go to bed at 8.30 pm or even 12.30 am, I'm awake each morning at 2.30 am sweating profusely and with my heart beating as wildly as it did when we crept towards that jungle clearing. In my dream I see the distressed looks on the dead faces of the women – looks of horror, confusion and fear – and I also see the look of terror that overcame one particular Japanese officer I killed without mercy or remorse. He died a brutal death, and even though the bastard continues to show up as an unwelcome visitor in my dreams, I compose myself by telling myself the same thing that I've said for 80 years. I say this: 'That bastard deserved what he copped – and then some more . . .'

26

Sanananda

If they asked me [about dying in battle] I would say, 'Well we're going to die sooner or later and our chances are it's going to be sooner. But, if we love the Lord we're right.'

**Ray Wotton (Padre), Senior Chaplain,
18th Australian Infantry Brigade**

I left Kokoda with the 2/33rd to pursue the enemy, and my blood was boiling as we trekked for a couple of weeks over the last of the steep mountains that led to the coast. I felt deeply unwell in both body and mind. I don't know if I was in a state of shock from the harrowing scene of the massacre site and The Believer's death, or if it was a side effect from my first bout of malaria, but I was out of it. I felt so lethargic and terribly sore. Indeed, I'm certain it was only my bloodlust for more revenge that gave me the strength to keep going. There was also no option except to dig deep and move, because if you collapsed you remained where you fell. The lucky ones might have received assistance from the troops or Fuzzy Wuzzies that came through behind us, but if you stopped it was a matter of fending for yourself.

While my mates looked after me as best they could, they couldn't do the walking for me, so I just focused on putting one foot in front of the other. When that became too hard, I tried getting rid of items from my pack to lighten the load. The first thing I dropped by the side of the trail was my Brodie tin helmet. It weighed 1.1 kilos, and believe me, even when I was fully fit and functioning it still felt like an iron anvil on my head. I was in such a bad way that I even disposed of the prized watch my parents had given me because it simply hurt my wrist too much to continue wearing it. Even though it had stopped working I thought I'd keep it until I returned home and get it fixed. However, my mind started to play tricks on me because I'd tell myself, 'This bloody watch is killing me,' and when I took it off, I felt instant relief. Of course it was all in my mind, but I still tossed it away.

Like many of the other men, I was so tired that it didn't matter if I fell into a puddle when we rested; I'd enter 'dreamworld' straight away. My body just shut down as soon as I closed my eyes. I was exhausted, and every moment of sleep I could get was priceless.

Food, or the lack of it, remained a major problem. There was never enough to satisfy anyone's hunger. Our supply lines were still a shemozzle, and we needed to preserve whatever we carried. That meant that whenever someone opened a tin of bully beef, six men crowded around to share its contents, just as we'd done on my 19th birthday. My mother would've been horrified because no-one used a fork or spoon to dole it out. We just dug our dirty fingers in and scooped it out before throwing it straight into our mouths – it was no wonder disease spread. We also had tiny tins of baked beans, but after dividing them between half-a-dozen men you were lucky to receive seven beans each. While we weren't as badly off as the Japanese, who'd resorted to eating bark and leaves and cannibalising the corpses of dead diggers and Papuans, we were wasting away due to malnutrition. I don't mind admitting that whenever I dug my fingers into the bully beef there was always the temptation to take more than my fair share, but my conscience wouldn't permit it. This was reinforced every time I looked at my five mates, all of whom were gaunt, hollow-faced and bug-eyed, and so physically weak it struck me that even though I was exhausted and hungry I figured those poor bastards needed the food more than me. Perhaps they felt the same – that another man's suffering was worse than their own – whenever they looked at me.

Despite feeling as though I was on the verge of collapse, I welcomed the opportunity to have another crack at the Japanese at Gorari. That was the battle historians later described as the last major engagement of the Kokoda Trail. As much as I loathed the Japanese, I'll give the bastards this much: they fought on this occasion like wild beasts caught in a trap. And that's what they were. They'd realised all too late that we'd copied their tactic and encircled them. While they hammered the 33rd's position with suicidal charges in their attempt to try and shove us off the trail, we didn't budge. My rifle worked overtime because my heightened fear of what the Japanese would do to our women if ever they invaded Australia drove me to kill as many of them as possible. The terror of knowing what they could do to our women awakened my killer spirit.

While the 2/33rd walked to the beachheads after the Battle of Gorari, Lieutenant Ryan and the other members of the 55th Battalion flew in Dakotas and Qantas aeroplanes over the Owen Stanley Range to the airstrip at Popondetta, near Buna. Those flights from Port Moresby were hops of 40 minutes or so, and they spared the men the energy-sapping 14-day trek.

After serving in the Gona area – and the horrific war waged there was reflected by the casualty lists – I met up with Lieutenant Ryan and the other men in time for the battalion's assault on the Japanese lines at yet another tropical sewer: Sanananda. It was without doubt among the vilest of Papua New Guinea's hellholes. After their losses in the costly battles of Buna and Gona, the Japanese Army and naval units had fortified this godforsaken place for their final stand. With nothing but the Coral Sea at their backs, they fought fanatically – and bravely – because there was nowhere for them to go. The Japanese had made the deteriorating battle at Guadalcanal their priority and left the wretched remains of their fighting force in Papua New Guinea to fend for themselves. Our fighter pilots dominated the skies, ensuring the defenders remained isolated by making it all but impossible for the Japanese Navy to either reinforce their numbers or resupply them with food, ammunition and medical essentials. Our opposition was rotting, but they were far from defeated. As the days turned into weeks, those bastards made us fight for every inch of that cursed swamp, and the price we paid for each small inroad was far too high.

The siege began on 7 December 1942, when I found myself standing shoulder to shoulder with my mates as we waited to assault the entrenched Japanese. I don't think anyone up there was ever 100 per cent fit but despite our terrible physical condition, shaped by constant exhaustion and starvation, we were considered fit enough to put on our packs and fix bayonets on our .303 for any hand-to-hand fighting. It seemed fitting that we used the same tactics that my father's battalion, and all the ANZAC units, had employed on the Western Front, because I imagined with its swamps, mud and pungent smell, Sanananda could quite easily have been a scene taken straight from the Somme. However, unlike the charges Dad and his mates undertook, we lacked any artillery support – because there wasn't any available. We all knew that meant there'd be many casualties before the day finished.

That's why I was pleased to play a role in ensuring that at least Titch wouldn't be among them. His boots had fallen apart during the lead-up to our assault, and his feet became infected from their exposure to mud that teemed with goodness knows what. It infuriated me that a blockheaded officer had cleared my friend to fight even though he could barely walk. Yet, Titch's was a solid character, and rather than complain about the unfairness of his orders, he stoically took his place in the line and prepared himself to give his all. However, it was impossible to miss that his feet were an angry red colour and terribly swollen. It was obvious Titch wouldn't have a snowflake's chance in hell of surviving, so

I called out to our Colour Sergeant Dave Swaney to take a look. When he came over I challenged Swaney to tell me a man in Titch's condition was able to fight. 'He can't even walk,' I said. 'How on earth can he be expected to fight like that?' Swaney, who'd served in the British military before migrating to Australia, was a tough but fair man, and it didn't take him long to order Titch to return to camp and get his feet treated by the medics. I'm not exaggerating when I say that Swaney's intervention – and his common sense – most certainly saved Titch's life that day.

Anyone who says they weren't scared about rushing into Sanananda, a place where even angels would've feared to tread, was lying. However, what I thought was remarkable as we prepared to charge blindly into the Japanese lines was that I saw no-one shirk their duty. I have no doubt quite a few of our men, especially those who were sick or wounded, felt envious of Titch when he was let off the hook, but they did what was expected of them. As the clock counted down to Zero Hour, the moment when we'd advance, Dick Kayess bestowed an unexpected honour upon me. 'When we get home, Reg,' he said in a cheery voice that was in stark contrast to the seriousness of the moment, 'I'm going to marry Isabelle . . . and, mate, I want you to be my best man.' It was news that made me smile, a welcome window to life beyond the impending battle, and I told Dick that I wouldn't miss it for quids. It also made me think of Betty. My mind was a whirlpool of thoughts and fears; one minute I'd tell myself that no matter what happened that day, I was going to survive and return home to her, but the next minute I'd hope that if I didn't make it Betty would move on and make the most of her life. I also thought about my mates. For some unknown reason, the universe had brought us together for this particular moment. I vowed to be as brave as I could for them, and no matter what followed I wouldn't let any of them down.

We received the order to advance. I moved forward with Dick Kayess on my left and James 'Davo' Davison on my right, where Titch would otherwise have been. Dick hadn't taken more than three steps towards the enemy before one of the snipers hiding in nests they'd constructed in the palm trees shot him through the brain. Dick was dead before he hit the ground; his wound didn't even bleed. I remember thinking, *Poor Isabelle.* After we took another step, Davo was also killed instantly by a bullet from a sniper in a different direction that went through his temple. And there I was, the man who'd been in the middle now standing all alone. The jungle was teeming with snipers, and I braced myself, waited for the third bullet to finish me off but, thankfully, it didn't come. There was nothing I could do for either of my friends, but I quickly worked out that I had no hope if I stood still, so even though there were bullets whining overhead or around me I just pushed on with the others. It helped that I was in a robotic state where it seemed doing my duty and taking the high ground from the Japanese were all that made sense. I know it seems strange, but at that moment doing my job was all that mattered.

To reach the river we needed to step over the dead Australians who littered the ground, and I'd find out a few days later that poor Norm Wolfson — the loner who befriended my group at Greta — was among them.

The Japanese poured deadly fire into our ranks, and from their position they couldn't miss. Whenever I'm asked to describe what it felt like to be in that situation, I say it was akin to opening a door to enter a room where you waited until someone killed you. You had no control over your fate – none whatsoever – but if you didn't keep moving you were a sitting duck. So I kept going, and even though every step could have been my last, I realised it was pointless to run back to our lines because we'd only be ordered to do it all over again.

By the time our advance came to a halt just 20 minutes after commencing the attack, we'd somehow pushed the Japanese back 100 yards – but it came at a terrible cost. The Australians had copped a mauling; in that 20 minutes of fighting we suffered 364 casualties across our entire frontline – sadly reminiscent of the Western Front. Nightfall was a nerve-shattering experience, not only because of the ongoing threat posed by the snipers and the fears the Japanese would mount a major attack at any moment, but because we could hear the anguished cries of our wounded as they screamed for help. It was something that challenged your humanity, because as much as you wanted to rescue them – and there were those who threw caution to the wind and tried – and died – a sense of self-preservation overcame us. Oh, those screams . . . At one stage I covered my ears to block them out. It was the same feeling of helplessness I'd felt when I'd been at the hospital listening to the dying men talk to the nurses in their final moments. It was cruel, but mercy eventually arrived in the form of the bravest souls in the jungle that night – the unarmed stretcher bearers. They had guts, and no protection at all; they were nothing more than targets for the snipers as they dragged those poor souls to safety.

The other heartbreaking postscript to 7 December was when others would ask if you'd heard who was 'brown bread' (dead). Hearing each name was painful, but the one that hit me hardest outside of Dick, Davo and Normie, was Lieutenant Ryan. He died as he'd lived his life: as an officer, leading his men and inspiring them to follow him. There was a rumour that Bill saw a puff of smoke from a sniper's rifle and he was killed as he tried to get at him, but a private, Geoffrey Shaw, wrote a first-hand account which was a testimony to the former rugby league star's gameness and guts. Shaw wrote:

> Bill Ryan was as great a hero as New Guinea will ever know. Armed with a rifle he led us into action along the Sanananda trail on the morning of December 7. Some of our men had Brens, Owens and .303s. Lieutenant Ryan jumped out 30-yards ahead of us and called for us to follow. When one of our Bren men was knocked, Bill threw down his rifle and took the Bren. Then he charged with the Bren, shooting up the Jap machine gun posts. It was wonderful to see him. Our men were getting knocked, but Ryan kept going ahead to complete the difficult task assigned to him and calling on us to follow. Side-stepping past Jap sniper and machine gun posts in real rugby style, he took heavy toll of the Japs. Having used all his Bren ammunition, he seized an Owen Gun and wiped out more Japs. He jumped into a trench, taking the Japs by surprise and

cleared them out of that. But as he chased a fleeing Jap a sniper high in a tree fired and tore a hole in his back. When our chaps raced up to Ryan he told us to carry on and not to bother about him. Almost at once he collapsed from blood loss and exhaustion. That man had the heart of a lion. He did not know what fear was. Whatever action may be, Bill Ryan has been awarded the soldier's VC by those who were at the spot to see . . .

Bill was a devout Catholic, and I'm sure it would've comforted his family to learn that two days before his death he'd arranged for the priest 'Nobby' Earl to say mass for the men of his denomination so they could receive their Holy sacraments. I don't know why, based on Shaw's account, he didn't receive a military honour because other men received the Victoria Cross or Distinguished Service Medal (DSM) for similar actions. However, Shaw's assertion that Lieutenant Bill Ryan would have received the VC if such decisions were left to ordinary soldiers is correct. He was a hero and is honoured still by the Newtown (Jets) Rugby League club as one of their bravest and finest, while I understand his photograph takes pride of place in the assembly hall at the beautiful St Joseph's College in Hunters Hill. I hope the footballers who play for Newtown, and the students at 'Joeys', draw strength from Bill's life and death. They can take it from me that he ought to be a source of inspiration for any young person making their way in the world. He represented the best of us. While he was a great and courageous officer who expected the highest possible standards from his men, Bill also never forgot that all of us were just that — men. He was big enough to accept that each of us had our shortcomings and our differences but he was good enough a leader to bring us together and follow him. And, as Bill Ryan proved during my battle with The Officer, and the time when Nugget and Bula bashed the MPs, he was man enough to stand by us when others would have walked away.

In the 80 years that have followed those events, I've thought about Dick, Davo, Norm, and Bill every day. I have no answer — or even a theory — as to why they died and I didn't. When it comes down to it, I can only attribute my survival to plain old luck.

A month or two after that horrendous day in December, I was reading the months' worth of mail that had accumulated for me in Port Moresby while I was in the mountains and then on the coast. There was one letter from Betty that I've kept all these years, and interestingly enough I only recently realised there was an eeriness to it:

Dear Reg,
I was very pleased to get your card and to know that you are well. We had a letter from Bruce [Betty's brother] today, and he said he may not be able to write for a while and Mum thinks he must be getting moved. I have been working fairly hard lately. I have been doing three nights a week overtime, and two nights ago I worked all night from 6 o'clock until 7. I had to come home this morning with ulcers in the eye, and believe me, it is terrible so you'll have

to excuse this writing, I have a shade over one eye. I often see your mother and [my sister] Myra down Marrickville of a Saturday morning and always ask how [indecipherable] and Jean [my sister] and Ken [my youngest brother] are. I was going to work that morning and saw your father waiting for a tram at Saunders Corner, Railway Square. I might close now, Reg, my eye is driving me crazy.

Lots of love from Betty

The letter's eeriness was pointed out to me only recently when I showed it to someone. They noted the date she wrote the letter ... 7 December 1942. We were both in the wars that day.

27

Ray of No Hope

Heaven is Java; hell is Burma;
but no one returns alive from New Guinea . . .
Japanese Imperial Army saying about New Guinea

In the weeks after that fateful 7 December, we lived no better than water rats in the swamps that surrounded the fortress of enemy bunkers. The Japanese engineers had started work on the bunkers when they'd landed in Papua New Guinea six months earlier. They'd used palm logs to construct them, but each was reinforced with 44-gallon drums filled with concrete. It was one of a number of ways they'd provided their soldiers with maximum protection. They'd also devised an intricate maze of trenches and tunnels which allowed their soldiers to move freely from bunker to bunker during an attack. While they weren't five-star hotels, the bunkers were far superior to what we lived in: hastily dug foxholes and small trenches with no cover at all. That meant it was open slather for just about every insect in the world that could sting or bite a man, and they went to town on us.

The misery of our situation was compounded by the fact that our dugouts quickly became breeding grounds for beri-beri, tropical ulcers and dysentery – each of them terrible afflictions which chewed on men from the inside out.

While there was always plenty of ammunition, hunger was a constant companion because the Japanese machine gunners and snipers made the job of resupplying us with food and medicine a dangerous one. On top of all that we became waterlogged, because living in a swamp meant that whenever the tide rose, our 'homes' filled with water. You could joke and say it was the ultimate in waterfront living – but there was nothing nice about our real estate. You had no alternative but to sit or crouch for hours in the foetid water because the sniping was so hot, it would've been certain death to crawl out to dry off. We tried to bail the water out of our foxholes with empty bully beef tins, steel helmets, or anything else that could hold liquid, but it was useless. We were covered in rashes, sores, slime and even mildew. Our clothes and skin stank of the swamp, and, like our boots, our clothes fell apart.

Another health hazard the snipers forced upon us was that we had no alternative except to urinate and defecate in the foxholes, the very place where we ate our meagre rations, slept and lived among the flies that were drawn to our lumps of waste. It was terrible, but living like that was better than having a bullet smash a hole through your skull.

Not that I've ever had a skerrick of sympathy for them, but the Japanese snipers had it no better. They lived in a 'nest', which was a big bamboo basket in the palm trees, and like us they ate in it, pissed in it, dumped in it, and slept in it. Their advantage over us was that they were dry (at least, when it didn't rain – and it always rained in sheets), and it was as frustrating for us as it was frightening that we had no idea where the bastards were hiding because if they weren't among the palm fronds on the top of palm trees, they lived in bunkers and machine gun nests which we didn't see until it was too late.

At Sanananda we were trapped in what was as much a psychological hell as a physical one. I tried to escape by thinking about Betty, Mr Fleming, the Dundee Cake Shop, and the other things I'd left behind. I talked about them a lot to the others because I wanted to remind myself that I was something more than a scared soldier caked in mud and slime. Talking about my memories meant I had a past, and, if I survived the war, a future. I'm certain some men questioned why *they* were stuck in such a nightmare, but it was pointless to play the victim because complaining wasn't going to change our situation. I only saw one soldier break at the front. He caved in when he saw the corpse of his best friend and he started crying. Rather than condemn him for being 'weak' many instead joined this man in crying. Seeing his reaction opened the floodgates to everyone's miseries and sense of loss. Some wept, others sobbed uncontrollably, a few bawled unashamedly. The noise we made that day could have passed for the chorus to the song of the damned.

The longer we remained pinned down the worse life became for us. Our health deteriorated to the point where everyone was sick, although I can't recall anyone ever complaining about a toothache or a headache. Those ailments that caused men to take sick days in civilian life were trivial when compared to the suffering that surrounded us in that swamp. We became desensitised to so much: living among the rotting corpses of friends and comrades, the ever-present feeling of fatigue and hunger that became as much a part of our life as eating and sleeping. One saving grace was over time our noses tolerated the offensive smells – man made or otherwise – that had made us dry heave during the early days of the campaign. The mosquitoes were as relentless as Milne Bay, and many men fell ill as a result of their stings.

Most of us disposed of the photos of our loved ones because the waterlogged conditions ruined them. And even though they were reduced to pulp, it was hard to get rid of them because it felt as though we were cutting ourselves off from our 'other' world – the one of hope and wonder. Regardless, I clung to the idea I'd have a happy life with Betty if I survived, but it only took the sudden crack of a sniper's rifle followed by the deathly cry of the solider who was shot for reality to bite. That reality was at just 19 years of age, I was waiting for my turn to die.

One week after the snipers killed Dick, Davo and Lieutenant Ryan, I received yet another terrible reminder of their accuracy. We'd slept in the jungle overnight and were due to go on patrol the following morning to continue our mission to locate the enemy. We were always trying to find the bastards so as to kill them when we could have simply sat back and let them starve to death. In the early pre-dawn hours we were woken by Ray's booming voice,

'COME ON, YOU BASTARDS, TIME TO WAKE UP!' This was a fatal mistake: he'd alerted the snipers to where we were. The instant Ray stood up a bullet hit his shoulder and the bloody thing almost cut his arm in half. He crashed to the ground, screaming and writhing in agony. He was pleading for help, and I shouted at him to shut up. Despite the danger, I couldn't leave him there to be picked off, so I yelled for our Bren gunner and the others to give me covering fire. As soon as I heard the gunner pour lead towards the palm trees I was up and away. I crouched as I ran to Ray, and, just like that terrible day on 7 December, I expected to be bowled over by a bullet.

I have no idea if the sniper peeled off any shots at me, but it was obvious Ray was a mess. His left arm was attached to his body by a few shreds of skin, and blood was gushing from it as though someone had turned on a tap. I said something like, 'Jesus, Ray ... this isn't so good.' Australia's frontline soldiers were issued with two field bandages, but in Ray's case the bleeding was so bad they may as well have been cotton balls for all the good they did. I knelt beside him, hoping a sniper wasn't lining me up, and wondered what the hell to do. Ray was now in shock, and I realised if I didn't do something – and quick – he was going to bleed out and die in front of me. Inspiration came in the form of his rifle, which was lying on the ground next to him. Our rifles had a sling which we used to carry them over our shoulder. I took the sling from both his and my rifles and used one as a tourni-quet and the other to tie his arm in place. While Ray was bigger than me, I managed to put him over my shoulder using the fireman's hold, and then I made tracks back to our casualty clearing station.

Getting Ray there as quickly as possible was his only chance. If the station was three kilometres away, this particular trip felt more like 30. Even though he didn't answer me, I continued to talk to Ray as I carried him through the mud and slush. I urged him to hang in there and joked that he was a lucky so-and-so because he'd be home in Marrickville before he knew it. When he didn't respond I figured he'd lost consciousness, but I kept talking . . . I think it kept me going, if nothing else. Even though he was heavy and the walk exhausting, I didn't dare put him down on the ground because I doubted whether I'd be able to pick him back up. Despite the upbeat nature of my comments, I was scared because my body was covered in his blood.

As I approached the mud-splattered white open tent that served as our casualty clearing station I screamed for help. Two orderlies dressed only in shorts ran to assist, and I felt relieved when they took Ray from me because I figured he was now safe. However, rather than care for him they just dropped my mate into the mud as if he was a sack of rubbish. My old demons resurfaced: how dare they do that to my mate? I was worried his arm might have come off when he landed. Of course, my reaction was to want to throttle them. As I clenched my fists and shouted abuse at the pair, one of them put his hands up and said quite calmly: 'Mate, he's dead. He's dead.' And they were right, Ray was gone. He'd died on my shoulders. I told them again that I thought they were bastards for tossing my mate into the mud as though he was nothing. But the fight in me was draining away and grief for Ray rushing in, so I told them to go before I did something I might regret. I just wanted to be left alone with Ray, and as they walked away, I knelt down beside my friend and whispered my farewell.

One of the most surreal things that happened to me at Sanananda occurred as I walked from the casualty clearing station back to the frontline after Ray passed away. I was still cursing the orderlies for dropping my mate into the mud when I heard a distinctive voice say: 'Hey, soldier, where are you going?' It was a shock to realise it was our leader, General George Vasey, who was addressing me. This meeting was made even more extraordinary by the fact that he looked as though he'd just stepped out of a department store catalogue! The general was spotlessly clean and immaculately dressed – in stark contrast to my filthy, haggard state. What surprised me most, though, was that he had no-one with him, and that he wasn't even armed with a gun. After all, when General MacArthur had turned up for his photo opportunity at Owers' Corner a few months earlier, he'd been flanked by American MPs who wouldn't have allowed a mosquito to get close enough to sting him. The general asked again where I was going, so after telling him I was headed to the front I also told him Ray's story and it made an impression on me that he seemed genuinely moved by my mate's death. It also gave me some comfort to see that he appeared appalled when I told him about the way the orderlies had treated

Ray's corpse. I'd learn much later on that his sympathy wasn't an act, as I read the first thing he did after a battle was to sit alone in his tent and read the casualty list. He used the time to come to terms with the fact that he, as the commander, was responsible for creating widows, leaving children without fathers, and mothers without their sons. General Vasey's conscience ensured he was not reckless with his men's lives, and when he died in a plane crash in March 1945, I was one of many soldiers who mourned the passing of a good and decent man.

Interestingly, I noticed that when I spoke to the general I unthinkingly called him 'Sir' on a number of occasions. This surprised me because that was the first and only time I addressed anyone by that title during my time in Papua New Guinea. He had an air of authority – and decency – that obviously impressed me. My surprise only deepened when he asked me – a humble private – for my assessment of our situation, and my view on the casualties we were taking. I told him the truth: 'The Japanese can't get out of their bunkers, Sir, and we can't get in. It's a stalemate, but we're throwing ourselves at them.' When he asked about our officers, I again told him how it was: 'Sir, they're all dead!' It appeared to me as though he hadn't heard this before. He said if this was the case, who was in charge? He was obviously listening to my observations, so I told yet another truth about the life of his frontline diggers: 'It's whoever is at the front of us, Sir. And when he's knocked over, the bloke immediately behind him takes charge.'

Vasey just nodded while he took in what I was saying, but it was clear he was concerned by the growing number of casualties – especially when I told him that whenever seven men were sent out on patrol, only four men were expected to return. When the general kept walking towards the front alongside me, I advised him that wasn't wise: 'If the Japanese see you, Sir, they'll lose half of their men just to get at you.' Vasey stopped then. As he turned to go back to wherever it was he'd come from, he told me reinforcements were going to come.

While the general proved true to his word, he unfortunately sent people who shouldn't have been on the frontline because they weren't properly trained for the infantry. Our reinforcements consisted of truck drivers, cooks, bakers, blokes off Bren gun carriers and others from the anti-aircraft guns that were based at Port Moresby harbour. They had no chance of learning the tricks of a deadly trade on the job, and while many of them died bravely the sad truth is they were nothing more than easy picking for the battle-hardened Japanese.

History allows us a more clear-eyed view of some of the decisions made at the time: had MacArthur taken on board General Vasey's request to allow his troops to fall back 15 miles so an Australian naval destroyer could sit off the coast and bombard the Japanese positions to rubble, it would've saved many lives and ensured a quicker victory. However, MacArthur refused this request, saying all available naval ships, Australian or otherwise, were employed to cover the American marines at Guadalcanal.

I thoroughly understand that our government was desperate when they agreed to put a foreigner in command of our forces, but I feel that many men paid for that decision with their lives because MacArthur's priorities were skewed towards America's interests. MacArthur was determined that the USA would save the South-West Pacific – whatever the cost.

28

Christmas in Hell

The boast of heraldry, the pomp of pow'r,
And all that beauty, all that wealth e'er gave,
Awaits alike th' inevitable hour.
The paths of glory lead but to the grave.
'Elegy Written in a Country Churchyard',
Thomas Gray (1751)

Despite the loss of more Australians in futile attacks, the Japanese remained entrenched in their bunkers and pill-boxes at Christmas time. It didn't matter how often we attempted to overrun them; our bullets, bayonets and the bravery of those who threw themselves at the defences made little, if any, impact. There were hundreds of bunkers, and something we begrudgingly admired about our enemy was that they'd made brilliant use of the terrain. It reduced the number of tactical possibilities that were available to General Vasey and his staff of officers.

When we weren't stuck in our foxholes we were out on patrols to find where the enemy were, and it was always a macabre lottery as to who would survive the network of Japanese snipers and machine gunners dispersed throughout the jungle – and who wouldn't. The snipers remained a curse, and the only reason we didn't scour the ground for telltale signs such as boot prints that would've given their positions away was because we were too preoccupied constantly scanning the tops of tall palm trees in the hope we'd spot them before they fired. In any event, we rarely saw them, because they camouflaged themselves so well they became as much a part of the tree as a palm frond or a coconut.

However, we quickly learnt tricks that increased our chances of making it back to camp in one piece. For instance, most of the men who still had their tin hats threw them away because, in an environment where silence could be the difference between life and death, the helmets were as loud as a brass band whenever they knocked against low-hanging tree branches. We also listened and learnt from the likes of 'Poppa' West, who 20-odd years beforehand had fought in the trenches of the Great War. With hair the colour of steel-blue grey, more wrinkles and creases in his face than a prune, and his short stature, Poppa looked to me as though he was 50 years old. However, he was strong and as brave as all billyo. As someone who'd been through the horrors of the Western Front, Poppa understood the business of war, and that included appreciating the need to improvise sometimes. And that's exactly what we did when we ran out of the oil that kept our rifles functioning. We cleaned the barrels with the oil and a 'pull through' which was stored in a hollow chamber in the wooden stock of a Lee–Enfield. When we exhausted our supply, Poppa shared a trick he'd learnt as a young digger, which was to urinate on the bolt of the rifle. It may have sounded like he was having us on, but he wasn't. The previous generation of ANZACs discovered in the mud and slush of the Somme that a man's piss could be used as a lubricant that allowed the weapon to continue firing when it should've seized up. Under Poppa's mentorship we also learnt to instinctively realise when something didn't belong in a setting, such as the smell of smoke from a cigarette. What he drilled into us was that in those cases, we needed to take cover or take action. As was the case during our time on the Kokoda Trail, our senses became supercharged and attuned to the environment. We also lived off instinct and adrenaline, and while that helped keep men alive, the state of being constantly on edge was exhausting.

While most young blokes dream of girls, we fixated on two things at Sanananda: food, and a warm bed. I think it's safe for me to assume that if any man in a foxhole was offered the choice between pocketing a thousand pounds or having a decent night's sleep and a grand feed, he wouldn't have baulked at taking the tucker and slumber. I know that would have been my choice. By then, we were little more than skin and bones through malnutrition, while wicked hunger pangs tortured our bellies. We also felt physically ill from sustained sleep deprivation, which I hadn't known was possible.

Each day started just before dawn when we 'stood to' in readiness for an attack. Even though groups of Japanese went 'hunting' after nightfall, and we took turns keeping watch overnight, the brass assumed if our enemy was ever going to launch a mass attack it would come at daybreak when they'd expect we'd be fast asleep. However, no-one ever really slept at Sanananda. The best we managed was a series of catnaps because you could never switch off. In my case, at night my mind constantly replayed the image of a Japanese soldier slithering from out of the jungle's foliage and slitting my throat while I slept. That's why even the slightest sound made me jump bolt upright, because it was so still at night that it's no exaggeration to say you could hear a leaf hitting the ground.

Regardless of whether we were in our foxholes or stuck out in the jungle during an overnight patrol, we'd go to sleep with our rifles aimed towards the Japanese – and always with one bullet up the spout. A man had good reason to be frightened while he was out on patrol at night; however, the worst experience was taking your turn as the sentry. It didn't matter if you were married or single, young or old, a father to three kids or an orphan, everyone took their turn – and it challenged even the bravest man's resolve. The sentry was situated only five yards from the others while they slept, and while that might not sound very far, it was enough to make you feel like the loneliest man on earth. It didn't matter who had the job, it was a struggle for the sentry to keep his eyes open because we were all exhausted. Whenever it was my turn I tried to keep awake by thinking of home: Betty; Mum; all of my siblings and friends; a hot meal on our kitchen table; Mr Fleming's freshly baked pies; my rabbiting trips with him at Ingleburn; watching a movie at the Hoyts De Luxe while holding Betty's hand; our first date at Manly and how we'd go back there when the war finished. I also thought of having a hot cup of tea on the porch of the family home while looking out onto Wardell Road. Sometimes my thoughts drifted to my father, and while Dad and I would never enjoy the 'Hollywood-style' father–son relationship even after the war ended, while I was on sentry duty I found that I sympathised with him in a way that I never could have done before I experienced combat. While my military service allowed me to understand what had led Dad down his miserable path, I promised myself that no matter what other horrors awaited me as a soldier, I would never allow alcohol to become the 'medicine' that dulled my pain. I didn't want Betty, or the children that I expected we'd have after we married, to experience what Mum and we kids endured due to Dad's war legacy: alcoholism and a violent temper. That said, I don't think I ever felt closer to my father than on those occasions when I was alone in the jungle. The fear that gripped me gave me some insight into the terror he must've felt while he lay wounded among the dead and dying at Passchendaele.

Another thing that made sentry duty so awful was the pitch blackness of the place. At first you saw nothing; I imagine it was the closest experience to being blind. However, after a while, when your eyes had adjusted, you'd see the faint outline of shapes, and there were times when I 'saw' things that made my finger instinctively curl around my rifle's trigger. As I peered into the great nothingness thoughts would flood my mind: *Fuck me, is that a Jap lining me up? . . . If I shoot and it turns out to be nothing I'll give our position away and we'll be done for . . . wait . . . wait . . . get ready . . . no, relax, it's nothing!* It was terrible, because in a situation where the person who shot first normally had the best chance of surviving, I was constantly second-guessing myself. Before firing my rifle, I needed to be certain that the Japanese soldier who I thought had moved in the darkness wasn't actually a bush or a rock. And when dawn finally broke – always a huge relief as it brought with it a sense of security – that's exactly what it would turn out to be!

There were times, of course, when the shapes in the dark were not so innocuous. When the Australian artillery arrived at Sanananda they really gave the Japanese curry, blasting the tripe out of them. The shelling did untold damage to the Japanese base. Rather than just sit there and cop it, the Japanese sent out units of men at night whose job it was to get to the artillery – even though they were miles away – to kill the crews and destroy all of the cannons. To reach them the Japanese needed to slip through our lines, and that led to all sorts of fun and games, especially for the poor sentries. There were soldiers in the Japanese Army who'd studied in the United States before the outbreak of war, and they spoke good English with an American accent. When someone claimed to be a US soldier, we were instructed to challenge them to pronounce words with multiple Ls in them because we were told Japanese people struggled to say the letter L. One night while I was on sentry duty I heard the chilling sound of movement in the jungle some-where in front of me, and I vividly recall how the hairs on the back of my neck stood instantly to attention.

'WHO GOES THERE?' I shouted in the direction of the noise, while clicking the bolt of my rifle in preparation for the worst.

'We're Americans, Joe. Don't shoot.'

'You're Americans?'

'Yes, Joe. Americans. Don't shoot.'

'ALRIGHT, YANK, SAY "WOOLLOOMOOLOO"!'

There was a deathly silence, and when I repeated my order it was obvious the 'American' wasn't going to attempt it because he couldn't! I fired my rifle in the direction of the voice, and the men behind me, having been woken by my exchange with the so-called Yank, joined in, firing blindly. When we stopped firing after a minute or so, we braced for the Japanese to have a crack back at us, but they'd melted into the darkness. Later that morning we scouted the perimeter looking for bodies or the telltale blood trails that would let us know if we'd at least winged one of them, but we found nothing. It appeared as though our friends the 'Americans' had escaped with nothing more serious than the same fright we'd received.

I had no idea it was Christmas Day 1942 until a Salvation Army officer appeared on the frontline. He was an affable bloke who, besides wanting to wish peace to all men at a time when we were hellbent on blowing one another's brains out, brought with him a large brown paper bag bulging with boiled lollies. We watched as he crawled from foxhole to foxhole, trench to trench, to dole out one lolly to each soldier. When the 'Sally Man' – as we called Salvation Army officers – reached us we figured the fact he hadn't already been 'knocked' by a sniper meant he'd used up his luck and it would be dangerous for him to go any further. We advised him to keep his head low and hand over the bag. When he did, we shared the sweets with the other men, and it speaks volumes about my C Coy mates that despite how hungry they all were, they took only one each. If anyone felt tempted to pinch an extra lolly – as I was when Titch passed me the bag – they resisted. No-one would have risked a mate missing out, but I also think we did it because as children of the Great Depression we were all familiar with tough times and sacrifice. It was a Christmas I've never forgotten, because besides receiving our lolly from the Salvo, our dinner was the same as my birthday meal: a mouthful of bully beef from a tin shared among six mates. We tried not to think about food, but we invariably spent the day reminiscing about the dinners we'd enjoyed at home with our loved ones, and how we hoped to be with them for Christmas 1943.

Our situation in the swamps only worsened when, after being pinned down for weeks, we found ourselves living among the dead. While some of them were our friends and it hurt to see them lying there, it would've been suicidal to try to bury them. The unbearable foetid smell of the swamp was gradually overpowered by something much worse – the stench of death. I'm not exaggerating when I say that it took months for that pungent odour to leave my nostrils. However, what really scarred us – and it was like a scene from a horror movie – was watching the corpse of a mate we'd once laughed, joked and shared our dreams with bloat in the humidity before starting to decompose with maggots crawling out of his ears and nose where he lay, all because we couldn't bury him. I often wondered to myself amid that madness how on earth any of us could expect to return home with our sanity intact. It was yet another image from the war that would haunt all of us. Thinking about Betty and the life we could have together *if I survived* remained my antidote to the craziness that infected others.

However, our dead mates helped us, because as we ran short on ammunition or fresh drinking water, we'd wait until dark and creep out from our foxholes to take whatever they had to share – their ammo, water bottles, any food. In death, our mates helped keep us going. We made a point of ensuring their personal items, such as wallets, paybooks, photos and any letters made it back to their loved ones. At the time, it was the only decent thing we could do for them as their friends.

There was one occasion when I thought I was certain to join the ranks of our ever-growing number of dead. It occurred while we were in a swamp and neck-deep in what I can only describe as putrid water because it was black. Each of us carried our rifles above our heads to keep them dry, and that meant we were helpless when the Japanese opened fire. The bastards only needed a few minutes to cut us to ribbons. They couldn't miss and we lost many men. It was horrific, and I can only remember flashes of the chaos: the chattering of the Japanese machine guns; our officers shouting for us to 'keep moving'; the volleys of bullets that whistled past me and whipped the water; men all around me falling and sinking beneath the surface before bobbing back up like corks; the flash of the Japanese guns. At some point during that bloodbath my mind returned to the zombie-like state it had entered during our catastrophic battle on 7 December. With my rifle still held high above my head, I kept moving through the water because I knew I'd die if I stopped. Somehow, and I have no idea how I did it, I managed to reach the relative safety of the muddy banks. I joined a group of the others who'd survived and we returned fire at the Japanese before beating a hasty retreat towards our lines.

Despite our heavy losses we went out on another patrol a few days later. On this occasion an officer warned us that if we couldn't return by 5 pm that evening we were to lie flat on the ground before the clock struck five and remain there until the following morning. If we failed to take notice of the time, we risked death from our own guns. A major from the 55th had scrounged some Vickers machine guns from the 2/1st Infantry Battalion and they were used to shoot thousands of bullets into the trees around our sector to clear them of snipers. Just before those powerful guns arrived I witnessed the death of one sniper who was responsible for many casualties at Sanananda when a bloke armed with a Bren gun went to work on him. The gunner had pinpointed the sniper's location in a particular palm tree and we watched as he poured two magazines' worth of bullets (60 in total) into it. His handiwork chopped down the top of the tree, and we cheered at the sight of the sniper tumbling 50 feet to his death. We knew that sniper had killed a few of our mates.

When we prepared to go out on patrol that day, we saw a line of Vickers machine guns had been assembled with their barrels pointed towards the enemy lines. They were going to light up the jungle by spitting hot lead into it. We took longer than expected that day and all of us kept an eye on the time. Just before 5 pm everyone lay down and waited for the sound of the guns opening up. And when they did, it sounded like an orchestra. I don't know about the other men, but as the bullets flew above us I buried my face as deep as I could into the mud to make sure I wasn't a casualty to what the modern media refers to as 'friendly fire'.

There were other things in the jungle besides the bullets, grenades and shellfire that were capable of killing a soldier stone dead – and I had the misfortune of coming face to face with one while out on yet another patrol. I'd heard something rustling in the undergrowth and I instinctively thought it was a Japanese soldier. I fell straight to the ground because I'd learnt that you hear someone's footsteps more clearly if you get as close as possible to the ground. The noise stopped suddenly, and to this day I have no idea why I looked up, but when I did, I froze, because a death adder was less than two feet away from me. Snakes have always terrified me; the red-bellied black snakes that baked on the rocks in the sun beside the Georges River were frightening enough, and they had nothing on this brute. I knew that a death adder's venom is extremely toxic and that if this snake bit me I wouldn't last 20 minutes. I reckon I moved so quickly I would've challenged Jesse Owens for the gold medal at the 1936 Berlin Olympics! After scrambling to what I thought was a safe distance it occurred to me that the snake might strike at one of my mates. It took all of my courage, but I went back to confront the creature. Well, that's if you call blasting its head off with a .303 a 'confrontation'.

There are few things in life as funny as irony, because in the end what almost killed me at Sanananda wasn't a death adder or even the fanatical troops who were willing to lay down their lives for their Emperor back in Tokyo. It was something the size of a pinhead, but as fatal as all sin.

29

Touched by an Angel

God bless 'The Rose of No Man's Land',
Who guides me through my night of pain.
And keep her safe throughout the storm.
A Prayer of Thanks – Anonymous

One of my last acts at Sanananda was to 'obtain' 200 pairs of American gaiters for my mates and other Aussie troops. These were coverings for our boots meant to prevent water, mud or anything else getting into them. There was an American base behind the lines and I somehow 'found' 200 pairs of gaiters that were tied together with a long piece of string. Unlike the Australian-made version, which simply funnelled water into our boots, the American gaiters were beautifully designed and of a far superior quality. They completely covered our boots and went much higher up the leg. The reason I snaffled them was because I realised they'd make life more comfortable for my mates. I never scrounged things for personal or financial gain – I wasn't a black marketeer or a thief. My efforts were always for the good of the group. That's why whenever I passed an Australian as I returned to our lines carrying my bounty I'd bail them up and say: 'Hey, mate, do you want some Yankee gaiters?' It didn't come as a surprise that everyone took a pair.

A few days after that, I staggered out of the Sanananda frontline suffering from the wildest headaches. My body ached everywhere, and was gripped by fever and chills. I wondered if it was the malaria coming back, because the doctor had told me it would resurface. Just like that time at Eora Creek, my world went black.

When I woke up I thought I'd been taken prisoner, because the first thing I saw was chicken wire above me, and I was scared. I must have muttered something, because all of a sudden an upside-down face peered at me and I then heard an Australian voice call out to Sister Campbell that I was awake. She made her way over and knelt down beside me before saying calmly: 'Just lie where you are, Chard, you're alright.' I recognised her from my last stint in hospital, and I immediately relaxed because I realised the wire above me was supporting the mattress of four army blankets on the bed I was under. I myself was on a stretcher. The second thing I learnt was that I'd been taken for my second stint in the 2/9th Australian General Hospital in Port Moresby and had been out cold for two weeks, ironed out by scrub typhus, a debilitating disease which is transmitted by the bacteria that's spread by a mite's bite. The third lesson was hearing Sanananda was finally captured by the Australians on 22 January 1943 . . . the day after I collapsed.

Like when I'd had malaria, I had a raging fever. It was worse, though, because at the same time as I was shivering and shaking, buckets of sweat poured from me. My temperature had apparently hit 40 degrees. In spite of all that, I was very fortunate, because I somehow pulled though. I later learnt that eight of ten people succumbed to the disease.

Sister Ruth Campbell, an angel if ever there was one, instructed some male orderlies to lift me from my stretcher and place me on what was a filthy bed. I simply didn't care about that – I was safe, and I was alive. Sister Campbell then washed off some of the muck from the swamps that still covered me; she cut my hair; brushed my teeth and also shaved my face. It was through her devotion that I started to get better, because after she finished her shift she returned to care for me. When I asked her why she was looking after me so well, I noticed tears well in her eyes when she answered: 'My brother is your age and he's serving in the Middle East. If anything was to happen to him, I'd hope that there was someone who would care for him if he needed your kind of help.' I didn't know what to say, but I felt the sting of a tear in my eye for the first time in such a long time. I credit Sister Campbell's dedication for saving my life.

My recuperation was complicated by another bout of malaria that almost killed me. Sister Campbell realised that if I didn't get to Australia for treatment the odds were against me pulling through. One morning she said, 'Chard,' – Sister called all of the men by their surname – 'there's an ambulance ship leaving today and we really have to get you onto it.' The problem was, the ship only took walking wounded, and I didn't even have enough strength to sit up without help. Sister Campbell must have sensed I was worried that

I wouldn't make it on board because she patted me gently on the shoulder and said in the most soothing tone: 'Don't worry, Chard, I'll get you on.'

I can only suppose the ambulance drivers were ordered to be strict about only allowing walking wounded onto what was called a Sea Ambulance Transport, because they scrutinised every one of us as we made our way to the waiting vehicles as though they were the judges at the Royal Easter Show's bull ring. Sister Campbell's plan wasn't bad, but it was open to me being caught out if one of my accomplices passed out or fell over. You see, on my right-hand side was a fellow with a walking stick, and on my left was a man who looked like an Egyptian mummy because he was covered in plaster of Paris! Dear Sister Campbell walked squarely behind me, pushing me forward. Somehow the three of them pulled and tugged me towards the ambulance, but when one of the drivers saw me stagger he said in what sounded like an accusing tone: 'What happened to that one?' Sister Campbell responded with what was perhaps the most officious voice I've ever heard, and was worthy of her official rank of lieutenant. 'He's obviously fallen over, hasn't he? Don't just stand there – get down and give him a hand!' And guess what? The driver did, and he assisted Sister Campbell as she made her way into the ambulance. She wanted to make sure I made it on board.

There were American air crews at the wharves and they were waiting to board the transport to go to Townsville for what they called R and R – Rest and Recreation. Even though they saw that the ambulance men were waiting to assist us onto the ship, they pushed past us and ran up the gangway. I didn't care, all I wanted was to get on and get to a hospital in Australia. Sister Campbell helped me up the gangway – she knew no-one would question her – and when we reached the top she simply said: 'Take care, Chard!' and made her way back to the hospital.

I don't know why, but when she said that, I felt the urge to bawl like a baby. I'd seen great friends killed in front of me, and I'd also witnessed the greatest horror of all at the massacre site, but it was something about that moment that brought me undone.

The sea ambulance weighed anchor, and it wasn't long before we found out why the Americans had rushed aboard – they wanted the cabins to themselves. However, when the ship's captain saw a mass of wounded and ill diggers lying on the deck he announced over the loud-speaker that all American personnel were to report on deck immediately. As they stood there, the ship's officers and crew threw the Yanks' duffel bags out of the cabins and then helped the wounded Aussies into them. There weren't any doctors or nurses on the ship. We had a few first aid men, and they were assisted by members of the ship's crew who treated us wonderfully.

When we arrived at Townsville all of the Queenslanders disembarked. Interestingly enough, the skipper made the Yanks wait for them to get off first. That evening the Sea Ambulance Transport continued south to Sydney. I occupied myself during the trip by reading the small sack of mail that had accumulated while I was at the front. One of the first things I read was a card from Betty which said: *Christmas Message – All good wishes for Christmas and the*

New Year from Betty to Reg. Mum and all the family wish to be kindly remembered to you. I felt even more excited to be going home after reading that. While I had no idea of what was to come, the one thing I was certain of was that I'd at least get to hug Betty again.

Later, my mother and Betty wrote to Sister Campbell to thank her for saving me, and for her wonderful efforts to ensure other mothers and sweethearts were reunited with their soldier. The three of them corresponded regularly, and when Sister Campbell sent the portrait of herself that my mother had requested it was hung in our dining room and always looked upon with reverence. She saved my life, and my mother made it clear through her letters that she would be eternally grateful for that. Sister Ruth Campbell passed away just a few days before ANZAC Day in 1984, and I grieved her passing because, like everyone who she cared for in Port Moresby, we'd lost someone who went beyond the call of duty for us. Her portrait hangs in my house, and after all these years I can't help but still call her the soldier's 'angel'.

30

Ward 27

Most of our patients were servicemen, and they were the best patients you could find. You might have a civilian who had had his tonsils out, who would be the greatest whinger. But the servicemen could have bullet wounds and be really very ill, and they wouldn't complain a bit.

Thelma 'Shirley' Grinyer,
113th Australian General Hospital

It was dawn when the Sea Transport Ambulance entered Sydney Harbour, and for the first time since we'd left Townsville for the frontline over a year earlier, I felt truly relaxed. When I saw the Harbour Bridge, and then the tall grain silos at Glebe Island where we dropped anchor, I knew I was thousands of kilometres away from the jungle. While I returned sick, looking more like a scarecrow than a soldier, and my sleep was now tormented by the most wicked nightmares, at last I felt as though I was safe.

The first thing I noticed when I looked over the ship's side were the lines of ambulances waiting for us on the dock. The soldiers who milled around the vehicles also caught my attention because they wore a peculiar, floppy style of uniform that I'd never seen before. It wasn't until I reached my ambulance that I realised the soldiers were *women* – and adding to my surprise was that they were our ambulance drivers! That was simply a reflection of the difference between 1942 and 2022. Before the war, I hadn't known a single woman who had a driver's licence, but I was soon to see that the events of 1939–45 had revolutionised our society. With so many men in the armed forces, women filled roles no-one would ever have thought them able or willing to do. They did what was traditionally men's work on the land, they made bombs in munitions factories and aeroplanes at Bankstown. History is right to note that they kept the country running in its darkest hour.

My driver greeted me warmly, but when she said we were going to the 113th Australian General Hospital at Concord, I baulked – I had no idea where that was. Incredibly, even though it's only ten kilometres from Dulwich Hill, I'd never heard of Concord, and asked if it was near the Blue Mountains! However, when we arrived I saw I'd been transported to a hospital that was nothing like the mud-splattered tent in Port Moresby with its dirt floor. This was a newly constructed, state-of-the-art, 2000-bed hospital which was the biggest in the Southern Hemisphere. It was very shiny and spotlessly clean, and I was happy to be there.

Betty and my entire family visited me the day after I arrived, and while I knew I looked terrible, my younger brother Ken articulated what everyone was thinking. 'He sounds like Reg when he speaks, but he doesn't look like Reg.' Ken was right; I looked nothing like the 18-year-old who'd just about broken his neck in the rush to sign up 15 months earlier. When I'd taken my oath of allegiance to King and country I'd weighed 65 kilos; now, as I lay in my hospital bed, I tipped the scales at barely 40 kilos. My legs were covered in ugly tropical sores, my face was gaunt and my body was a sack of bones. However, the only thing that mattered that day was the look I saw in Betty's eyes. If she was horrified by the physical toll my time in New Guinea had taken on me it didn't show, because I only saw love – and that's what I needed.

Concord Hospital turned out to be my sanctuary, and when I look back on the time I spent in Wards 29 and 27, I know it was the only place where I ever felt safe during the war. We had four nurses to each ward; two were on duty throughout the day, and the other pair did the rounds overnight. If any man made even the slightest movement or noise they rushed over to check on him. They were the most marvellous women, and reminded me of Sister Campbell.

I remember waking one morning at 2.30 am after what was by then the familiar nightmare involving the Japanese soldier who I killed at the massacre site. One of the nurses – Sister Stearman – raced over to ask what was wrong, but I didn't tell her about the dream because there was nothing she could do to help me with that. However, I said that I was starving, and while I forget what meal I requested, I ate like a king. In those days the hospital's kitchen staff were on duty 24 hours a day, and if a soldier wanted a meal of steak, eggs, chips, and a dessert of ice cream, custard, cream and steam pudding, then that's what the kitchen prepared. Every meal reinforced that the deprivations of Sanananda were far behind me, but with them came some guilt because I couldn't help but think of how Titch and the others were faring 'up there'.

After a few months convalescing I was discharged and, in May 1943, was sent back to Townsville by train to join C Coy as it prepared to head to the Solomon Islands. While I felt excited in 1941 to be choofing off to defend Australia from our enemies, I wasn't as enthusiastic – or so bloody gung-ho – about returning to the frontline. The time I'd spent in Sydney, even though most of it was in Ward 27, meant I enjoyed time with Betty, Mum, my siblings and friends, and it made me realise how much life I'd missed out on while I was in the army. So, I wasn't happy to be returning to the tropics – none of the soldiers on that train were – but I also knew our job was only half done. Despite the success we'd enjoyed at Milne Bay, Kokoda, the Beachheads and on other battlefields in Papua New Guinea, the Japanese were still within a thousand kilometres of Australia. Knowing the evilness they were capable of unfortunately meant that – as tough as it was to say goodbye to our loved ones – we had no choice but to grab our rifles and head back.

When I arrived in North Queensland there was tension between Titch and the other boys and an Italian farmer who grew watermelons in a patch near our temporary camp at Alligator Creek. The boys wanted to buy a couple from him, but the farmer had developed a taste for American greenbacks – or more to the point, for the way in which the Yanks foolishly splashed their cash about – because he demanded one pound per watermelon – highway robbery! He wouldn't budge even when our blokes explained that Australians weren't paid at the same rate as our allies. I thought I could reason with him, but he was a miserable old coot with a terrible attitude. When I tried to argue that we just wanted some watermelon before leaving to fight the Japanese, he said, 'Bad luck,' and slammed his front door in my face. Of course, I saw red, but rather than flatten him I decided it'd be more satisfying to hit him where it would hurt him . . . the hip pocket.

When we returned to camp I asked Lieutenant George Wearne if I could borrow a truck. George had been my witness at Greta when I had my showdown with The Officer who wanted me to become his personal chef. George was a good man and besides the late Bill Ryan he was the only officer who I'd ever have asked for help. I liked that George only grinned when I admitted he wouldn't want to know why I wanted the vehicle.

Later that afternoon I gathered a group of blokes together and said we wouldn't merely raid the greedy man's patch; we'd strip it of every bloody watermelon he'd grown. We had two solid blokes who I didn't know but they were built like rugby props, and as darkness fell they stood guard on the back and front doors to ensure the farmer remained locked inside in case we woke him. The rest of us proceeded to pick each and every watermelon – and there were hundreds of them over a paddock the size of a football field. While most of the boys loaded the melons onto the truck, a few of us used the bloke's rakes to remove the distinctive prints our heavy boots left in the dirt. We then drove the truck into town where we divided all of the fruit between the local hospitals and a couple of children's homes – we didn't keep even one for ourselves. We then washed the truck clean of dirt, and by the time we climbed into our beds it was almost time to get up with the rest of the camp. We were tired, but we'd agreed it was worth teaching that farmer a lesson about the price of being greedy.

That wasn't the end of the story, though, because later that morning there was an announcement over the loud-speakers for everyone to fall in on the parade ground *immediately*. It didn't surprise me to see the farmer standing there, looking as glum as a cane toad with food poisoning. However, standing alongside him was what looked like half of the Queensland police force and a team of eager detec-tives. When no-one confessed to plundering his patch, the cops sprang into action, tipping over every garbage tin on the base as they searched for evidence, but try as they might they didn't even find a watermelon pip! When I walked past the farmer I couldn't help but hurl his own words back at him when I said, 'Sounds like you had some BAD LUCK, mate . . .'

I'd only been discharged from Concord for a few weeks when I was struck down yet again with malaria during a sightseeing trip to Magnetic Island off Townsville while I was taking photographs of American naval craft. After I regained consciousness, the attending doctor said he couldn't understand how anyone thought I was fit enough to return to the war and he said I needed further hospital treatment. I was put on a train, and when it reached Brisbane I had yet another relapse and they shoved me into Greenslopes Hospital which, like Concord, was for returned servicemen. After a few days there I was put on another train bound for Sydney, and as it made its slow journey south, I reread a letter Betty had sent me after we'd said our most recent goodbye. It saddened me because it made me realise how deeply my decision to run off to war had affected her. Betty wrote that she'd been so upset the night I left to rejoin the 55th in North Queensland, she hadn't been able to eat her dinner because she feared we'd never see each other again. When I'd first read that in Townsville, I'd sent letters to her, Mr and Mrs Banham and my parents informing them that when I returned Betty and I would have our wedding. Her words had made me realise it was time to start planning our life together as husband and wife, not soldier and sweetheart.

However, before we'd walk down the aisle I'd spend another stretch in Concord – 13 long months in Ward 27 – and the doctors pumped so much of that vile-tasting liquid quinine into me I would've bled the stuff if I'd cut myself. The quantities I consumed worried me, and when I asked the doctor in charge about the effect it might be having on my system, his reply chilled my blood. He said in a dismissive tone that I'd either make a significant improvement and get better – or I'd die of heart failure. When he saw my expression he said, a tad too nonchalantly for my liking: 'Well, it's alright ... after all you men have been through, I'll be surprised if any of you make it to 60.' I couldn't help myself, and with my temper rising at his lack of empathy – or common sense – I growled through gritted teeth: 'That's all well and good, doc, but I'm only 19.' When the good doctor realised I was about to explode he suddenly remembered he had rounds to do.

I didn't want to die – I had a wedding to attend and a life to live – so I focused on getting better. And, despite our illnesses and the traumatic experiences we'd been through, the other men and I were able to relax and have some good times while we were in hospital. Some of the antics in my ward showed me that laughter really is the best medicine of all. There were some real hoots among us, and one wag – the boldest of us all – organised a Miss Concord Hospital beauty pageant. It was nothing more than a bit of fun, and something that kept hundreds of bored minds occupied. However, it was also kept top secret because no-one wanted the nurses to know about it through fear it might offend them. (It's important to note that I saw nothing but respect for the nurses from the men. I have no doubt if a soldier crossed the line and acted inappropriately towards any nurse he would've had a dozen men line up to knock his teeth out.)

As much as I thought the Miss Concord Hospital was innocent fun, I ruled myself out of voting because it felt wrong to get involved when I only had eyes for Betty. However, the ones who were 'in' made their way from ward to ward on the pretence that they were visiting a cobber. After making their mental notes, they returned to their own ward and cast their votes. For what it's worth, the winner was a lovely young nurse who worked in our ward named Joan Long.

However, of all the laughs I had in Ward 27, one of the heartiest was courtesy of the General Blamey–endorsed 30-page booklet titled: *What to Do in the Tropics*. It contained quite a lot of information about malaria, but it mostly proved to those of us who'd been there how out of touch the likes of Blamey and his staff officers were about life on the frontline. It was side-splitting material that we felt had to have been written by a team of comedians, because among their pearls of wisdom was to: (a) wash your socks every night; (b) change your underwear daily, and, most importantly, (c) to shower. It was a completely unrealistic view of jungle warfare because there were times at Kokoda, and then of course at Sanananda, where we didn't take our boots off for weeks at a time, and our socks became embedded into the soles of our feet. My underpants were a stinking biohazard that had no idea they were meant to be in a relationship with laundry soap; and, as for a shower, well, we had those when it rained – and it always rained – or when we fell into a river. Indeed, there were times when it was beneficial to your overall health to keep the mud smeared across your face up there, because it provided camouflage from the Japanese.

The men who I shared the ward with became my friends, and because some of them were from Western Australia, Victoria and South Australia, they didn't receive any visitors and it was quite lonely for them. That's why when my family came to see me they'd spend some of their time chatting to these men and asking whether they needed anything. The families of Ward 27's other Sydneysiders did the same thing, and it worked wonders in helping to lift their morale.

Unfortunately for Betty, her nightly visits provided her with an unwelcome insight into the reality of war. Sometimes, the evening after she'd spoken to a particular patient she'd ask me whether 'that nice man, Ken' was having a shower because she'd noticed his bed was empty. Whenever I told her that Ken had passed away in the early hours of the morning – or Albert – or Tom – or Bruce – she'd gasp in genuine disbelief. I'm afraid that it happened so often Betty refused to visit me in the ward unless I was too sick to leave my bed. We'd instead meet in the hospital's canteen – which is still there – to talk.

As for me, there was always the risk of learning the horrors of what was happening to my mates back at the front, even when doing something as innocuous as reading the sports pages of the *Sydney Morning Herald*. I was doing just that on 18 May 1945 when a small item buried among the army snooker results, a report on Manly rugby team's new fullback, the greyhound racing news, and the Law Notices for Today, stopped me in my tracks:

SWIMMER KILLED

News has been received of the death in action on Bougainville of Lieut. Geoff Valentin, who won the State 110 yards swimming championship two years ago while on leave in Sydney.

No-one who has been in combat ever escapes the war, but reading that brought so many memories flooding back that it made me feel sick. It also made me realise I hadn't said a proper goodbye to Titch, Bluey ... 'Miss Valentine' ...

and the others before I was packed off to Sydney and they headed to the Solomon Islands.

After I recovered, I left Concord for a big convalescent home in Wahroonga called Bonnie Brae. It was owned by a wealthy man who lent it to the Red Cross to provide wounded and sick servicemen a peaceful place to recuperate. It was a beautiful home which had acres of gardens, a swimming pool, a full-sized billiard table and dozens of bedrooms that were so large they could accommodate 20 beds. It was a wonderful place and I wouldn't have minded staying there longer.

Eventually I was discharged and sent to the Sydney Showgrounds in Moore Park. Soldiers waited there to be transferred to their unit, and it was mind-numbingly dull because there was nothing to do except sleep in the disused pigpens or horse stables. The way it worked was that if you weren't called to get on a train by 3 pm, you were granted a leave pass from then until 7 am the following morning. In the meantime, you needed to find things to do to occupy yourself until 3 pm. As a scrounger, I whiled away the hours by walking around the big halls where I'd turn the doorknobs to see if they'd open. It took a few days, but I struck paydirt when I opened a side door to the Hall of Industries and discovered boxes and boxes of tinned salmon stacked to the ceiling. It was a bonanza, but my challenge was getting it from the Showgrounds to Dulwich Hill without being nabbed by the MPs. I remembered there was always a line of ambulances inside the showground, so I went over to them to see if I could find an accomplice. The first driver looked too much like a stickler, so I made my way down the line until I saw a younger girl who was laughing and chatting. 'Excuse me, Miss,' I said, trying hard not to sound sleazy. 'But would you like something for nothing?' When I explained what that meant, she was all in. We loaded up the ambulance and I lay on a stretcher as the car was waved out of the showground by the MPs. The driver was a great sport because when I said she could drop me off at the tram stop she insisted on driving me back to Dulwich Hill – and we divided our loot between us outside my family home. As I've said, my scrounging was always for the greater good, and a great number of the tins went to a pregnant woman in the street because my mother insisted she and her unborn child needed the protein.

I was flat out on my back with malaria in Ward 27 on 15 August 1945 – the day World War II ended. I was taken to hospital after suffering another relapse and I felt numb when the nurses came in shouting and singing that the Japanese had surrendered and it was all over. However, they stopped mid-sentence because not one of the 45 men in that ward made a sound. It was deathly quiet, and the poor nurses couldn't hide their confusion because they thought we'd be jubilant. They walked out silently to leave us alone with our thoughts. A few hours later, Joan Long asked why I wasn't happy when I heard it was all over, and while my response was truthful, it was depressing. 'I was 18 when I joined the army,' I replied. 'Now I'm 23-and-a-half, and I have no home, no job, no money, no clothes. When you said that it was over, all I thought was: "What am I going to do? I don't even own a handkerchief.'" Funnily enough, two weeks later when the same nurses told us we were going to start taking quinine tablets rather than the unpalatable liquid form, we all yelled 'HOORAY!' Now, that was a good day!

Nurses who'd been POWs to the Japanese were repatriated to the hospital, and they were perhaps the most pitiful sight I saw while I was there. We heard some of the stories about what they'd been through at the hands of the enemy, and it was soul-destroying. I was asked by one nurse, Sister Thompson, to speak to one of these women because she was having 'problems'. When I sat with her, the first thing the woman asked me was if I could tell her the worst thing I did during the war. I think she wanted to know if I understood pain and torment. I told her about the way I killed one of the Japanese officers at the massacre site, and how what I'd done tormented my dreams. She nodded in a way that suggested she understood, so I asked her to reciprocate and tell me her worst thing. This woman looked me straight in the eye and said that after they were taken prisoner the commander of their POW camp wanted her and the other nurses to service him and his officers. He wanted them to be his white 'comfort women'. This courageous woman was a few years older than the other nurses – and me for that matter – and she told the commander she'd do it if he promised to spare the younger ones from having sex or being raped. He agreed, and after she stripped, the nurse apparently bent over a chair, picked up a book and read it. She then did her best to hide that she was terrified by looking bored by the whole process. Then, when she looked at the commander, she scoffed and laughed at him, saying there were young schoolboys in Australia with bigger penises than his. He was humiliated, and he bashed the tripe out of her. He was so embarrassed by her comment that she and the nurses were left alone.

When she finished speaking, the woman started to cry because she said no-one would ever marry her. When I told her that I would, if I wasn't getting married myself, she did a double-take as if trying to work out if I was being sincere. I was, but I was too young to articulate my feelings properly. What I wanted to say was that she was so admirable a woman, and so strong of character, it would be easy for any decent man to fall in love with someone like her. I should have told her that I thought she was the bravest person I'd met, because I did think that. The 23-year-old me simply told her not to worry and that everything would be alright. However, I left that meeting with a recharged hatred for the enemy who had inflicted such misery on good people.

At 5 pm on Saturday, 6 October 1945, Betty and I became husband and wife when we married at St Clement's in Marrickville. The Reverend Stephen Denman officiated as I made good on the promise I'd given my mum when I first saw Betty breeze past our house on her bike all those years ago: 'I'm going to marry that girl one day!'

Betty looked beautiful – radiant – and I'd never felt happier in my whole life than I did that day. We had family and friends around us and there was plenty of good cheer. Even my father behaved himself because he appreciated the significance of the day. We had a brilliant reception at Dulwich Hill, and the centrepiece of the room was the most incredible cake, which Harry Fleming made as his and Jean's present for us. It really was a work of art, but I couldn't stop laughing when I thanked him again for a job that obviously took a lot of work because the old Scotsman whispered into my ear: 'Aye, but just don't fucking well tell Jean I did it for free, alright!'

Betty and I left for our honeymoon to the Jenolan Caves early on Sunday morning, but on Monday morning I was back at bloody Concord after being floored yet again by malaria. I just couldn't escape the disease.

My health wasn't good. By then I'd had 36 bouts of malaria and one of scrub typhus, and I eventually became a guinea pig for the doctors. They tried all sorts of medication on me; they had me eat certain foods to see if diet was a factor in beating malaria; they also monitored my sleep and my bodily functions. However, even though I'd signed on for the duration of the war and 12 months thereafter when I was a keen teenager, I now wanted out of the hospital and out of the army. I was married, and Betty and I needed and wanted to get on with our lives.

On 15 June 1946, a doctor drove me to the Department of Veteran Affairs for my assessment to see whether I was entitled for a TPI (Totally and Permanently Incapacitated) pension. I took my numbered ticket, sat on a seat and waited to be called in. Looking back on it, I must've looked like a swagman because I wore my slouch hat, a pair of tattered shorts and my old slippers. There was an elderly man sitting opposite me resplendent in a suit, tie and a stylish hat, and when he caught my eye he said cheerily enough: 'Good morning.' He then pointed at my slouch hat and asked whether I was a reinforcement. When I told him I was an original member of the 2/55th Infantry Battalion he seemed genuinely surprised that I was still in the service. Well, I took that as an invitation to tell him my story, ending with the fact that I was in Concord Hospital and they wouldn't release me because I was a malarial guinea pig. He calmly asked whether I wanted to get out, and I replied that of course I did; I'd done my bit and wanted to get on with my life with my wife. With that, he took out a notebook from the breast pocket on the inside of his suit jacket and jotted down my name, unit, serial number and the hospital ward I was in. I thought he was nothing more than a big-noter who was humouring me by taking down my details, but I thanked him for listening when he was called in for his appointment.

It was finally my turn to see the civilian doctor who'd decide whether I was entitled to a pension, and when I walked into his office he was busy filling out a form. As I sat down, he peered over the pair of spectacles hanging off the tip of his nose and said tersely: 'Who told you to sit?' I told him my feet were sore and I needed a rest. He replied that he hadn't given me permission to sit. I knew he wanted me to stand, but I'm stubborn, and I couldn't have realised how staying put in the seat was going to cost me. I'd made an enemy of the wrong person, because despite all I'd been through, he denied me a war pension.

Naturally enough, I gave him a piece of my mind and made threats, but he was unmoved. Later, another doctor, from the army this time, examined my file, and he was flabbergasted that I'd been knocked back. He appealed on my behalf, but it went around in circles. I was eventually given a 'burnt-out' pension, which means I get less than a third the amount a TPI would have entitled me to. However, it wasn't all bad news, because a week later, on 26 June 1946, a nurse handed me a handwritten note on letterhead from the Tattersall's Club – which was one of the clubs where Sydney's wealthy met. The note simply said:

Dear Chard,
Hope everything has worked out to your satisfaction.
Yours sincerely,
Major-General Herbert Lloyd

I had no idea what it all meant until later that day when I received the news that I was being discharged. The man I'd dismissed as a big-noter actually had plenty of military and civil clout, and his intervention set me free. My final duty as a member of the 55th Infantry Battalion was to head to the Sydney Showground, where I walked into the Engineers Hall as a soldier and walked out a civilian. It was a clinical process; there were no thanks, no parting words. Nobody asked me what I was going to do, or if I needed help to get a job. Like the other men who'd served, I was on my own, and while I was free of the army, it'd take a long time for me to realise that was a good thing.

31

The Peace

A man disturbed two thieves when he returned home at 10pm yesterday. He is Mr Reginald Chard of Norton Street, Leichhardt. Mr Chard had opened his front door when he saw the thieves in the hallway. He challenged them, but they ran from the house escaping over the back fence. A mantle radio and clothes were missing. Detectives Anderson and Hansard, of Leichhardt, are searching for the men.

The Daily Telegraph, *15 August 1946*

At Villawood, people were waiting from as early as 6am, and women called 'You beauty' as Her Majesty was introduced to Mr. and Mrs. Reg. Chard and their two sons, Robert, 10, and Gary [sic], 2. Mr. and Mrs. Chard showed the Queen Mother to the front door of their neat two-bedroomed home. Mr. Chard picked up Gary, who had begun to cry a few minutes before the Royal visitor arrived. The Queen Mother took Gary's hand and said, 'You're a lovely boy. What have you got to be crying about?' Gary immediately stopped crying.

The Canberra Times, *25 February 1958*

Betty and I made our marital home in half a house at Norton Street, Leichhardt. We leased the two front rooms and the lady who owned the place lived at the back. Our two rooms were sparsely furnished, and that was because after five years in khaki, I left the army with 350 pounds in the bank and 100 pounds that I'd invested in a war bond certificate. I know there are people today who'll think that was probably enough to buy a harbourside mansion in the 'olden days', but take it from me, it wasn't — and not by a long shot.

What I quickly discovered were the many unexpected costs associated with a soldier's return to civilian life, including having to shell out a small fortune for a new wardrobe of clothes. I hadn't given clothing a second thought since I enlisted because I was used to dressing in whatever the army told me to wear. And it was for that reason I'd told Mum to pass on all of my civilian clothes to my brother Ray when he grew big enough to wear them, and Ray had shot up so much there wasn't even a thread left for me at Wardell Road. A lot of ex-servicemen had no alternative but to wear their old army tunic and trousers because they couldn't get clothes, but I wanted to leave the army and Papua New Guinea behind me. So I paid a salesman at Murdoch's menswear in the city an exorbitant price for a jacket, a few shirts and couple of pairs of pants. I felt guilty when I handed over the money because I would've preferred to put it towards saving for our house and future. After being denied a TPI pension, my priority was to find a job that would provide Betty and me with some security.

There was no shortage of work because Australia's contribution to the war had resulted in almost 50,000 men and women being killed or wounded, and those losses were felt heavily by the nation's business and industry sectors during the immediate post-war years. Mr Fleming had offered me my old position back straight after I was discharged from hospital. It was a generous offer on a few fronts, not least because I had left Harry in the lurch with the Manpower department when I'd raced off to join the army. Plus, he now had two young apprentices working for him so he was effectively creating a position for me. While I wanted to accept because I still had a passion for the bakery trade, I declined for two reasons. One was monetary: I'd be back on my apprentice's wage for six months and Betty and I wouldn't be able to get by on that. The second reason, and for me it was just as important, was for Harry's sake. My legs were covered in ugly scabs which a doctor had loosely diagnosed as 'tropical dermatitis', but he confessed he'd never seen anything like it in his career. The sores looked shocking and I asked Harry whether he honestly believed his customers would feel comfortable buying cakes and pastries from a baker with hideous, weeping wounds all over his legs. Mr Fleming said it wouldn't worry him, but I figured the health department would have a different view if – or when – someone complained.

So over tea and apple pie I politely declined Harry's offer, and when I left the shop that day, the old Scotsman shook my hand and said something that made me think long and hard: 'It's a pity that you joined the army when you did, Reg, because after you went away the Bakers' Association of New South Wales were set to name you the state's top apprentice baker for the state in 1941.' At a time when I was uncertain about my future, it made me wonder what could've been if I'd listened to Betty and Mr Fleming when they'd advised me to finish my apprenticeship before going away. However, something I've learnt over the years is that there's no point dwelling on things that might've been, or the things in life that can't be undone.

I eventually took a job as a furnaceman at J.K. Foundry in Wentworth Avenue, Botany, but I underestimated the toll riding my bike the ten kilometres from Leichhardt to Botany would take on my body. It was brutal, and on the first day I was so stiff and sore by the end of my shift that the three fellows who owned the foundry – Jack, Tony and Ray – had to lift me onto my bike because I couldn't do it myself. They then had to push me along to help get me started. It took me a while to get used to that bike ride because of the poor condition my body was in due to the war, but I managed.

I enjoyed my time at the foundry, and in 1947 we had a young cricketer named Les Favell join the crew. He was a great character, very sure of himself in a likeable way, and he was a good singer. I used to tell him: 'I know when you're singing, Les, because you make your voice shake.' He left after a few years for Adelaide, and it was from there the foundry's one-time warbler worked his way into the national team after forging a reputation as a daring batsman for South Australia.

While it was hard work, I also took night shifts at a bakery in Enmore every Monday, Wednesday and Friday. It was tiring, but Betty and I made it work. When I returned home from the foundry on those nights, I ate the light meal she'd prepared and slept until midnight. Then I got up and rode my bike to the bakery, and when my shift finished I rode from there to the foundry. It was a regimented life, but the reward was that Betty's and my nest egg continued to grow.

However, for every person who was prepared to roll up their sleeves and earn an honest dollar, there were those who were determined to get ahead by underhanded means. Unfortunately, Betty and I fell victim to two such criminals and they took almost everything we had. We'd been out for a walk along Parramatta Road, which in those days was full of businesses and colourful shopfronts. We'd stop outside some of them and imagine how one day we'd have the furnishings on display inside our dream house. When we returned to our place that night the lights were on in our two rooms, and my blood ran cold. I told Betty to go straight to the nearby police station and tell the sergeant our home was being burgled. I was walking up the side passage of our place when two blokes ran out of the house and almost bowled me over. I chased one of them across the old tram lines on Norton Street and walloped him. When the police came, he was on the ground, and because he was banged up one of them asked: 'What happened to him, did he fall over?' So as not to risk being charged for assault I just nodded and said, 'Yeah, the bastard fell over.' I don't know why *The Daily Telegraph* reported both thieves escaped, but the one I nabbed was an old jailbird from Melbourne.

The police arrested and charged the man and we got some of our things back, but his accomplice escaped with all of my clothes, our bankbook, a 100-pound war bond, my army statement, our wedding certificate and a mantle radio that Betty loved listening to. The police were confident they would get everything back for us, but I sought advice from someone who I figured would have a better understanding of how these things worked. This was the father of my late mate Normie Wolfson, who still ran his pawn shop in Sydney. We first spoke about Normie, whose loss was still raw for us both. Then I asked for his opinion, and Mr Wolfson said I should just kiss our things goodbye because I'd never see them again. Unfortunately, he was right.

My brother Jack had also returned home, but unfortunately it turned out that my mother had been right – my brother wasn't cut out for war. It was a damned pity we hadn't been able to serve together because he came back from the battles of El Alamein, Finschhafen and Scarlet Beach a shell of a man. He was what we called 'gone', and was sent to Kenmore – a war neurosis hospital – in Goulburn for ten months. While the hospital saved the lives of some of the patients who were sent there, there were unfortunately men like Jack who never recovered. Like my father before him, he turned to alcohol, and it wasn't a kind friend to him or his wife Phyllis. Their marriage lasted for about five years before she could take no more.

In February 1995, 50 years after the war ended, I received a phone call from Sydney Hospital to inform me that Jack had been admitted and he wasn't well. By the time I got there the doctors said my brother was in a serious condition because he'd climbed out of bed and hit his head on the corner of the nurse's desk when he stumbled. The doctor explained that Jack's brain had stopped functioning. When

I saw him, he looked terrible, and I feel it was a small mercy that he didn't last long in what was an unresponsive state. It was very sad, but the truth is I lost my brother long before that day.

Thankfully, things were a little brighter for my older brother Herb. Having survived his stomach cancer, after the war he was appointed the chief carpenter for Qantas, and he often travelled to London to inspect and work on the homes that the airline owned and used to accommodate their flight crews. His colostomy bag never stopped him from doing the things he wanted to do. Herb lived until he was 91.

While I was happy at J.K.'s I left there after a few years to continue work as a furnaceman at Drummonds foundry in Chapel Street, Marrickville, because it paid higher wages. The work was just as every bit as hard as it was at Botany, and it was as hot as all blazes. As a matter of fact, when the Drummonds' furnace reached a certain temperature everyone was sent home, even the office lady. However, the pay was much better than what I made at J.K.'s, and I made extra money during the Christmas break by relining the furnace, which involved replacing all of the bricks that had been damaged by the heat.

I still worked a second job, but I left the bakery in Enmore to load trucks overnight because it paid more. After 14 productive years at Drummonds I changed career once again and went to work for my brother-in-law, Jack Seaton, who had opened his own trucking business. I became an interstate truckie, starting off on the English-made Bedford trucks before finishing in 1984 in the driver's seat of a Mack.

Even though I was kept busy, and life with Betty and our boys really was tremendous, I had bouts of what I can only describe as 'dark thoughts' about the war. While I didn't follow the formula my father used to drown his pain, I escaped by driving along the backroads as I transported goods all across the nation. When I was home, I chose to deal with it by loving Betty and my kids.

As I settled into 'Civvy' Street (military slang for civilian life) I suffered from what I imagine they'd describe these days as 'anxiety' because for 18 months I worried about anything and everything. I didn't show it outwardly, but I was a mess on the inside. My reaction when Betty spoke about us starting a family was to be gripped by the irrational fear that something terrible would happen to her during childbirth. While I spared Betty from hearing about my war experiences because they would have troubled her, I explained I was terrified something would happen to her while she was in labour. However, Betty wouldn't hear of it. She wanted us to have a family of our own, and I'm so grateful she insisted because both Robert and Garry are wonderful sons who I love dearly. Becoming a father to them stands alongside marrying Betty as my greatest achievement. I'm extremely proud of the men they are and that they themselves embraced fatherhood. We have a large family, and I often find myself wishing Betty was here to see the beautiful and loving people our grandchildren, great-grandchildren, and even great-great-grandchildren have grown to be. She'd have been so proud.

After the war, I left everything about my time in the military behind me. Except for 1946, when Dad asked for Jack and I to join him, I have never marched on ANZAC Day, and I didn't keep in touch with any of the men who I fought alongside. However, through driving trucks I happened to run into two of them. The first was the only soldier I knew at Sanananda who had shot himself to get out of the front-line. He was hammered by the men for what he did – some branded him a 'coward' – but when I saw him at a truck stop I wanted to say hello and see how he was. However, the look of shame that crossed his face when he recognised me stopped me dead in my tracks. I saw him quite a few times during my travels, and because it was obvious to me that he, too, was trying to escape his demons, I left him in peace.

The other man I bumped into was Titch, and it made me so happy to see him. I was driving my truck when I saw him riding a bike one day. I slammed on the brakes and jumped out. He was working in the building game, married, and had a couple of kids. We made plans to have a barbecue at his place in Sydney's south, but it was cancelled at the last minute because he fell ill. We said we'd meet up, but our paths never crossed, and it's only through doing research for this book that I believe my best army mate died in 1996, aged 73.

I couldn't help but keep tabs on another old mate because he was frequently in the sports pages. While Betty and I often went to Leichhardt Stadium to watch the boxing and wrestling, I never saw The Pugilist fight. However, I read plenty about him because he was as colourful in the ring as he was an unwilling conscript. In one newspaper report he was said to have been about to 'turn it up' at the end of the eighth round in one bout because he had internal bleeding in his mouth and nose. The referee apparently coaxed him to get back out and fight because he was leading by a big margin on the scorecards. The referee's advice can't have been appreciated by his opponent, who The Pugilist knocked cold in the 11th round, and it made a few headlines. The man who I last saw being escorted from the parade ground as we all doubled over in laughter at his attempt to feign a fit retired from boxing in 1953 with 40 victories from his 68 bouts.

In 1955, Betty, Robert, Garry and I moved into our two-bedroom Housing Commission home in Villawood, a suburb in Sydney's south-west. Betty made it her castle: it was always spick and span and she was extremely house-proud. Eventually we bought it from the government, and not only was it the perfect place to raise two boys, we had a royal visitor on 22 February 1958 when Queen Elizabeth The Queen Mother visited our home! Her Majesty was in Australia to attend a conference on behalf of Queen Elizabeth, and some bureaucrats thought it would be a good idea for her to visit some ex-servicemen to see how we were adapting to life after the war. We had someone from the government come to our house before the visit, and they laid down the rules. No-one was allowed to touch our VIP; we were to address her as 'Your Majesty' the first time we spoke to her, and then 'Ma'am' thereafter, and we couldn't have family or friends in the house while she was there. We were also told she would be in our home for three minutes because she was on a tight schedule.

Well, even though it was a fiercely hot day, a large

crowd gathered outside our home in the early hours of that morning. The government sent out three bodyguards and they made sure no-one went past our letterbox. Betty looked like a princess, and I was dressed in my best woollen suit and sweating profusely as I waited for Her Majesty to arrive. I didn't see it, but Robert, who was ten, was ordered to remove chewing gum from his mouth in the countdown to the Queen Mother's visit. We knew she'd arrived long before she and the official party made their way to the steps of our humble abode because an almighty roar went up from the hundreds of people who had by now gathered in our street. Robert recalls that the Queen Mother had three strings of pearls around her neck, and that her skin was the colour of milk. However, I remember meeting a woman dressed in a summer frock and hat, along with white elbow-length gloves, who seemed to enjoy chatting to Betty. I liked her. She even asked questions about our towels because she liked the bright colours, and she was very complimentary about how beautiful Betty had made our home – and while I agreed wholeheartedly, I may have forgotten to say 'Ma'am'. The Queen Mother was aware of my military service, saying she knew I was in the infantry and that I'd fought in the jungle. She was a gracious woman, and before long her scheduled three minutes had extended to 20! The visit could have gone for even longer if a lady-in-waiting had not prevented Her Majesty from accepting Betty's offer of a cup of tea. It was a special day for my family, and when people ask me about it I simply say that while the Queen Mother was lovely, there was only ever one Queen in our house ... and she didn't come from England.

★

While Dad's life after the war centred around his mates and the ANZAC Club, mine was all about Betty and the boys. Dad and I had different views about fatherhood, but in his own way, my father prepared me well for life in the era I lived in as a young man. His alcoholism also steered me away from consuming alcohol and smoking, so I owe that much to him. However, he showed a generosity towards my sons – his grandsons – that I never experienced as a boy. Betty and I would go to Marrickville every Saturday morning to visit our parents, and whenever Dad saw Robert and Garry he gave them two shillings. That always made me smile.

As Dad grew older he would sit in his bedroom and read books, but he was slowly losing his mind to dementia. One day when I asked Mum how he was going, she said he was well but that I ought to go into his room and ask him what he was 'watching'. They didn't have a television, but I dutifully went in and asked the question. Dad seemed surprisingly happy. He told me to sit down and look at the pictures on the wall. So I sat down, and he described the people he could see on Bondi Beach, and how they were all laughing and having fun; kids were throwing balls at one another and there were people bathing in the ocean. He went downhill from there, and one day I phoned Dad's doctor and asked him to come and examine him.

'Mr Chard,' the doctor said to my father after talking to him, 'I think it's time we go on a holiday.' Dad was taken to Gladesville Hospital, and all was well until the day Ray and I received calls from a nurse that Dad was missing. We searched the grounds until we found his lifeless body under the Gladesville Bridge. The coroner's autopsy found that the shrapnel that had rested next to his heart since 1917 had moved, and Dad had died when it severed an artery. Passchendaele had finally finished off Herbert Hercules Chard.

I was overwhelmed by a great sadness. Dad was cremated at Rookwood Cemetery in February 1968, and it was a sad day. My father was 80 when he died, and despite his troubled ways I knew I'd always loved him. He suffered for his service, and my hope is that he found peace.

My mother followed him almost three years to the day, aged 82, and that was an awful blow. My mother, despite the ill health that plagued her for most of her life, was a strong woman who kept her family together under the toughest of circumstances. If my father taught me to survive such things as Sanananda and Kokoda by having a hard heart, my mother taught me how important it is to have love in our lives. I miss her to this day.

In the 1960s, Australia sent troops to Vietnam to assist the United States in stopping the spread of communism through South-East Asia. But the conflict escalated, and in time Canberra introduced conscription. To my horror, Robert's number was drawn in the lottery no parent wanted their son to 'win'. Betty was distraught – she understood how war affects those who fight in them – and I felt the same way. However, in the end, the job Robert was doing as a carpet layer saved him. He passed every aspect of the army's medical but his knees let him down – his use of the knee kicker tool to stretch the carpet had ruined the joint. He was ruled medically unfit, and that meant I didn't have to go through with my plan to break my son's leg, because I had no intention of letting Robert go to war. It had done enough damage to our family. And I wouldn't have hesitated to do the same to Garry if the army had called him up. All I can say is that I loved my sons too much to let them see the things that have scarred me.

In 1984 I retired from trucking and received $5000 in superannuation. However, as was the case with the 350 pounds I left the army with all those years earlier, it wasn't enough after I'd bought two things I'd long promised Betty – a new fence, and the engagement ring I'd never had the money for when we were kids. At 51, I needed to find a new job. I was advised there were jobs at the University of Technology at Broadway for exam supervisors, and they were paying a decent wage. I spent 16 years there, and it was an eye-opener. Sometimes I was called upon to make tough calls during exams if the professor couldn't be contacted. On one occasion the students weren't sure what one of the figures was that they needed to use to calculate an answer because of a misprint. I stopped the exam, and when the professor couldn't be found – he was playing golf – I asked the students to decide what they thought the number was. And the professor and markers had to accept it. You just needed to have common sense, which I've learnt isn't that common!

I retired from UTS in 1997, because it was high time Betty and I finally spent as much time together as we possibly could.

32

It's Hard, But Life Goes On

CHARD, Betty Passed away peacefully May 21, 2011. Late of Villawood Aged 88 years Loving wife of Reg. Cherished mother of Robert and Garry and their families. Forever in our hearts . . .

The Daily Telegraph, *25 May 2011*

During our time together, Betty and I lived a simple, but happy, life. She was an incredible woman blessed with the rare gift of being able to roll with life's punches. When the thief's accomplice escaped with everything we owned when they burgled our place in 1946, Betty didn't dwell on the setback or the loss because, even at a young age, she was able to put things in perspective and see them for what they were. While I counted the cost, she was grateful that neither of us had been hurt – or worse.

Dealing with the trauma of wartime experiences is handled very differently today. Back then, when it went largely unacknowledged, I coped with the darkness that sometimes flooded my mind by getting on with things, and especially by going on interstate truck trips for work. Even though I was miserable, Betty always greeted me upon my return home with a kiss and a hug and she'd ask how the trip had gone, even though she knew how I'd respond – I'd mutter 'good' as I walked past. My disposition wouldn't . . . *couldn't* . . . let me speak to her – or to anyone – for a couple of days after these episodes because something inside of me said I needed to be left alone. Sometimes Betty would break the silence by saying: 'Oh, you're a cranky bastard, Harold [her pet name for me, which normally brought a smile to my face],' and that occasionally helped bring me 'back' to the present from the massacre site, or from the foxholes where we watched our dead friends rotting before our eyes because we couldn't bury them, or from the mud where I was kneeling next to Ray after the orderlies had dropped his lifeless body. When I finally returned to a better frame of mind I'd always explain to Betty that my silence wasn't because I was angry at her or the boys; I just found that if I didn't speak to anyone for a while I could get past the images that clouded my thinking.

As awful as the silence must've been for Betty, she never condemned or criticised me for those times when I chose to lie low when life didn't feel right. She never said, 'I don't know what's wrong with you,' because she knew. It was simply further proof that my wife not only knew me, but she loved me despite my flaws. For my part, I never raised my hand to Betty or the boys; I would've cut it off before doing that, because I'd seen enough as a boy when my father returned home intoxicated and angry to know that domestic violence is among the most despicable acts a man can bring into the family house.

I would've liked to have gone on more holidays. The first Christmas after I started at Drummond's we took a trip to Tuggerah on the New South Wales central coast. We stayed at an old house that didn't have hot water, and it was the last break we had together as a family for 20 years because I worked non-stop so we'd get ahead. After I retired, Betty and I regularly travelled to Tweed Heads to stay with my brother, Ray, but while we loved the Gold Coast, Villawood was home. Betty played tennis well into her old age – it was her passion – and she was quite good at it. We also enjoyed going out to the occasional dinner at a number of licensed clubs and then seeing acts we liked.

One great memory was the time when we went to Bankstown Sports Club to watch the American group, The Platters – they were a pretty big deal back in the day. One of my quirks is that whenever I go out somewhere I have to arrive early. I don't know why, I just do. We arrived at the club really early before the concert and when we walked into the auditorium the lead singer, Herb Reed, was in there running through the show with other band members while their road crew set up their equipment. I introduced myself and told Herb that Betty's all-time favourite song was the band's hit, 'Smoke Gets In Your Eyes'. Herb smiled when he heard that, and he made his way to where Betty was sitting. He welcomed her to the show and said that when the time came for him to sing her song during the concert, he'd look towards her as his form of a dedication. He struck me as a great bloke, and when he sang Betty's favourite tune he was true to his word because he looked straight into her eyes. That song reduces me to tears these days because whenever I hear it I can see Betty so clearly it hurts.

In January 2010, after Betty had not been feeling well for some time, our GP sent her to a specialist at Kitchener Parade, Bankstown. This time, after a series of tests, we'd learn it was Betty who was fighting for her life. When the specialist told Betty she had bowel cancer and the prognosis wasn't good I felt numb, but Betty didn't even flinch. She just took the news in and accepted her lot with a rare grace and incredible courage.

There was one positive thing that came from our trips to Concord Hospital, a place where we'd already spent too much of our life. Whenever Betty finished her appointments there we'd cross the road to where the Canada Bay Council, in conjunction with benefactors and RSL clubs from around the state, had opened an 800-metre path called the Kokoda Track Memorial Walkway. It links Concord Hospital to Rhodes railway station, and what struck me from the first day I went there was the peacefulness of the place. It's located on the banks of the Parramatta River, but there are parts of the walk that are landscaped in such a way that it's easy for me to feel as though I've been transported back to New Guinea – although unlike the dark, sinister images I see in my mind when I recall *that* jungle, the setting at Concord is bright and vibrant. There are 22 stations along the Walkway which combine audio and photographs to explain the various military engagements which occurred along the Kokoda Trail, and the places that I know only too well: Milne Bay, Eora Creek, and the Beachheads. I can't explain why, but whenever I went there at that time – even with all that was going on with Betty's appointments – I felt a deep sense of peace.

After finishing at the hospital, we'd go to the canteen at the track and have a sandwich, a cup of tea, and a talk before returning home. Sometimes Betty would tell me to go for a walk while she rested, and there were occasions when I heard the volunteer guides on the Walkway tell schoolchildren things about the campaign that made me wonder where on earth they'd got their information from. As much as I wanted to correct them, I didn't think it was worth making a scene in front of the kids.

Betty wasn't well, but we made every minute count and we often laughed about things from the past. During one of our last cups of tea at the Kokoda canteen, I'd been thinking about the first time Betty whizzed past our house in that blur of colour and curls when she and I were kids of 16, and how I told Mum I'd marry that girl one day, when I realised something that had evaded me for over 70 years. It dawned on me that Betty had gone out of her way to ride her bike past our place because my street was nowhere near hers ... *she* had been trying to catch *my* attention! When I told her my theory she just scoffed and told me to stop talking rubbish – although the initial look on her face was a bit like a kid caught with their hand in the biscuit tin!

Betty's only request when she was diagnosed with cancer was that she stayed at home and I looked after her. I did that until I showered her one morning. Whenever I washed Betty I'd prop her against the wall while I set up the chair that she sat on. But on this morning I heard a thud and I saw she'd slid down the wall on account of her being so terribly weakened by the cancer. I attempted to lift her, but because she was so frail I was terrified I'd pull her arms out of their sockets if I dragged her up. I phoned the ambulance for help and thankfully they were there within three minutes. They took her to Liverpool Hospital and the doctors decided she should stay there to recover. She had her 88th birthday in that ward, and just as Betty did during all of the tough times throughout her life she made the most of it. Anyhow, I was by Betty's bedside at 7 am every morning and I'd stay with her until 8.15 pm every night. I'd help feed her, and one day ... 21 May 2011 ... she said that I never seemed to eat anything. She told me to go to the cafeteria to have a pie and chips while she had a 'little sleep'. I hadn't even reached the elevator when a nurse came running towards me. She told me to return to the ward urgently, but Betty was gone by the time I got to her. The only blessing was I know she went peacefully. I could write chapter and verse on Betty's battle, but it hurts too much. Of all the terrible things I've witnessed during my lifetime, her death is the toughest of them all.

We were very blessed to grow old together, but I floundered in a sea of loneliness when Betty passed away. She had the beautiful send-off she deserved, and her farewell was an outpouring of absolute love from me and her family and friends. At the same time, it was also a celebration of a life that was well lived. However, when I returned to an empty home that night, and felt the loneliness of the days and nights that followed, I felt as if I was the most isolated man in the world. It affected my mind because when I had my nightly dream about the massacre site and I saw the Japanese soldier's face as I killed him, it was even more vivid and far more disturbing than usual – if you can believe that possible. I did my best to keep going, but my mind was a whirlpool, dredging up so many awful memories I'd spent a lifetime burying. I thought I'd never experience a pain that was as bad as that time in Kokoda when it hurt just to wear the wristwatch my parents gave me, but I was wrong. The pain that was associated with Betty's death was unbearable. One morning when I dragged myself out of bed I realised I couldn't cope with it anymore. I got up, showered, shaved, dressed myself and got into my car, then I started to drive to The Gap near Watsons Bay, an area of sheer ocean cliffs. At 88 years of age, I planned to hurl myself off the cliffs and onto the rocks below. It truly felt like it would be a mercy to finish things off.

On the way to my death, I decided to go to the Walkway for one more visit. As a non-religious man this place was the closest thing I had to a church. As I walked along the pathway I told Betty, Lieutenant Ryan, The Believer, Ray, Dick Kayess, Davo, Miss Valentine and Norman Wolfson to prepare a place for me at the table, because I'd be with them soon. I looked at the cenotaph in the middle of the memorial, which has large chunks of granite displaying different images from Kokoda. In one, a wounded digger is being assisted to the casualty clearing station at Sanananda by a Fuzzy Wuzzy Angel.

As fate had it, there were two women there when I reached it, and I heard one of them say that she wondered whatever happened to the wounded man. Thinking it would be my last kind act before dying, I said, 'Excuse me, ladies, would you like to know what happened to George Whittington, the man you're wondering about?' They turned to me and asked how I knew, and after I explained that I had been in the same campaign, I told them that the Fuzzy Wuzzy who helped George was named Raphael Oimbari, and that he was made an Officer of the Order of the British Empire. I noticed that they looked sad when I told them that while George had made it back to safety, he had later died of scrub typhus, the same disease that almost killed me. The women were fascinated, and asked me if I would like to have a cup of tea with them back at the café.

I decided to accept their offer and we spoke for hours. One of the women knew Alice Kang, the woman who has devoted her energies to looking after the Walkway, and they asked her to come over from her office in the hospital to meet me. After I spoke to Alice, she asked if I would like to be a volunteer guide to take schoolchildren and groups, such as war widows, on tours, and to share my experiences with them. It struck me as being the best idea put to me by anyone that day – it was much better than taking my own life – and so I agreed. The events of that day gave me the purpose I needed to keep going. Those women, and Alice, didn't know it at the time, but they saved my life. Since that day I've had 11 more years of life, and at 98, I hope to have a few more.

★

When I started volunteering, there were 22 guides who had served in World War II. After Dick Payten, Lloyd Birdsall and Ray Gentles – Ray was also a 55th/53rd man – died last year, I find myself the last man standing. We'd all become good mates, and I miss them dearly. We have other guides now – some were in the Vietnam War, some were National Servicemen – and we're all doing our part to keep the spirit of Kokoda alive by helping take up to 5000 schoolchildren and other visitors along the track each year.

My day at the Walkway starts when I arrive at 7.30 am. I drive myself there early so I can go up and down the path and inspect it. We've had a lot of damage there over the years. Some of it is caused by Mother Nature – some big winds once uprooted a tree and it blocked the path – but I'm afraid most of the damage is man-made. There was a period where vandals used red paint to deface the stations – I have no idea of the symbolism behind their actions – so I'd take petrol with me and a bottle of turps to remove it. Another time at the Myola station one genius threw into the river the railway sleepers that were used as steps to allow people to get to the riverbank. The schoolkids loved being able to get to the bank because they were able to see the little crabs running around. The council bolted the sleepers back down, but by the end of the next school holidays they were gone again. It was three years before we discovered the high water mark belongs to the Maritime Services Board, and the land back from the water mark belongs to the council, but neither party wants to know about it because, I imagine, of the costs involved to repair it. The shame about that is the kids miss out on seeing the crabs.

Volunteering has allowed me to meet some incredible children, and as a result of my interaction with them I believe Australia's future is in good hands. They're different from my generation – their access to technology and information would have been unimaginable in my childhood – but overall, the majority I've come across have been brilliant. I also learnt early in the piece not to be a harsh judge of them. There was one day when a young girl at the back of a group I was taking seemed especially uninterested. I must have been in a cranky mood, but it struck a nerve in me because I'd just been talking about how boys not much older than her had sacrificed their lives so she and her friends could grow up in a free country. She appeared to be more interested in an ibis bird nearby, so I said: 'To the girl at the back – yes, you, the one looking at the bird – can you tell me what I just said?' She dropped her head and said she was sorry because she couldn't. So, I repeated it word for word. What I found was that throughout the rest of the tour this girl edged closer to me and was quite respectful. Later, when the kids had their lunch, a teacher told me the girl I had singled out was the most painfully shy student she'd ever taught, and she probably only said she didn't know what I'd said because of her bashfulness. Oh, I felt terrible. I had been a shy kid myself, and I knew what I'd done was punish her for no other reason than being herself. As the group prepared to leave I gathered the kids together and said: 'When I'm wrong about something, I apologise, and I have an apology to make. I won't mention any names, but I know the young lady in question will know this apology is for her. I asked this young lady to repeat what I said and she said she didn't know. I apologise to you, young lady, because it's been pointed out to me that you are very shy, and there's nothing wrong with that. I'm very sorry I singled you out.' I received some nice letters from the students a few days after that visit, and alongside the name of the young girl who I'd made an example of was the message: *I'm the shy one*. It made me smile.

I've learnt as a volunteer guide that children need to know they matter. On another occasion I had a group of so-called 'bad kids' – children with behavioural problems – visit the pathway. Someone said they were a difficult mob, and when I was told there'd be seven male teachers accompanying the group of 14 I wondered what the hell I was in for. However, I treated them no differently from any other child, and by the end of the visit they were saying 'please' and 'thank you'. The teacher in charge said that if they could get that behaviour for ten minutes a day they'd be happy. Although, I also think the pathway has a calming effect on people. I find when people hear a little bit about the story of Kokoda, and the men who fought there, they naturally want to know more.

We've had all manner of people visit us over the years; politicians, military officials, business leaders and sporting teams. The New South Wales police commissioner used to bring a team of about 20 officers annually to present them with the cape, raincoat and bedroll they'd take to New Guinea with them as they walked the trail. While writing this book the Sydney Thunder cricket team that plays in the Big Bash League came to visit, and I told them some of the stories that have appeared in this book. The cricketers reminded me of C Coy because while their squad consisted of all sorts, I could see they were bound by a great camaraderie and that they were working towards a common goal. Sadly, in this age it seems only war, sport and bushfires achieve that.

I worry about the future of the Kokoda Track Memorial Walkway. The people who run it – and it's not for profit – have bought state-of-the-art virtual reality glasses for the day when we no longer have guides. In late 2021 the state premier, Dominic Perrottet, allocated the memorial $600,000 over four years because he wants future generations to appreciate the sacrifices that were made in Papua New Guinea. I worry about what will happen after that, though. Who'll fund it?

The Memorial Walkway really is a place for all, something I made clear when a few cheeky boys came to me during a recent school visit. I knew they were up to something from the moment their ringleader said: 'Hey, Reg, guess what?'

'What?' I replied.

'We've got a Japanese girl in our class,' he said boldly as his mates struggled to contain their grins. They were hoping to get a rise out of me. 'A *Japanese* girl, Reg.'

'Is that so? Well, you'd better bring her to me,' I said, feigning sternness. 'Go on then, go get her.'

A few minutes later the young girl came to me and she looked terrified as she waited to hear the old man start shouting at her.

'I'm . . . I'm the Japanese girl, Reg,' she said timidly. 'The boys said I'm in trouble for what my great-grandfathers did.'

The innocence of what she said brought me to the verge of tears. I just looked at her and smiled.

'Why would you be in trouble? You're a lovely young girl who hasn't done anything wrong. I asked the boys to send you over because I just want you to know you're going to hear some terrible things about the past during your visit here. This all happened in a war that happened many years ago, and it was a war you and your parents had *nothing* to do with. It was a different time. Please don't listen to the boys – if boys can be anything, they can be foolish. I want you to know you're welcome here, love, and I'm very happy you're here.'

With that she held my hand briefly as we walked towards the first of the stations. It all went well until we neared the end of the tour and stopped at the station which commemorates the Battle of the Beachheads. As I've done on so many other occasions, I told the children the story of Sanananda, and how I lost many good friends there. I felt the tears welling in my eyes; they always do at this point on the Walkway because I see Ray, Dick Kayess, Davo, Bill Ryan, Norm Wolfson, and all the others who died in that terrible swamp. As I tried to wipe my eyes without any of the children seeing it, it felt as if someone was looking at me. When I looked down I saw it was the little Japanese girl. She must have sensed my sadness because I was greeted by a beaming and beautiful smiling face. I found myself smiling back. We then walked back together with all the other children and their teachers towards the café. We didn't say much, but I know there was a mutual understanding between us of the stupidity of war and the price people pay – even innocent young Japanese–Australian girls – 80 years after hostilities.

That moment reinforced for me a lesson I learnt a long time ago, when my brother Dave died in a motorbike accident on his way home from the beach, and in the days that followed I watched as my father put his deep grief aside and went to work to provide for his family. It allowed me to push on in Papua New Guinea and many years later when I lost Betty. I think it is a good message to finish my story on because if nothing else it puts *everything* I've been through into perspective, and it might even help you, the reader, during your own challenges. It is this:

Make the most of life, because no matter how bad something may seem, life goes on – just make sure you go with it.

Acknowledgements

Reg Chard acknowledges the wonderful friendship and support of his extended family, especially his son Robert, and Maria Leetham; his friends and associates at the Kokoda Track Memorial Walkway, including Alice Kang, Charlie Lynn, Karen Camage, the late Rusty Priest and Jennifer Collins. He has never forgotten the compassion and care of Sister Ruth Campbell of the 2/9th Australian General Hospital, who went beyond the call of duty in helping those diggers who could not help themselves. Reg salutes the men he fought alongside from the 2/55th Infantry Battalion – the Mice of Moresby.

Daniel Lane wishes to offer his thanks to a number of people who helped him in the production of this book especially Reg for trusting him with his incredible story; Camille; Ian Heads; Bernard McCarthy; Nicholas Lane; Peter Morrison; the many veterans, authors, and journalists who have written about the Kokoda campaign. He singles out two: Paul Ham whose book *Kokoda* remains the benchmark, and former colleague Peter FitzSimons who captured the true spirit of the diggers in his offering on Kokoda.

Both Reg Chard and Daniel Lane are grateful to Pan Macmillan publisher Alex Lloyd, who, from the outset, grasped the importance of this story; the wise guidance of Danielle Walker; and the expert editing of Brianne Collins – she deserves a medal!

Credits

Page 96:   Transcript of interview with Francis Rowell (Frank),
           10 June 2003, Australians at War Film Archive (Archive
           No 451) http://australiansatwarfilmarchive.unsw.edu.au
           retrieved 17 March 2022

Page 141: Transcript of interview with Joseph Dawson (Joe),
           16 March 2004, Australians at War Film Archive (Archive
           No 1592) http://australiansatwarfilmarchive.unsw.edu.au
           retrieved 17 March 2022

Page 161: Transcript of interview with Keith Irwin (Scoop), 6 May
           2003, Australians at War Film Archive (Archive No 17)
           http://australiansatwarfilmarchive.unsw.edu.au retrieved
           17 March 2022

Page 171: Transcript of interview with Errol Jorgensen, 3 February
           2004, Australians at War Film Archive (Archive No 1554)
           http://australiansatwarfilmarchive.unsw.edu.au retrieved
           17 March 2022

Page 303: Quote used with kind permission from *The Canberra Times*.